Urban Environmental
Management

Urban Environmental Management

ENVIRONMENTAL CHANGE
AND
URBAN DESIGN

Rodney R. White

JOHN WILEY & SONS
Chichester · New York · Brisbane · Toronto · Singapore

Copyright © 1994 Rodney R. White

Published by John Wiley & Sons Ltd,
 Baffins Lane, Chichester,
 West Sussex PO19 1UD, England
 Telephone National Chichester (0243) 779777
 International +44 243 779777

Other Wiley Editorial Offices

John Wiley & Sons, Inc., 605 Third Avenue,
New York, NY 10158-0012, USA

Jacaranda Wiley Ltd, 33 Park Road, Milton,
Queensland 4064, Australia

John Wiley & Sons (Canada) Ltd, 22 Worcester Road,
Rexdale, Ontario M9W 1L1, Canada

John Wiley & Sons (SEA) Pte Ltd, 37 Jalan Pemimpin #05-04,
Block B, Union Industrial Building, Singapore 2057

Library of Congress Cataloging-in-Publication data
White, Rodney R.
 Urban environmental management : environmental change and urban
design/Rodney R. White.
  p. cm.
 Includes bibliographical references (p.) and index.
 ISBN 0-471-95001-7
 1. City planning—Environmental aspects. 2. Urban ecology.
I. Title.
HT166.W513 1994   94-9553
307. 1'216—dc20   CIP

British Library Cataloguing in Publication Data

A catalogue record for this book is available from the British Library

ISBN 0-471-95001-7

Typeset in 11/13 Palatino from author's disks by
Mathematical Composition Setters Ltd, Salisbury, Wiltshire
Printed and bound in Great Britain by Biddles, Guildford, Surrey

Contents

Figures

Tables

Preface

Cities are both victims and culprits in the unfolding drama of human-induced environmental change, which has recently expanded to include the changing composition of the atmosphere. Humans constantly modify their environments, both built and natural. But now the urban environment itself is profoundly changing the entire global ecosystem, with consequences that we have only just begun to imagine. In order to understand the environmental role played by cities, the damage done, and the measures that may be taken to reduce the damage, it is necessary to see the city *as part of* the environment.

Part of our cities' difficulties lie in the fundamental metabolic problems of circulating nutrients, energy, air and water, and extruding wastes. Unlike the ant-hill and beehive, cities have remained essentially two-dimensional smears across the landscape. Our efforts to build our cities by making use of the third dimension are very costly in terms of finance, amenities and energy. Skyscrapers and elevated highways are impressive feats of engineering, but they are environmentally and socially unfriendly. Subways are expensive to construct compared with roads on the surface. Our underground circulation systems for water, gas and electricity are difficult to maintain without constantly digging up the surface for repairs and extensions. Estimates of water wasted in the delivery pipe vary, but 30% is often mentioned, especially in cities in the developing South. We bury our wastes in the ground, but we now know that liquids leaking from landfills may threaten crops and human health.

The aim of this book is to examine the problems of urban planning and management from an environmental perspective. The city is analysed as part of the cycle of organisms, elements and nutrients that make up the natural environment. Thus we can identify the metabolism of our cities—the ways in which they ingest, process, and extrude elements of these natural cycles. The general conclusion is that we need to manage our cities more 'intelligently', meaning that the city lives symbiotically within the environment, rather than at its expense. This has become steadily more apparent as the planet reacts to the stress that humans have placed upon it, unknowingly and uncaringly for the most part.

My own appreciation of the depth of the problem has grown out of many experiences both in the university and in the consulting world. My intellectual debt to the people who began to operationalise an approach to understanding the city as part of the natural environment is evident in the citations in the text. The importance of the work of Blair Bower, Stephen Boyden and his colleagues, Ian Douglas, Andrew Goudie, and Abel Wolman should be very obvious. That I have been most intrigued by James Lovelock's Gaia hypothesis and its implications for the evolution of urban systems can be seen in Chapters Two and Seven, especially. Peter Hall's interpretation of the last hundred years of urban planning provided a very useful framework for Chapter Four. It was through David Harvey's writing that I first became aware of Leon Krier's interest in the creation of an 'ecological city'. A less visible debt is the one I owe to my colleagues in Project Ecoville—the urbanisation component of the IFIAS Programme for Analysing Biospheric Change (ABC), which was supported by the Institute for Environment Studies at the University of Toronto. In particular I have benefited from a long association with Ian Burton, Richard Stren and Joe Whitney, and from several other colleagues at the Institute, and at the Department of Geography.

In addition to regular contact with colleagues at Toronto I have also learned a great deal from a number of specialised conferences, and in a sense this book is an attempt to gather some of the material that we will need to respond to questions that were posed at those conferences—note, I am not yet confident enough to speak of 'answers' to those questions. I began to understand the linkages between a large number of environmental problems from my association with the IFIAS–ABC project, especially at a concluding meeting that was held at the then headquarters of IFIAS, outside Stockholm in 1986. There John Firor spoke of the 'big three' problems of acidification, stratospheric ozone depletion, and the greenhouse effect in a way that made the linkages much clearer, especially in relation to the work that we were doing at Toronto on the urban contribution to environmental change. The first conference that encouraged me to revive my interest in Abel Wolman's work on urban metabolism was a conference on The Pathology of Urban Processes, hosted by the Institute for Space Economy at the University of Warsaw 1987, to which I was invited by my old friend Richard Switalski. The conference also allowed me to see something of the impact of industrialisation on the Polish environment, so I was not totally surprised by the revelations that followed the demise of the Communist Government.

Toronto was the scene for a particularly useful conference on Cities and Global Change, organised by Jim McCulloch in 1991, on behalf of the Climate Institute, Washington DC. For the first time I realised that a lot of people coming from a variety of fields were beginning to look at cities in a different light—as part of the natural world, rather than as simply the built environment created by humans. It was interesting to see the puzzlement of the atmospheric scientists, at the conference, when confronted by civil engineers who told them what information *they* wanted out of the climate modelling exercises. Turbulence and wind-sheer estimates in a warmer world would be useful to know, they said. The modellers explained that they were still working on globally averaged temperature change, and it would probably be quite a while before they had anything on wind speeds. It was at a second run of the Cities and Global Change conference, held at the Royal Geographical Society in London, the following year, that Dr Luis Manuel Guerra posed a question with which I am still struggling: 'Given that modern urban technology is the product of the first industrial nations, do they now have anything remedial to offer?' All I have so far is a 'maybe'.

I was very fortunate to spend 1991–92 on sabbatical at the School of Geography of the University of Oxford. It was the first year of operation of the Environmental Change Unit and I was able to meet many fascinating and helpful people, especially through the encouragement of my friends Brenda and John Boardman who sensed, perhaps, that I might otherwise just spend the year reading and writing. I am grateful they did not let me do this; instead they phoned me up, wrote to other people on my behalf, suggested journals I should publish in, and took me to meetings they thought would be of interest. Through the good services of David Satterthwaite at the International Institute for Environment and Development, in London, I was invited to a very interesting workshop on Planning for Sustainable Urban Development, organised by Carole Rakodi of the Department of City and Regional Planning, University College of Wales at Cardiff. There I sensed the divergence of interest between those development specialists whose concern was with the daily environmental problems, such as the provision of clean water in developing countries, and the scientists involved in the problems of atmospheric change. From my association with IFIAS I had taken it for granted that all these problems were linked, and that it was not a question of one being more important than another. It was useful to have this assumption challenged. It was also at the Cardiff conference that I first met Adrian Atkinson whose stimulating work on political ecology has, I hope, left a visible mark on this book. However, he also saddled me with the challenging concept of the bioregion, which I still do not know what to do with, as I have admitted in Chapter Seven.

Most of my work, through the university and through consulting, has been focused on Africa, indeed on a handful of countries in West Africa, and it is only recently that I have begun to extend my interests in urban and regional infrastructure planning to cities of the richer Northern countries. I am fortunate to be living in Toronto, which has been a leader in the drive to find less environmentally destructive ways of redeveloping an urban system. The City of Toronto and the Municipality of Metropolitan Toronto are among the leaders of the world's cities in developing comprehensive plans to reduce carbon dioxide emissions by modifying buildings, land-use planning, and transportation planning. Toronto is also the headquarters of the Canadian Urban Institute and the International Council for Local Environmental Initiatives, both of which have led the way in disseminating information on ways to reduce the impact of cities on the environment. I am grateful to my colleagues Virginia Maclaren and Danny Harvey for introducing me to a variety of people who have helped me to appreciate what is going on in the city that has been my home for most of the last twenty years. At the same time, I am trying to keep in focus the needs of both the cities of the South and those of North, as countries become linked ever closer by their environmental problems. I have been encouraged to do that through the opportunities and stimulus provided by Peter Paproski of the Canadian International Development Agency and by Mario Polèse of the *Villes et Développement* Centre of Excellence, Montreal.

While I was in Oxford, Brenda Boardman and Adrian Atkinson suggested that I take my proposal for a book to Iain Stevenson who was in the process of building up an impressive environmental 'list' for Belhaven Press[1]. I am very grateful for their advice as Iain provided encouragement and ready support for the project when it is was still in an embryonic state. Once I had a completed draft to work on, I asked my colleague Barry Adams, at the Department of Civil Engineering and the Institute for Environmental Studies of the University of Toronto, for his reaction to the 'combined utility trench' (proposed in Chapter Seven). He very kindly explained to me what had already been done in this field, what else could be done now, what might be done under certain circumstances, and what was most unlikely ever to be done due to the engineering constraints. This he did very succinctly, and my proposal now looks quite different as a result. The person who had the greatest hand in rescuing me from my naïvities, obsessions, and various knowledge-gaps was Blair Bower who most generously gave his time to apply his unique expertise (and much ink) to an earlier draft of the book. The fact that he did this with tact as well as with his characteristic thoroughness is very much appreciated. There must be errors left in such a broad

---

[1] Belhaven Press was acquired by John Wiley & Sons in 1993 and is now integrated into Wiley's environmental science publishing.

approach to urban ecosystems and there must be important contributions to the field of which I am unaware. For these errors and
omissions I alone am responsible.

To my wife, Sue, I owe the greatest debt, as she endured another
book with good humour and provided much encouragement.

Rodney White
Toronto, January 1994

Acknowledgements

The author would like to thank the following for their kind per-
mission to reproduce various figures: Dr Stephen Boyden and his
colleagues at the Australian National University for Figure 3.3,
taken from *The Ecology of a City and Its People: the Case of Hong Kong*
(Australian National University Press); the Municipality of
Metropolitan Toronto for Figure 3.4; Figure 7.6 is reproduced
from Ebenezer Howard—*Garden Cites of Tomorrow*, published by
Attic Books, Powys LD2 3JY, UK; Friends of the Earth for Figure
7.7 taken from *Reviving the City—Towards Sustainable Urban
Development*; and the Board of *Environment and Urbanization* for
Figures 5.1, 8.1 and 8.3. Both the Municipality of Metropolitan
Toronto and the City of Toronto kindly provided me with access
to internal documents. While every effort has been made to contact copyright holders some enquiries remained unanswered at
the time of going to press; it is hoped that any further
acknowledgements may be added in future editions.

Acronyms

HABITAT	United Nations Centre for Human Settlements
IIED	International Institute for Environment and Development
IFIAS	International Federation of Institutes for Advanced Study
IPCC	Intergovernmental Panel on Climate Change
MAB	Man and the Biosphere Programme (part of UNESCO)
OECD	Organisation for Economic Cooperation and Development
OPEC	Organisation of Petroleum-Exporting Countries
REQM	Residuals and Environmental Quality Management
SCOPE	Scientific Committee on Problems of the Environment
UNEP	United Nations Environment Programme
UNESCO	United Nations Educational, Scientific and Cultural Organisation
WHO	World Health Organisation

Other Abbreviations

Btu	British thermal unit
CFC	chlorofluorocarbons
CO_2	carbon dioxide
CO	carbon monoxide
m^3	cubic metres
GHG	greenhouse gases
GDP	Gross Domestic Product
GNP	Gross National Product
ha	hectare
Hc	hydrocarbons
kg	kilograms
km	kilometre
kWh	kilowatt hours
lpppd	litres per person per day
m-atm-cm	milli-atmospheres-centimetre (see the Glossary, under 'ozone layer')
MTOE	million tons of oil equivalent
NO_x	nitrogen oxides, NO and NO_2
O_3	ozone
p	pence
pass/km	passengers/kilometres
Pb	lead
pc pa	per capita per annum
ppm	parts per million
SO_2	sulphur dioxide
km^2	square kilometres

A Note on Language

A book of this kind inevitably draws on the language of many disciplines from the social and natural sciences, planning, management, ecology, and engineering. Every effort has been made to
use specialised terms in the context for which they were first
developed, although this is not always possible where the term
has passed from one discipline to another and been modified in
the process. Terms such as 'system' and 'dynamic' mean
different things to different people. In cases such as these my
preferred point of departure is the field of systems ecology, as for-
malised by Howard Odum in his book of that title (1983). A glossary has been added to clarify the meaning of certain terms, as
employed in this book. As far as possible I have resisted the temptation to enclose in quotation marks those words that might
appear in an unfamiliar context. However, I have hyphenated
words like 'bio-geochemical' and 'air-shed' as they might look
unfamiliar to some readers otherwise.

No attempt has been made to distinguish between what is urban
and what is not urban. Although cities are the focus of this book,
their impact on the environment is only part of the impact of our
modern, technologically-dominated society, whether urban or
rural, industrial or agricultural. In the West the village almost
invariably depends on the same technology as the city—motor
vehicles, electricity, the use of large quantities of water, and the
creation of large quantities of waste *per capita*. Agriculture is
rightly referred to as the agricultural industry, and often depends
on distant sources of water and nutrients, and caters for distant
markets. As an example of the similar impact of urban and rural
life on the environment we can note that both urban traffic

congestion and fertiliser-dependent farming contribute to impacts on the nitrogen cycle. However, it is nonetheless useful to look at cities separately at this stage for, in the context of climate change, not only are they significant contributors to environmental degradation they are also likely to be foremost among the victims, especially with reference to global warming if only because of the concentration of cities along the coastline where they will be vulnerable to the impacts of sea-level rise. There is no formal definition of the term 'environment', as it is taken simply to mean the physical, observable, breathable world in which we live.

I have tried to avoid the use of the term 'consumption'. The meaning of the term is quite clear in commerce, economics and economic geography where it refers to goods that we purchase, use, and then ... Then what? The problem is that, in physical terms, the materials of which the goods are made are simply transformed and deposited somewhere else in the environment, as waste. I have been persuaded by Blair Bower that the term 'consumption' contributes to our avoidance of this fact. Having consumed something, it has disappeared. Right?

Wrong—it is still out there, somewhere in the environmental system. Therefore, wherever possible, I have substituted the word 'use' for 'consumption' and 'consume'.

1

The Urban Environment

'Great cities are biologically parasites in their use of the vital resources, air, water and food, in urban metabolism. The bigger the cities, the more these systems demand from the surrounding countryside and the greater the danger of damaging the natural environment "host"' (Douglas 1983: 11).

The main purpose of this book is to help urban planners and managers think of an urban system *as a whole*, at least with regard to its physical attributes, and hence its impact on the landscape and the biosphere. That may seem like a very tentative objective but it is a difficult task, even without detailed consideration of the political and social forces which have made our cities what they are. A further purpose of the book is to understand some of the opportunities available to urban planners and managers at a time of environmental change. It is written in the belief that the recently observed trends in the biosphere (especially the build-up of greenhouse gases, the depletion of the ozone layer, acid deposition, and the long-range transportation of many pollutants), oblige us to completely rethink the way we have encouraged our cities and our societies to evolve during the industrial age. Thus the possible magnitude of the impacts of these processes, coupled with the uncertainty that surrounds them, should encourage us to re-examine the long-standing problems of poor air and water quality, the accumulation of wastes, traffic congestion and, generally, the inordinate wastefulness of all those societies which have passed through the industrial revolution.

My enquiry is focused on urban settlements because our urban and industrial technology is the source of many of the problems, and there the most immediate improvements can be made, both for technical and political reasons—technical because urban society is extremely wasteful, political because urban governments are taking the initiative on environmental issues more readily than are national governments. Thus, although many of the observations made in the book may be discouraging, or even alarming, the message is generally an optimistic one. Human society urgently needs to rethink its relationship with the planet and the relationships between its various members, especially between rich and poor. There is a job to be done, and much of that job can best be done within the urban system, both to improve the immediate environment and to reduce the negative impact of our urban society on rural areas, the oceans, and the atmosphere. Despite the huge literature that has been spawned on the need for environmental rehabilitation, relatively few books pay much attention to the opportunities available to decision-makers and citizens within urban areas. It is hoped that this book will help to fill the gap.

This chapter continues with a brief survey of the spread of urbanisation in the last 200 years, beginning in the countries often referred to as the North—where the rate of population growth is now quite low. In the poorer countries of the South, where population growth is still rapid, urban conditions are very different. These contrasts between North and South are briefly examined. Next, recent developments in the process of environmental change are introduced, to be followed by the main elements of an analytical approach to the subject. The chapter concludes with a note on the organisation of the rest of the book.

Urbanisation and the industrial revolution

Prior to the industrial revolution the mortality rate in cities usually exceeded the birth rate. Congested living and the lack of systematic liquid and solid waste management assured that people would constantly be prey to contagious diseases, even in those years when they were not swept by major epidemics. Demographically, the cities kept going because they were refuelled by migrants from the rural areas. However, the upsurge of prosperity brought in by the industrial revolution permitted the improvement of urban infrastructure (health and education services, water supply, and waste management), to the point that the urban mortality rate fell below the urban birth rate and cities began to grow from their own demographic vitality. The negative feedback of diseases was replaced by the positive feedback of healthier living. Yet the cities still acted as a powerful magnet for migrants from the countryside. Under these circumstances, far from struggling to maintain their population, cities began to grow rapidly.

A growing demand for hands to run the new labour-intensive industries absorbed increasing numbers of the new urban-born workers and their rural cousins. But not all of them. Furthermore, the improved services first developed in urban areas diffused through the rural areas, where mortality rates also fell. As long as birth rates remained at their previous level, a rapid growth of the total population—urban and rural—was inevitable. Thus the early industrialising countries of Western Europe experienced a demographic explosion. Fortunately for them, this event occurred at a time when Europeans were colonising 'new lands', in temperate parts of the world, that could absorb both rural and urban labour. It is estimated that, between 1846 and 1932, about 40% of the rise of population in countries such as Britain, Italy, Portugal and Spain emigrated (World Bank 1984: 58–9). The absence of a similar safety valve should always be kept in mind when we examine the options for the South today.

In the twentieth century, new impacts of the larger cities of the industrial world became apparent. Improved water supply called on increased supplies from groundwater, to the extent that water tables began to fall (Goudie 1986: 168–73). Air quality was often so poor that the health of the people was affected. As the cities grew, the typical journey to work lengthened and the provision of infrastructure became more expensive. Urban sprawl consumed more and more land, to the detriment of both agriculture and recreation. However, the populations of the early industrialised countries of the North began to stabilise as birth rates fell, generally in response to the decline of mortality rates. Nevertheless, the more slowly growing (or stable) populations continued to demand more goods and create more waste as their wealth increased. Paradoxically, as the cities grew, they covered over their own supplies of building materials, such as brick earth and gravel pits, and these materials then had to be imported from other regions (Douglas 1983: 26–8).

Two problems have become apparent as outcomes from this first period of the industrial transformation of society. First, the richer societies are now producing goods and creating wastes on such a scale that the composition of the atmosphere is changing, with alarming implications. Second, the countries of the South are now urbanising very rapidly and are changing the environment on a scale comparable to cities in the North. The difficulty lies in the fact that the cities of the South are creating Northern-type environmental problems while their economies remain in grave difficulty, such that they are not producing the financial surpluses to deal with any of these impacts—neither the traditional environmental problems such as poor water supply and inadequate waste management, nor the new problems of atmospheric change. Furthermore, it is still widely assumed that pollution and the use of ever more resources are part of the price that one must pay for a higher standard of material well-being.

Low-income cities in the second half of the twentieth century

An important feature of cities, as they evolved out of feudal Europe, at least, was their freedom and independence. They regulated their own citizens, collected their own taxes, and indeed paid taxes to the central authority. As the industrial revolution went on, and the nation state became paramount, more and more administrative functions passed to the central government. In many countries of the North the original position is now reversed. The city is only the residual legal authority taking care of the simpler, housekeeping tasks of government. The central authority collects the lion's share of the taxes and hands a portion of this to the cities for their housekeeping role, while adding to that task by imposing higher environmental standards. In the older industrial regions of the United States the dismemberment of urban government has gone further. There the richer urban people moved out to the suburbs where they created separate jurisdictions, while they left the central city, bereft of wealth, to rot (Jacobs 1962). Even in Canada, where city centres have remained more prosperous, it has been shown that the political role of city dwellers, *as citizens of cities*, was extinguished (Isin 1992).

What has happened in the cities of the South is a different story with an even more problematic future. Other than China, and a handful of much smaller countries, the present states of the South were created as European colonies where the central authority was both paramount and overseas. In these circumstances there was little opportunity for urban authorities to develop much autonomy, either legal or financial (Stren 1989: 21). Today they remain heavily dependent on the central authority for most of their funding. In the face of very rapid population growth they have been overwhelmed. In the early stages, in the 1950s and 1960s, they maintained control by force such as by restricting the right to migrate to urban areas, and by bulldozing the illegal settlements of those who did so anyway. However, gradually, the number of newcomers became too much, and the immigrants from the countryside seized land where they could.

'This illegal process, by which most new city houses and neighbourhoods (in the South) are developed, has been evident for many decades and yet very few governments are prepared to acknowledge it. Most governments mix indifference with repression; some illegal settlements are tolerated while others are bulldozed' (Hardoy and Satterthwaite 1989: 15).

Despite this difficult beginning in the so-called developing world, there persists a strongly ingrained assumption among development theorists that the countries of the South can, and will, follow the same path as the North, employing industrial technology to raise productivity in both rural and urban economies, thereby reducing mortality rates and completing the demographic transition. However, this becomes less and less likely, as can be seen by a graph of the projected size of the world's largest cities (Figure 1.1). Those in the South are already, in some cases, much larger in population and areal extent. They are also much poorer and they are growing faster (White and Whitney 1992: 37). During the 1990s Mexico City is projected to overtake Tokyo/Yokohama in size; Shanghai will surpass New York; Calcutta and

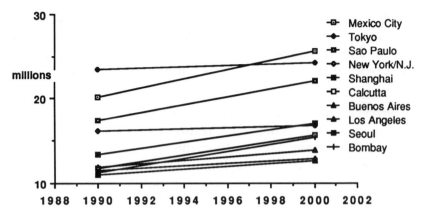

Figure 1.1 The Ten Largest Cities in 1990. *Source:* Based on Girardet 1992: 182–5

Bombay will each become larger than Los Angeles. Meanwhile, not only have the rural economies of many countries in the South not passed through an agricultural revolution, some are actually stagnating and are producing less food than before. In these circumstances the poverty of the rural areas assures a steady stream of migrants to the cities.

From the atmospheric viewpoint, we can distinguish a transition from poverty, through economic growth to relative prosperity. The poorest countries are still suffering from high levels of particulate matter in the air, from household fuel, bush-burning, rubbish burning, and dust; while cities in the newly industrialising countries (or middle-income countries), are following the early stage of the development path of the North, with heavy emissions of sulphur oxides as an unwanted by-product of industrial activities. Vehicles are major contributors to carbon monoxide, nitrogen oxides, and particulates. The richest countries have reduced the production of both particulates and sulphur, but they are steadily increasing their output of carbon dioxide from the ever increasing use of fossil fuels (Figure 1.2). These are just examples of the impact of urbanisation on the atmosphere. Similar impacts are felt on the ground and throughout the hydrological cycle. For example many cities—especially in the middle-income phase—are drawing down aquifers, on which their economy rests, beyond the safe yield level. These and other

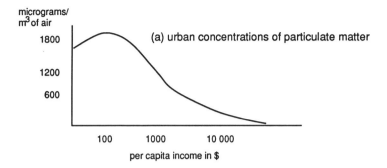

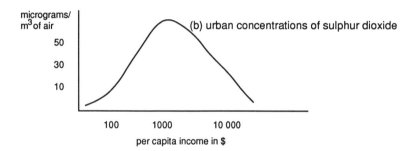

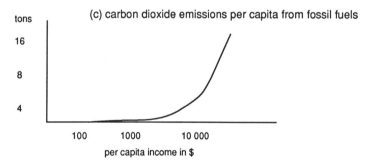

Figure 1.2   The Pollution Transition: from Poor-country Pollution to Rich-country Pollution. *Source*: Based on the World Bank 1992: 11

impacts are not simply physical problems, but symptoms of a wider social and economic malaise.

Whatever policies are proposed under the title of 'urban environmental management', they must respond to the global situation squarely. Until now people in the development field have acted on the assumption that the observable problems in the cities of the South could be treated with the technology of the North—land-use planning, traffic management, emission regulations, and so on. When these approaches were overwhelmed by rapid urban growth in the 1970s (with urban populations sometimes doubling within a decade), faith shifted away from the government and its planners to the market, and even to the informal sector—forces hitherto shunned by the governments and the development agencies. But this was a shift based on desperation, not on any comprehensive theory. Once cities surpass a certain size, neither the informal sector nor the market can mobilise sufficient resources from the community to cope with certain key elements of urban infrastructure. This phenomenon has been seen time and again in the history of urbanisation, whether the problem is water supply, sewage disposal, or universal primary education. Now that humanity is facing the prospect of global climate change it is even less probable that the spontaneous responses of local communities or markets will be adequate to deal with the scale of the problems that will arise.

In spite of the development of this situation many governments in the North have also simply assumed that some mix of privatisation and decentralisation will remedy the problem in their own countries, just as the development agencies have done in the South. Again, this assumption is simply a reaction to a financial problem rather than a rational policy based on needs and means. As national governments face an escalating debt (equalled in countries like Canada by comparable debts for provinces and for some public utilities), cities have simply been left to fend for themselves. One assumption has simply been replaced with another.

Instead of casting the problem initially in financial terms, we must conceptualise the problem based on the measurable physical features of the environment. How do our cities function as physical entities, and what is their trajectory in terms of the quality of life of their citizens and their impact on the global environment?

Current views on environmental change

It is only recently that urban systems have been associated with the environment at a global scale. For most of our history the 'urban environment' referred to conditions in the city itself, variously partitioned into the household environment, the workplace environment, and the ambient (or outdoor), environment. The principle problems were those associated with air and water quality, and their impact on human morbidity and mortality. This problem set will be referred to as the 'traditional urban environmental agenda'. People can grasp, intuitively, the nature of the traditional agenda because it encompasses the factors of everyday life at the level of the household. Water, energy, air quality, and solid-waste management are tangible issues. Even problems of subsidence (following the draw-down of the aquifer), may impinge on the household directly.

However, the new environmental agenda is focused on the much less tangible problem of the changing composition of the atmosphere, principally the 'big three' problems of greenhouse gases, stratospheric ozone depletion, and acid deposition (Firor 1990: viii). Linked to atmospheric change are older environmental problems such as deforestation (in the context of carbon dioxide uptake), as well as newer complications like the vulnerability of marine life to global warming and to increased ultra-violet radiation. (All of these problems are discussed in more detail in Chapter Two.) In the poorer countries of the South there is little concern about these new problems because, understandably, people are still preoccupied with basic needs, such as the supply of food, fuel, and water, and the safe disposal of solid and liquid wastes. Even in the North there is widespread scepticism about the assumption that a fundamental response to atmospheric change is urgently required (Beckerman 1991). Again, there are more immediate preoccupations such as unemployment, violence, drugs, mounting public debt, and political fragmentation.

Yet the scientific consensus on the likelihood of climate change has remained firm, despite the reluctance of governments and the scepticism of the critics. As John Firor remarked, in private the scientists are even more convinced of the reality of impending climate change than they indicate in the official documents (Firor 1990: ix). Likewise, the message from other sources, is quite clear:

If current trends continue, climatic conditions will change more quickly in the next few decades than they have in the last several millennia. Some

of the effects—such as the increases in average temperature and average
sea level—will be felt worldwide and can be predicted today with confi-
dence (Mintzer 1992: 3).

In this context the environmental priorities of North and South
may seem to be very far apart (White 1992a: 199; 1993a: 179–80).
Certainly the Earth Summit at Rio de Janeiro, in June, 1992, dis-
played little impression of political consensus, but rather was
dominated by recrimination and reluctant compromise on a few
very limited actions. However, if we move from those lists of priorities to a *systems view* of the human occupation of the planet,
then the linkages become very obvious. At that level of generalisation there is only one agenda, and that concerns the whole of
humanity, its technology, and its society (Goodland, Daly and El
Serafy 1992). The combined impact of energy consumption,
global income inequalities, and continued population growth can
be grasped only with a holistic vision. This viewpoint will be examined, briefly, in the urban context.

From a holistic point of view, there are three principal implications of environmental change for urban planners and managers.
The first is that the physical environment must now be treated as
dynamic, not as a given store of resources that may be pillaged
with impunity. The concept of equilibrium (the very lynchpin of
the market price mechanism), can no longer be taken as given,
other than in the very short term. Although there is disagreement
about what kind of climate change we might be facing, there
is virtually no disagreement that the future will be more uncertain than could previously be assumed (Graedel and Crutzen
1990: 23).

Second, many of the anticipated changes will be *irreversible*, at
least in the time frame of human civilisation. Greenhouse gases
and CFCs have a lifetime in the atmosphere of about 100 years;
so, unless some means can be found to retrieve them from the
atmosphere, the quantities *already released* will have a long-term,
unknown impact on climate and incoming ultra-violet radiation.
Other ground-level impacts such as tropical deforestation and
species extinction are, likewise, irreversible. Even in officially
commissioned documents, referred to above, it is assumed that

some change is already inevitable:

'Even if stringent measures are taken to reduce greenhouse gas emissions, some changes in climate and sea-level will occur anyway—a "climate change commitment". This is due to time-lags in the climate system response to changes in greenhouse gas concentrations that have already occurred. (Executive Summary of the First Report of the United Kingdom Climate Change Impacts Review Group, prepared at the request of the Department of the Environment' (Parry and contributors 1991).)

Third, even considered simply as a physical artifact, the urban system has developed serious defects. Some of these, such as traffic congestion, poor air quality, and poor water quality,

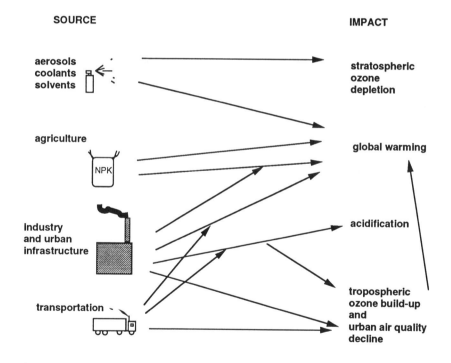

Note: A more detailed version of this diagram, which identifies the various gases, appears as Figure 5 .1.

Figure 1.3 Impacts of Human Activities on the Atmosphere

showed up in the early stages of industrialisation. The new environmental agenda will underline the deficiencies of modern urban technology in that it, too, results from an *energy-profligate land-use pattern* which paid virtually no attention to the physical environment in which the urban system evolved (Owens 1986; 1991). This generalisation is true both for the heating and cooling demands for buildings and for our dependence on motor vehicles for private transport. Figure 1.3 illustrates how the same sources contribute to a varied range of atmospheric problems from air quality near the ground to the accumulation of greenhouse gases and CFCs. Any useful approach to one of these problems, in an urban context, should take into account the other effects as well. This makes the choice of policies more complex, but it also means that a policy can serve more than one end. It also brings an additional advantage: if some of the environmental trends, like global warming, turn out to be less catastrophic than expected, then these mixed-ends policies will still be worthwhile. Such options are known as 'no-regrets' policies. One of the interesting results of approaching the city holistically is that we can find a surprising number of such policies. The argument thus implies that we should not let the uncertainty of the climate change scenarios be used as an excuse to delay the necessary changes to our urban-industrial technology. Rather—to the extent that the current scientific consensus is likely to be correct—we have every reason to intensify our search for improvements.

An analytical approach to an interdisciplinary problem

Environmental problems, by their very nature, require an inter-disciplinary approach which in turn requires an interdisciplinary language. One candidate for this role is the language of systems theory as applied to ecology (Odum, E. P. 1989; Odum, H. T. 1983). At the heart of systems theory is the definition of a system in terms of its boundary, the flows across the boundary, and the linkages within the boundary. Changes in the status of the system depend on positive feedbacks which enlarge or otherwise enhance the system, and negative feedbacks which reduce it. Elsewhere, I have described the application of this approach to environmental problems at many scales from the global to the individual and therefore that ground will not be retraced in detail here (White 1993a: 22–34).

At the global scale environmental change is best studied as a set of bio-geochemical cycles, following such key elements as water, carbon, nitrogen, sulphur, and phosphorous—and the other nutrients on which plants and animals depend (Munn 1986; Lovelock 1991: 107–32; Nisbet 1991: 4–50). The rate at which a particular particle moves through a cycle may be measured through the study of environmental pathways which show how much time a particle may stay in the various environmental media (Mackay 1991). One aspect of this study, of interest to plant and animal health, is the tendency for harmful residues to accumulate in fauna and flora—a process known as bio-accumulation or bio-magnification. On a global scale, this accumulation occurs in sinks, such as the atmosphere, the ocean, or the vegetal mass of plants and trees. On a smaller scale these accumulated residues become the dose in the dose–response relationship which is used to describe impacts on the health of human beings and other species.

So far, the language sounds more or less biological, but it can easily be transformed into something more familiar to the engineering world when the cycling particles are treated as physical materials, the mass of which may be traced from one system to another, such as from an upstream branch of a river system to a downstream confluence, or, further downstream, from the drainage basin to the ocean. The 'materials balance approach' to estimating these movements, and the transformation of energy, can be used to describe problems on a regional scale, such as the pollution of the Delaware Valley, the Ljubljana urban region, or the North Sea (Basta et al. 1978; Bower 1977; Dekker et al. 1987). In this book a variation of this approach will used to describe the mass movement of resources into an urban system and the extrusion of wastes. This approach has been presented as a form of urban metabolism (Boyden, et al. 1981; Meier 1970; Wolman 1965).

The impact of human activities on these natural environmental cycles first became apparent at the local level—wherever people cut down forests, excavated minerals and left wastes. However, it was in urban settlements that these effects were most marked, especially once humans had embarked on large scale industrialisation. This impact changed over time, first as the global population began a long period of continual expansion at the beginning of the nineteenth century, then as individuals used more goods *per capita* and lived longer. Thus the human population went through various transitions—a demographic transition from high birth rates and high death rates to low death rates and low birth rates; an energy transition from fuelwood, through coal to oil and natural gas; and a diet transition from local cereals and vegetables to one with an ever-increasing percentage of protein coming from meat and from fish. All of these transitions—to longer life, greater wealth, heavier dependence on fossil fuels, energy, and meat—imposed a heavier and heavier burden on the environment. Today that burden has passed through to the major biogeochemical cycles that affect the entire planet, such as the all-important carbon cycle.

Some of the decisions that have to be made by managers and planners can be analysed using traditional economic tools like cost–benefit analysis (Barde and Pearce 1991; Pearce et al. 1989; Pearce et al. 1990; World Bank 1991). But their application rests within a fairly circumscribed set of decisions for which the costs and benefits can readily be translated into monetary terms, and where the time frame is too short to be much affected by discounting. However, many of today's time frames are intergenerational, as the physical impacts of decisions taken today could endure for the foreseeable future. The situation is further complicated by the fact that the degree of uncertainty as to what these impacts will be is very large. Furthermore, as many writers have argued, this new situation implies that we must recognise that the economy rests upon the environment, and that the environment is not something external to the economy (Daly and Townsend 1993; Goodland et al. 1992; Pearce et al. 1989). Such recognition may come slowly, however, once it is understood that this situation implies that we may have to forego some resource depletion in the present in order to leave a viable resource base for future generations.

The symbiosis of the environment and the economy

The World Bank, a major player in international economic relations, has now accepted that:

> 'Economic development and sound environmental management are complementary aspects of the same agenda. Without adequate environmental protection, development will be undermined; without development, environmental protection will fail' (World Bank 1992: 25).

Yet, so far, the policy debate surrounding environmental change has made little progress at the level of national governments, despite widespread support among the industrial countries for the curtailing of CFCs, more limited support for reductions of carbon dioxide emissions, and the emergence of concern for deforestation, biodiversity, and the pollution of regional seas like the Mediterranean. The debate quickly runs into an *impasse* as one interest group, or another, feels threatened by the prospect of unpredictable, large scale changes in the way society organises itself. The temptation is to seize the very uncertainty of the outcome as an excuse for postponing all decisions. Yet, given the amount of inertia in the physical systems we have disturbed, to delay is to court disaster. Furthermore, major decisions are made in the face of uncertainty every day (Maunder 1989). Indeed such decisions are the very basis for the insurance business—one of the major growth sectors of a modern economy.

Again, as we make long lists of problems and priorities the difficulties are very apparent. But, if we think in systems terms, the issues begin to open up into possibilities for resolution, or at least mitigation, of the impacts. For example, the commonly held, negative assumptions which inhibit the development of environmental policy are that *any* environmentally positive step will:

- cause unemployment,
- cost money,
- render a company or country less competitive.

Yet there is abundant evidence that such policies can create jobs, save money and enhance a company's or country's competitive position. One need only look at the two fastest-growing economies in the post-war period—Japan and Germany (as the former Federal Republic)—to see a strong positive correlation between economic growth and an improved environmental record in some areas (OECD 1991a: 37). Obviously, pollution regulations could close factories and terminate jobs, but those same regulations will probably create new jobs elsewhere.

In the transportation sector, policies which benefit both the environment and the economy have been dubbed 'green and gold' policies (Goodwin 1991). For the industrial sector, a book was written over ten years ago, called *Profit from Pollution Prevention* (Campbell and Glenn 1982). When the details are examined there are many examples of environmentally benign policies which entail other benefits of an economic or social nature (Frosch and Gallopoulos 1990). As noted above, such opportunities are called 'no regrets policies'. Even if the spectre of environmental change were to fade tomorrow, such policies would still be worthwhile. Thus, a principal objective of this book is to incorporate the environmental change agenda into the practice of urban management and urban planning in the belief that the new concerns will intensify the search for remedies for some long-established defects in the urban-industrial system.

The organisation of subsequent chapters

Chapter Two reviews current thinking on global climate change, with an emphasis on the implications of recent findings for the management and planning of urban systems. It emphasises the interconnections between all living things and the ways in which they modify the environment in which they live. This chapter also examines the degree of uncertainty which surrounds predictions on climate change. However, it will be shown, that, despite the uncertainty, certain conclusions regarding the implications for managing urban systems are unavoidable.

Chapter Three looks more closely at the inside of the city, to understand exactly *how* it modifies its immediate environment— its own sources of water and energy, and its available sinks for the disposal of wastes, including the quality of its air-shed. The concept of urban metabolism is introduced, linking the city back to the most primitive organisms that modified their environment by processing resources and extruding wastes. One point that is emphasised throughout the book is that, even if public belief in global warming wavers during a run of cool summers, the long-term problems that are embedded in our urban technology and society will remain. The threat of global warming, due to the human contribution to greenhouse gases, is just the latest reminder of the precarious nature of the human tenancy of the planet.

The problems encountered in this enquiry are not simply phys-ical, and thus perhaps susceptible to remedies such as cleaner technology and the recycling of more materials. The deep problems are social, and they reside in the competitive and acquisitive drives that direct the course of Western industrial society, and all those other societies which are now being reshaped in the Western image. These complex difficulties are often bundled together under the seemingly innocuous term 'life-style', but there is nothing harmless about their implications for social injustice today and for future generations. For this reason Chapter Four examines the ways in which urban systems, despite some successes, have often failed to provide support for many members of society. In a sense, the physical blight of the urban fabric is a symptom of the failure of the social underpinnings of the system.

Chapters Five and Six return to the physical variables that define the urban system, in the context of the revisions to planning and management practice that are implied by increased environ-mental awareness. Chapter Five deals with the whole range of discharges to the air illustrated in Figures 1.2 and 1.3, including those discharges that affect local air quality, those that have long-distance impacts, and those that are changing the chemical com-position of the atmosphere. Chapter Six examines the complex impacts of discharges to ground and water, including both per-mitted discharges to landfills and unregulated discharges.

Throughout the debate on the best response to our environmental problems in and around the cities there is something of a chasm between those who structure the argument in terms of social and political factors and those who concentrate on the physical aspects of urban planning—such as slope, drainage and setbacks. The more socially critical observers decry the tendency among physical planners to reify the city, as if it somehow acts independently of human society. The critics point out that this tendency encourages a management and planning style which emphasises the physical instruments that are available to policy makers, while ignoring the social variables that shape those instruments. Much of this book is indeed organised in terms of physical variables (for example, Chapters Three, Five and Six). Thus Chapter Seven, on the concept of an ecological city, is designed to go some way to redress this apparent imbalance, although it should be taken as given, that, for humankind to live in harmony with nature, it must first live in harmony with itself.

The ecological city is a proposal for a new kind of urban system —one that can exist symbiotically with its environment, drawing on resources and producing wastes on a scale which the biosphere can absorb without undergoing rapid and major modification. This type of city will have to be 'intelligent' in the sense that the human body is intelligent, with an efficient circulatory system that nourishes all parts of the system and removes wastes, with a nervous system that immediately signals malfunctions in the system and makes the means available for the necessary repairs. This may sound a little futuristic, and it does not address the problem of the depletion of non-renewable resources. However, given the rate of environmental change to which we have now committed the whole planet, it goes without saying that the cities we *need* are going to be very different from the cities we have right now, and even more different from the cities we are likely to have, if present trends are allowed to continue.

Some parts of the book are designed to encourage the reader to think about the future in a way that might seem a little luxurious given the immediate problems faced by most urban planners and managers. However, the climate change scenario gives us little choice but to think in terms of a fifty-year time frame, at least. Similarly, other parts of the books take a look into the past to see how human society developed the techniques of urban living, and it even takes a brief look into the history of the earth, before the human impact became important. Despite all this, the book is focused on the problems of the present, and on what urban decision-makers can and have done about the environmental challenge. To underline this point Chapter Eight brings together all these problems in the context of Toronto, where it examines responses to environmental concerns at various levels of government. One of the encouraging themes from this chapter is that human organisations are capable of rapid response once consensus has been reached on the nature of the problem.

Further reading:

Douglas, I. (1983). *The Urban Environment*. London, Edward Arnold.

Firor, J. (1990). *The Changing Atmosphere. A Global Challenge*. New Haven, Yale University Press.

Friday, L. and R. Laskey, Eds. (1989). *The Fragile Environment. The Darwin College Lectures*. Cambridge, Cambridge University Press.

Goudie, A. (1986). *The Human Impact on the Natural Environment*. Cambridge, MIT Press.

Kristensen, T. and J. P. Paludan, Eds. (1988). *The Earth's Fragile Systems. Perspectives on Global Change*. IFIAS Research Series. Boulder, Westview Press.

Mintzer, I. M., Ed. (1992). *Confronting Climate Change. Risks, Implications and Responses*. Cambridge, Cambridge University Press.

Nilsson, A. (1992). *Greenhouse Earth*. Chichester, John Wiley & Sons.

Nisbet, E. G. (1991). *Leaving Eden. To Protect and Manage the Earth*. Cambridge, Cambridge University Press.

Scientific American (1990). *Managing Planet Earth. Readings from Scientific American*. New York, W. H. Freeman and Company.

2

Environmental Change

'The conclusion that greenhouse warming will soon outweigh other natural climatic fluctuations is very strong indeed, unless some very unusual natural event occurs' (Nisbet 1991: 307).

Within the debate surrounding development and the environment or, in other words, the human use of natural resources to create material goods and wastes, there are two deeply opposed sets of assumptions. One set emphasises the potential for development, the other set the constraints imposed by the environment. According to the former, development has been possible due to the capacity of human beings to learn and to adapt. At no time has the species, *taken as a whole*, failed to do this, although, locally, some groups have failed to adapt and they have paid the price. Given this track record there is no reason to assume that human inventiveness is now about to fail to meet the environmental challenge. According to the latter, the salient fact is that the planet is finite. Furthermore there is a growing weight of evidence to show that human numbers and their consumption habits are seriously disturbing the ecosystems on which humans and other life-forms depend.

This debate over the ability of the earth to support human activities and human responsibility for environmental degradation has a long history. Indeed it can be found in the writings of Plato and his contemporaries (Glacken 1967: 121). Despite the abundant evidence of the negative impacts of human activities on the environment, despite the impressive sales of *Limits to Growth* (Meadows et al. 1972), and despite the scare thrown into the world economy by the OPEC oil prices increases in the 1970s, the optimism of those who believed that a significant number of human beings will continue to survive and prosper has usually won the day. The optimists included those who believed that the price mechanism, which encouraged human inventiveness, would always ensure that resources would be available to fuel economic growth.

However, there is increasing evidence to suggest that the time for blind optimism is running out. The change was signified by an important shift in perception which took place in the 1980s, when environmental concerns moved from resources, or environmental 'sources', to the capacity of the environment to absorb our solid, liquid, and gaseous wastes in its various 'sinks'. Marine pollution and acid deposition have become problems of increasing concern, but people's attention has been claimed in a dramatic fashion by the depletion of the stratospheric ozone shield and the build-up of greenhouse gases, with the attendant danger of the heating up of the climate. The debate has moved on from environmental damage as the necessary price of progress, to global environmental change and the potential cost of catastrophe. The combination of all these interactions between humans and the planet has led to a call for 'sustainable development', as spelled out by the World Commission on Environment and Development in its report, *Our Common Future* (World Commission on Environment and Development 1987). This appeal is based on the assumption that more 'development' was still needed to provide for the unmet needs for the world's poor, and that this could be accomplished in a sustainable manner, such that the needs of future generations will not be compromised. Since then the implications of sustainable development have been vigorously debated (Brown 1993; MacNeill 1989; MacNeill et al. 1991; Redclift 1987; Rees 1992; Starke 1990). Some argue that the term 'development' is defined in so many different ways that the phrase 'sustainable use of resources' is more helpful (Bower 1993) and that is the phrase I have used in this book.

Some of the more alarming projections for environmental change, such as global warming, may not unfold as expected. The warming effect may be negated by some as yet unforeseen natural process, or human society may restructure itself so dramatically that it can curtail the warming effect within manageable limits. However, what is important from the physical planning perspective is that even without the threat of global warming, a great deal of preventative planning needs to be done to face up to the traditional, or established, agenda for urban planners. This agenda includes traffic congestion, affordable housing, poor air quality and poor water quality, noise, inadequate disposal of wastes, and inadequate recreational opportunities. What the new concern for environmental change does is to intensify the need to search for a better response, from planners and managers, to these long-standing problems.

Certain aspects of environmental change are more contentious than others. Thus, while large scale changes like regional acidification and stratospheric ozone depletion are already well-established in the high school curriculum, the even more alarming problem of potential global warming receives more cautious and limited treatment even in university-level texts. Some books on environmental management ignore the topic completely or give it only a passing mention. Despite this circumspect treatment by textbook writers there is a very large literature of governmental and quasi-governmental documents on climate change, with the emphasis placed on carbon-dioxide build-up and the associated prospect of global warming. Since the late 1980s the popular literature on the subject has become voluminous, which is not surprising because the consensus is that climate change is already underway. Indeed, only recently over 1600 senior scientists ('including 102 Nobel laureates—a majority of the living recipients of the Prize in the sciences') signed a two-page document titled *World Scientists' Warning to Humanity*, which stated:

> 'A great change in our stewardship of the earth and the life on it is required, if vast human misery is to be avoided and our global home on this planet is not to be irretrievably mutilated' (Union of Concerned Scientists 1992).

Despite the level of concern that is now being expressed by many scientists, some politicians, and members of the public, it will probably be a long time before such opinions become the accepted wisdom. A plausible explanation for this lag in response has been proposed by Paul and Anne Ehrlich in the context of the related problem of rapid global population growth:

'One of the toughest things for a population biologist to reconcile is the contrast between his or her recognition that civilisation is in imminent serious jeopardy and the modest level of concern that population issues generate among the public and even among elected officials. Much of the reason for this discrepancy lies in the slow development of the problem. People aren't scared because they evolved biologically and culturally to respond to short-term "fires" and to tune out long-term "trends" over which they had no control. Only if we do what doesn't come naturally—if we determinedly focus on what seem to be gradual or nearly imperceptible changes—can the outlines of our predicament be perceived clearly enough to be frightening' (Ehrlich and Ehrlich 1993: 56).

The reluctance, in some quarters, to accept that global warming is already inevitable is understandable as the implications of the threat strike at the underpinnings of our entire urban-industrial civilisation, based as it is on cheap energy derived from fossil fuels. Nowhere is the general reluctance to face up to this problem better captured than by John Firor's observation, based on numerous public lectures on atmospheric change:

'The question I received most often was not about detail; it was about a request for judgment. "All that science is okay," people seemed to say, "but tell us straight—are we in trouble or not?"' (1990: vii).

He devotes a chapter to this simple question (to which there is no simple answer) in his lucid book, *The Changing Atmosphere*, and concludes:

'the best efforts of the world's scientists foresee a rapid heating of the climate, and a vigorous search for reasons not to be concerned has so far failed' (1990: 96).

In the last 40 years we can look back and see that some adverse environmental changes have been reversed. For example, in the United Kingdom, we have the Clean Air Acts, the return of trout to the Thames, and the gradual replenishment of groundwater in the London Basin aquifer. Some endangered species have been nursed back from the brink of extinction. Indeed, there are even suggestions of the possibility of major changes in urban policy with regard to the private car which could alleviate a lot of environmental problems simultaneously (Goodwin 1992;

Parkhurst 1992). In cases such as these we can see to what extent the environmental balance was restored simply by halting the adverse human activity (e.g. burning coal) and to what extent it required positive rehabilitative actions (e.g. restocking the Thames with trout). The time and cost (direct and indirect) could also be estimated. Some of these examples might suggest that some aspects of environmental change—once recognised by decision-makers as adverse—may readily be reversed. Unfortunately some changes would take a very long time to reverse; others are so poorly understood that the best course of action is not clear; and some changes may not be reversible at all.

Natural environmental change

A major objective of this book is to persuade the reader that there are no quick technological fixes to the environmental problems that humankind has blindly created. A long-term view is essential if ameliorative actions are to be initiated and maintained. A less anthropomorphic view of the world would also help. In order to gain such a perspective it might be useful to review, very briefly, the natural evolution of the environment before the influence of people was felt, indeed from the beginning of the history of the earth. This might also serve to illustrate how much the environment can change with regard to such basic components as the composition of the atmosphere and the distribution of land and sea. Of course these major changes took place very slowly, from the perspective of the human time frame. Indeed, what is alarming about the current predicament is not just the changes that are implied by a human-induced doubling of atmospheric carbon dioxide, for example, but also the extreme rapidity with which such changes are projected to occur. Yet sceptics on global warming usually point to the relatively small changes in temperature that are predicted, and to the apparently slow rate of change that is predicted. I think the reasons for this divergence of opinion may be attributed to several factors which condition the debate. First, very few of the sceptics are natural scientists, so they tend to compare these predicted physical changes with the rate of change of human systems, such as rates of change of employment, interest, or inflation. Second, the natural scientists who have developed the predictions are by nature extremely cautious. They tend to say not 'when' but 'if'. And the 'ifs' and the double negatives multiply if the documents are written by a committee or repeatedly reviewed by panels (as is usually the case). As John Firor remarked: 'many of the authors I know well hold much stronger, more definite views than emerge from their committee endeavours' (1990: ix). In order to stand back and put the human impact on the environment in context, people, as members of an increasingly urban-industrial world, must see themselves as part of the natural world, just as their forbears did. (For interesting treatments of this subject, from different perspectives, see Crosby 1986; Glacken 1967; and Thomas 1983.) Now however, we need to see ourselves not only as part of a cultural landscape, domesticating some animals and exterminating others, cutting down forests and planting crops, but as a species that can rapidly change the composition of the atmosphere. In others words we must see the world as one interconnected system in which people are playing a major catalytic role.

Over the last few years James Lovelock has advanced the Gaia hypothesis, which states that the earth may be viewed as a single living organism which is not only becoming an increasingly complex entity but is also 'a system that has the capacity to regulate the temperature and the composition of the Earth's surface and keep it comfortable for living organisms' (Lovelock 1988: 31). (The following brief description of earth's history draws on *The Ages of Gaia* and *Gaia—The Practical Science of Planetary Medicine* (Lovelock 1988; Lovelock 1991).

The first billion of the Earth's 4.6 billion years were devoid of organic life. Radioactivity was high, vulcanicity was much more widespread than today, temperatures were much higher, and the atmosphere consisted mainly of carbon dioxide. For obvious reasons this time is referred to as the Hadean period. The origins of the bacterial life that emerged in the succeeding, Archean, period remain disputed. What is generally accepted is that these first, unicellular organisms produced oxygen as a by-product of photosynthesis and this oxygen combined with hydrogen to replenish the store of water which might otherwise have been lost to space, and thus left Earth as dry as Mars is today. Carbon dioxide became less dominant in the atmosphere as fermenting bacteria produced methane. Lovelock suggests that oxygen was present in the atmosphere only in trace amounts, less than 1%. More complex multicellular organisms in the Proterozoic period replaced methane with oxygen and so laid the foundation for the modern composition of the atmosphere and thereby made possible the evolution of animals, as well as more complex plants, in the current, Phanerozoic, period. Now oxygen accounts for 21 % of the atmosphere and it is carbon dioxide which has become the trace gas. All this is mentioned only to underline the dynamic aspects of the biosphere. It has changed before: human beings are in the process of changing it again, principally by discharging heat-trapping gases to the air and removing the forests which act as a sink for carbon dioxide.

The human impact on the environment

Since the Neolithic era when people shifted from hunting and gathering to farming, and to living in permanent settlements, they have had an ever deepening impact on the natural environment. In so doing they have secured themselves a dominant niche in all of the world's habitable ecosystems, from the tundra to the tropical rainforest. In the last 600 years people grew steadily in number until the time of the industrial revolution; then the growth curve shifted from steady to exponential. *The world's human population has doubled since 1950 to reach 5.5 billion in 1992.* (See Figure 2.1) (Thus, it has doubled in the lifetime of this author, his publisher, and presumably many of our readers.) No-one can predict where this remarkable biological expansion may end, although there is a growing realisation that this trend is not sustainable. The growth of the human population and its evolving technology are the driving forces behind the major changes in the biosphere.

In the early stages of the industrial revolution, in nineteenth century Europe and North America, some side-effects of population growth, urbanisation and technological change were very visible. The industrial landscape was dotted with slag heaps and littered with depressions from gravel pits and subsidence from mining (Goudie 1986: 204). In the major industrial centres air quality was

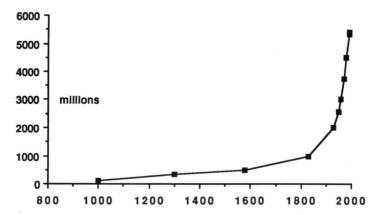

Figure 2.1   The Growth of the Human Population. *Sources*: Brown et al. 1992; McKeown 1976

poor and aquifers were depleted to meet the demands of cities and factories. However, although these impacts were widespread they were also quite local. The beginnings of environmental concern in the mid-twentieth century led to some remedial actions such as Clean Air Acts. Higher chimney stacks also improved local air quality, although the more widely scattered deposits of sulphur oxides and nitrogen oxides resulted in acidification on a regional scale beginning in the 1950s and 1960s. Slowly a technological response has emerged to curb some of these emissions through the installation of filters or scrubbers on chimney outlets and by switching to less-polluting types of fuel.

Hard on the heels of the acidification problem came the discovery that the use of the synthetic compounds known as CFCs (for chlorofluorocarbons) was depleting the stratospheric ozone layer which shields the earth from ultra-violet radiation. (See Figure 2.2.) This radiation is highly inimical to most plant and animal life, from phytoplankton in the ocean to human beings on the beach. The fear of skin cancer and eye damage brought a fairly rapid response from international leaders and a protocol was signed in Montreal in 1987 to reduce the production of CFCs. This action took place only thirteen years after scientists first published their findings on the CFC impact on the ozone layer (Benedick 1991; Roan 1989). In terms of political response to scientific warning this reaction was very swift.

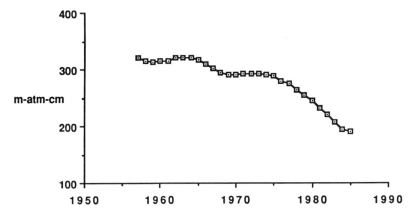

Figure 2.2 Stratospheric Ozone Depletion, Halley Bay, Antarctica. *Source*: Based on UNEP 1987: 23

While reluctant steps were being taken to address the acidification issue and more rapid action taken on CFCs, a consensus on global warming was emerging. The Intergovernmental Panel on Climate Change (IPCC) was established in 1988; it published its first report in 1990 and it has continued to update its assessment continually since then. Despite the momentous implications of the global warming hypothesis, the consensus emerged quickly and has continued to firm up. In the words of the panel the overall conclusion is that:

> 'Findings of scientific research since 1990 do not affect our fundamental understanding of the science of the greenhouse effect and either confirm or do not justify alteration of the major conclusions of the first IPCC Scientific Assessment, in particular the following:
> - emissions resulting from human activities are substantially increasing the atmospheric concentrations of the greenhouses gases: carbon dioxide, methane, chlorofluorocarbons, and nitrous oxide;
> - the evidence from modelling studies, from observations and from the sensitivity analyses indicate that the sensitivity of global mean surface temperatures to doubling CO_2 is unlikely to lie outside the range 1.5 to $4.5°C'$ (Houghton et al. 1992: 5).*

The most famous of the observations referred to above are the measurements made of carbon dioxide in the atmosphere at Mauna Loa, Hawaii, begun by Charles Keeling in 1957 (Figure 2.3). This 35-year record has since been corroborated from the

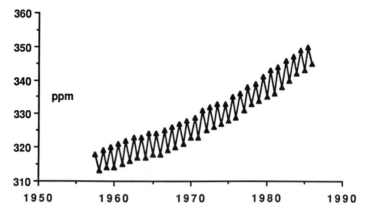

Figure 2.3 Carbon Dioxide Build-up, Mauna Loa, Hawaii. *Source:* Based on Firor 1990: 50

very beginning of the Industrial Revolution, based on the analysis of samples of air trapped in the polar ice caps (Figure 2.4). Carbon dioxide is the principal greenhouse gas, although methane, nitrous oxide and CFCs also make significant contributions (Figure 2.5). The growing presence of these gases in the atmosphere is not disputed even by the most sceptical critics of the global warming projections.

In order to underline the strength of the consensus reached

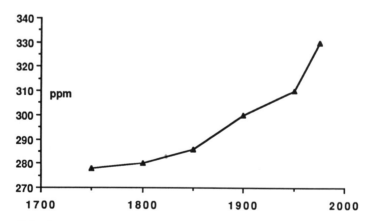

Figure 2.4 Carbon Dioxide Build-up from Polar Ice Cores. *Source:* Based on Firor 1990: 51

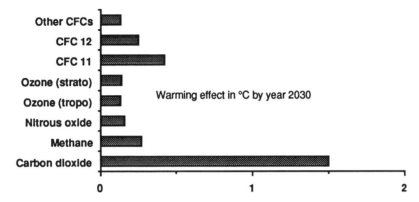

Figure 2.5 Relative Warming Impact of the Greenhouse Gases. *Source*: Based on UNEP 1987: 25

on the matter, the editors of the IPCC report noted, in the Preface, that:

> 'The conclusions ... are based entirely on the supporting scientific material published here, which has been prepared by leading scientists and exposed to a widespread and thorough peer review. ... Generation of the background papers involved ... 118 scientists from 22 countries. A further 380 scientists from 63 countries and 18 UN or non-governmental organizations participated in the peer review ... It can therefore be regarded as an authoritative statement of the contemporary views of the international scientific community' (Houghton et al. 1992: xi).

The change in the degrees Centigrade may seem small to some readers, but it needs to be compared with the temperature difference between today and the depth of the last ice age, which was only 2.5°C. As James Lovelock summed up the situation:

> 'We have changed the atmosphere more *already* (my italics) than took place between the last glaciation and now. The consequences, a rise of temperature comparable to that between the glaciation and now, are inevitable' (1991: 168).

Associated with the increased temperature is an estimated sea-level rise 'due to oceanic thermal expansion alone' (Houghton et al. 1992: 17) of 2 to 4 centimetres per decade. This projection does not include the impact of the possible melting of glaciers or either of the polar ice caps; thus, this is a conservative projection.

The implications of the anticipated changes in the composition of the atmosphere and the rise in sea-level will be examined throughout this book and will not be taken up in detail here. For the time being the range of impacts for cities can be briefly divided into impacts *on* the inputs that are brought in to keep urban systems functioning and the impacts *of* those wastes that are sent out, either inadvertently (like gases) or more deliberately (like liquids and solids).

First, let us look at the inputs. Global warming will have major impacts on agricultural productivity and hence on food security. Local and regional impacts are still difficult to predict but the global harvest is likely to be seriously reduced if the cereal-producing continental heartlands suffer a decline in rainfall—and this is one of the most consistent regional predictions of the climate change models. The same disruption in the rainfall patterns could reduce water availability for cities also. Some coastal aquifers would suffer from saline intrusion due to the rising sea-level, which will compound the problems in those coastal areas where the aquifer is already overdrawn. A warmer world is expected to increase the frequency of storms, which in turn will increase the danger of floods. Some hydroelectric sources may be diminished by low-flow problems in the river basins on which they depend. However, despite all the uncertainties involved in estimating probable impacts, many detailed studies of the implications of global warming have already been carried out (Houghton et al. 1992; Kellogg and Schware 1981; Mintzer 1992; Parry and contributors 1991).

Energy is the key element, both as an input (for transportation, space heating and cooling, and industrial processing) and because the carbon dioxide by-product of fossil fuel combustion must be curtailed in order to lessen the impact of global warming. Carbon dioxide is currently contributing nearly half of the enhanced greenhouse effect (Figure 2.5). The use of fossil fuels always produces carbon dioxide, which is why the global warming strikes at the heart of our urban-industrial technology, all of which is based on the availability of cheap fossil fuels. In retrospect, the 1970s' energy crisis, which was caused by OPEC's unilateral increase in oil prices, may prove to be a dummy run for the full impact of the need to permanently reduce fossil fuel use.

In the end, the power of OPEC was broken by bringing in new oil fields by non-OPEC producers. But the lesson is clear: our urban-industrial society is extremely vulnerable to sharp increases in the price of energy, especially in the transportation sector. In some countries the industrial sector has significantly reduced its energy use per unit of output, although much more could be done. Households in the richer countries have tended to increase their energy consumption, both for air conditioning and for the proliferation of appliances, such as freezers, dishwashers, and electronic goods. The broad picture shows that industry has already begun to respond to the new emergency, but households and the transportation sector—as a whole—have not.

As noted in Chapter One (Figures 1.2 and 1.3), other gaseous wastes from cities have been creating problems since the onset of the industrial revolution, and even from the domestic burning of coal before that time. As all the fuel uses and all the wastes produced are interlinked it makes sense to develop an integrated policy on discharges to the air, rather than focusing on a single problem, even on one with such major implications as the enhanced greenhouse effect. An integrated policy on discharges to the air is the subject of Chapter Five.

There are also serious problems associated with the discharge of solid and liquid wastes to the ground and to the water, although the impacts may be less far-reaching in their possible consequences. The landfill crisis has been building up inexorably around the world's major cities as disposal sites become more difficult to find, even for ordinary household wastes. This problem has been signalled repeatedly as communities adjacent to the cities have refused to accept new landfill facilities, and thus the search for sites has grown steadily wider, and is now international in scope. Although these problems are not usually included in the term 'environmental change', they nonetheless represent an important stage in evolution in the human occupation of the planet, and are an important aspect of urban environmental quality management. As populations increase and the urbanisation trend continues, cities grow in size and they become less efficient transformers of materials. Our technology and our way of life must change in order to deal with these difficulties. In general this implies a shift away from the traditional dynamic of a

Western economy which consists of creating a supply of goods to meet ever-expanding demand. What is beginning to be addressed now, especially in the supply of water and energy to cities, is the management of demand, where 'management' is a euphemism for reduction. This will not be achieved without significant changes in the modern urban lifestyle found in the richer countries.

Unresolved issues related to global warming

Although the nature and implications of the greenhouse effect are well understood at a certain level of generality, many aspects of the phenomenon remain unclear. The speed at which the warming will take place (the 'transient scenario'), is probably the most fundamental unknown factor. The IPCC and similar bodies prefer to state their projections in terms of the impact of a carbon dioxide presence in the atmosphere when that quantity is double what it normally is without human interference. Then a timescale for this doubled CO_2 is affixed according to whether the human output of the gas will continue to increase at the present rate, at a higher rate, or at a lower rate. As the human response to the prospect of global warming is highly uncertain this is as close to a prediction as one can come.

Several other aspects of the science of the greenhouse effect are also difficult to anticipate. For example, it is believed that the increase in sulphur dioxide (a principal cause of acidification) in the atmosphere has a cooling effect on surface temperatures. Thus, if we reduce the acid rain problem we may increase the warming problem. Similarly, it is now believed that CFCs (which contribute to warming in the lower atmosphere) may have a cooling effect in the upper atmosphere. Therefore, the net impact of CFCs on air temperatures becomes more complex. The net impact of clouds on temperature is also disputed because, although their water vapour will trap outgoing long-wave radiation, they will also reflect away some of the incoming short-wave radiation.

To complicate matters still further, although most predictions (as noted above) suggest a drying out of the mid-latitude continental interiors, estimates of the regional impacts are highly speculative. As long as the regional effects are unknown then decision-makers in all countries may continue to hold out the hope that global warming will be beneficial to their patch of the globe. In countries where the agricultural growing season is constrained by low temperatures (rather than low rainfall), this may seem like an enticing possibility. But even here the net effects are as yet impossible to predict because, although a longer run of frost-free days will encourage plant growth, the warmer temperatures will reduce soil moisture through higher rates of evaporation. Of course, increased rainfall might compensate for that moisture loss. Then again, pests might grow more rapidly than cultivated plants.

One thing that is certain is that the level of uncertainty will go up, and, in general, uncertainty is costly for farming, for transportation, and for all aspects of the operation of a technically intricate society. Higher temperatures will probably increase the frequency of storms, and higher sea-level will threaten coastal regions. The combination of higher sea-level and more storms has clearly negative connotations for settlements and agriculture in coastal regions, as well as for offshore oil rigs. All of these factors have implications that relate specially to the planning and management of urban systems and the hinterlands that sustain them.

Implications of global warming for urban systems

This section serves as an introduction only, as other aspects of the implications of global warming will be developed in later chapters. For these introductory purposes, the implications may be categorised, from the human perspective, as:

- the physical impacts on cities,
- the health implications for humans, and
- the economic implications for humans.

Some of the physical impacts have already been noted. The most far-reaching is certainly sea level rise, which is projected by the IPCC to vary between 2 and 4 centimetres per decade under the business-as-usual scenario. This may not seem much but one has only to reflect on the damage that was caused in the Netherlands in 1953 in a once-in-a-century storm and accompanying floods, or the more recent and even more horrific floods in Bangladesh, to realise just how vulnerable coastal societies are to more frequent floods. Some countries have already commissioned studies on the need for improved coastal defences to combat rising sea levels (Delft Hydraulics 1988; Environment Canada 1986; Environment Canada 1987). A less dramatic (but just as costly) impact will be felt through the additional work that will have to be done to ensure the evacuation of rainwater and liquid wastes from coastal and estuarine cities. Figure 2.6 sketches some of these hydrological relationships, which are examined in more detail in Chapter Six. The purpose of the sketch is to emphasise the fact that although sea-walls can be built to reduce the encroachment of the sea on the surface, this does not resolve the problem of sea-water intrusion under the waterline, by infiltration into the groundwater. Such infiltration could occur if the water table falls below sea-level, which could result from either the overpumping of the groundwater or a rise in sea-level, and especially through a combination of the two. This reverses the direction of groundwater flow which normally runs from the land to the sea. Long Island, New York, and Southern California are two coastal regions of the United States that have already had to resort to recharging their aquifers, artificially, to compensate for overdrawing local groundwater. Of necessity, the water needed for the recharge operation must be brought in from more distant sources.

The increase in surface temperatures will be in addition to the

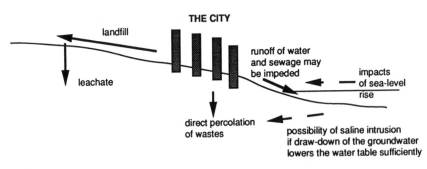

Figure 2.6 Some Implications of Sea-level Rise for Urban Discharges to Ground and Water

already measurable heat-island effect which is found in all large cities. This will increase the demand for cooling and hence the demand for energy and for CFCs or CFC-substitutes. Increased evaporation will also increase the demand for water. Under the present technology, living in warmer cities, possibly with water shortages, has mostly negative implications for human health, both directly through heat stress and indirectly through the respiratory implications of poor air quality. Disruptions to the drainage and sewage systems will further exacerbate the risks to health. In the richer countries of the North the increased costs of dealing with these problems might be manageable, at least in the first few decades of what has been called the coming 'greenhouse century' (Schneider 1990). The impacts in the poorer countries of the South will be much more severe as conditions for the majority of the people are already marginal. Air quality is already having severe health impacts, and water shortages are the norm. The escalation of these problems, and their growing impact on prospects for economic development are signalled by the devotion of the World Bank's *World Development Report* to environmental issues in 1992 and to health issues in 1993 (World Bank 1992; World Bank 1993).

Some of the economic implications have already been indicated. There will be substantial public sector costs for infrastructure maintenance and extension. Poorer health means more workdays lost and lower productivity from those who are at work. The World Bank has recently begun to measure the 'global burden of disease' attributable to premature deaths and to disability (World Bank 1993: 25). In addition to these measurable impacts there are intangible costs due to the negative impact on private investment which may stem from the uncertainty that is ushered in by environmental change. It is likely that the price of fuel, water, and agricultural products will rise to reflect both scarcity and uncertainty. All of the above rather discouraging statements are based on an extrapolation from the present trends which conform to the business-as-usual scenario, whereby greenhouse gas emissions are expected to grow proportionately with the global population and the global economy. However, one of the objectives of this book is to identify practical alternatives to this scenario.

If it is accepted that there are likely to be heavy costs attached to inaction then perhaps investment in ameliorative measures will seem more attractive. First, in concluding this introductory assessment of the probable implications of environmental change for urban systems, it can be said that cities are both a victim and a perpetrator of the processes at work. This, and others aspects of the problem, mean that urban managers and planners must take a holistic view of the situation. There is little to be gained by piecemeal technological fixes. Second, the global nature of atmospheric change means that international cooperation on the problem is essential. Individual national efforts to curb global warming and other major environmental changes will have only symbolic value. Lastly, a strong consensus has emerged on the likelihood of atmospheric change, and this means that the room for honest doubt is now extremely small.

Despite the consensus on atmospheric change and despite the measurable costs of past environmental neglect the way forward is far from clear. Holistic urban management and international cooperation will not smoothly slip into place to steer humanity onto a safer course. Serious environmental problems have been well known for decades before action is taken. Among the obstacles to action is the lack of congruence between ecosystem boundaries—such as coastlines and watersheds—and administrative boundaries, both local and international (Bower and Koudstaal 1986). Thus, although the next chapter examines the role of urban systems within the natural ecosystems in which they exist, it is not assumed that simply recognising this physical dependence of the city on the biosphere will readily bring us to a point where holistic urban management can be put in place.

Further reading:

Bradbury, I. (1991). *The Biosphere*. London, Belhaven Press.
Firor, J. (1990). *The Changing Atmosphere. A Global Challenge*. New Haven, Yale University Press.
Goudie, A. (1986). *The Human Impact on the Natural Environment*. Cambridge, MIT Press.
Gribbin, J. (1990). *Hothouse Earth. The Greenhouse Effect and Gaia*. New York, Grove Weidenfeld.

Houghton, J. T., Callander B. A., et al., Eds. (1992). *Climate Change 1992. The Supplementary Report to the IPCC Scientific Assessment.* Cambridge, Cambridge University Press.

Lovelock, J. (1991). *Gaia. The Practical Science of Planetary Medicine.* London, Gaia Books Ltd.

Mintzer, I. M., Ed. (1992). *Confronting Climate Change. Risks, Implications and Responses.* Cambridge, Cambridge University Press.

Nilsson, A. (1992). *Greenhouse Earth.* Chichester, John Wiley & Sons.

Schneider, S. H. (1990). *Global Warming. Are We Entering the Greenhouse Century?* New York, Vintage Books.

Scientific American (1990). *Managing Planet Earth. Readings from Scientific American.* New York, W. H. Freeman and Company.

3

Urban Metabolism

'The metabolic requirements of a city can be defined as all the materials and commodities needed to sustain the city's inhabitants at home, at work and at play. Over a period of time these requirements include even the construction materials needed to build and rebuild the city itself. The metabolic cycle is not completed until the wastes and residues of daily life have been removed and disposed of with a minimum of nuisance and hazard.

As man has come to appreciate that the earth is a closed ecological system usual methods that once appeared satisfactory for the disposal of wastes no longer seem acceptable. He has the daily evidence of his eyes and nose to tell him that the planet cannot assimilate without limit the untreated wastes of his civilisation' (Wolman 1965: 177).

In the previous chapter reference was made to the input of materials and energy necessary to sustain a city and reference was also made to the output of its wastes. Early attempts to model these flows were based on input–output tables that had been developed to predict the impact of inter-sectoral demands within an economy (Isard 1972; Leontief 1970). Initially the flows were treated as linearly dependent on one another and unchanging over time. In other words the technological coefficients that described how much one sector drew from another were treated as linear and fixed. Later, more complex versions of the basic input–output model dropped both these assumptions. It was soon found, however, that this kind of framework was ill-suited to even the simplest treatment of environmental processes, because of the complexity of the feedbacks between the various physical impacts of urban systems on the environment. A different approach was developed which attempted to measure all the major physical flows entrained by economic activities. This became known as the 'materials balance approach' or sometimes as 'residuals and environmental quality management'—'REQM', for short (Basta and Bower 1982; Basta et al. 1978; Bower 1977). The most important 'materials' were energy, water, and nutrients. (For an analysis of these flows see Douglas (1983), Chapters Four, Five and Six, respectively.) Later, toxic substances, like PCBs and dioxin, were recognised as being significant outputs, even though the quantities produced were small. It is not always necessary to measure these quantities directly because the financial value, or better still, the actual tonnage of goods produced can be used to give a rough idea of the output of residuals, if one is prepared to make assumptions regarding the type of technology employed.

Blair Bower defined a 'residual' in the following way:

> 'All human activities—households, farming, manufacturing, mining, transportation—result in the generation of residuals. This is because no production or use activity transforms all the inputs to the activity into desired products or services. The remaining flows of materials and/or energy from the activity are termed non-product outputs. If a non-product output has no value in existing markets or a value *less* than the costs of collecting, processing and transporting it for input into the same or another activity, the non-product output is termed a residual. Thus, residual is defined in an economic sense' (Bower 1977: 2).

The focus of this approach is ambient (i.e. outdoor) environmental quality, which can be measured by such indicators as:

> 'concentrations of dissolved oxygen in a river or lake; biomass of fish per unit volume of a water body; concentration of nitrates in ground water, concentration of sulphur dioxide in the urban atmosphere; hectares of land disturbed by surface mining; and hectares of land having uncontrolled dumps of solid residuals' (Bower 1977: 1).

From the beginning, the REQM approach combined an engineering and an economic perspective on the effect of human activities on the environment.

REQM evolved alongside the development of the concept of urban metabolism, where metabolism is defined as 'the sum of the chemical reactions that occur within living organisms' (Oxford University Press 1992: 189).This metabolism analogy helps us to put together the many complex subsystems within a city and to anticipate some of the problems that might occur as the system, as a whole, becomes larger. For example, James Lovelock described the evolution of the first multi-cellular organisms and noted:

> 'a spherical community of cells, larger than a few millimetres in diameter, would have difficulties in sustaining the supply of oxygen, and the removal of carbon dioxide from its interior' (1991: 105).

This is very similar to the problem that cities develop beyond a certain size (whatever their degree of wealth and infrastructure). Water and power become more expensive to bring in, and wastes to flush, or haul out, as distances from the centre to the periphery increase. The most visible disadvantage to many citizens is the lengthening journey to work and the degeneration of the rush hour into a day-long traffic jam. A less visible waste is the spoilage of food supplies:

> 'In New York and London about 50 percent of the fresh vegetables and fruits are spoiled before they reach the customer. Losses of 30–40 percent are common in cities of a few million inhabitants, while those of a few hundred thousand report much smaller losses when their market is independent of metropolitan wholesale markets' (Meier 1972, quoted in Douglas 1983: 69).

Some biological solutions to this kind of difficulty, as noted by Lovelock, are two-dimensional flat organisms, open-mesh three-dimensional sponges, and the development of circulatory systems. (All three of these strategies are of relevance to cities, as will be shown in Chapter Seven.)

Nonetheless, despite the mental stimulus provided by these biological metaphors, cities differ from biological organisms in at least one important respect—organisms have a known cycle of life, death, and decay. Such a cycle may be described for some cities in the past, but it cannot be proposed for cities that are still evolving. Thus:

> 'the organism analogy does not greatly help in understanding city change. However, the metabolic analogy is useful, reminding us that great cities are biologically parasites in their use of vital resources, air, water and food, in urban metabolism' (Douglas 1983: 11).

The rest of this chapter will explore some applications of the concept, because I agree with Ian Douglas that this parasitic aspect of cities is an important key to managing the impact of cities on the biosphere. One can imagine that a city could live in symbiosis with its surrounding region, each element—urban and rural—producing goods the other element needed, and recirculating their residuals in a fairly sustainable way. Indeed before the modern phase of industrialisation most cities had little choice but to operate in this manner for all their everyday needs like food, water, energy, and building materials, because only luxury goods could support the high cost of long-distance transportation in pre-industrial times. Even today, lower-income cities have far less impact on the biosphere than do the richer cities (Meier 1970; White and Whitney 1992). Indeed one can readily show that cities extend their dependence for inputs to ever-more distant regions if they grow richer, as did most cities of the North from the nineteenth century onwards (Girardet 1992: 48–9).

The problem we now face is that it seems clear that the biosphere cannot support even the world's present 5.5 billion people in this manner. The question then arises: 'Rather than the poorer cities trying to emulate the richer ones in their pattern of consumption, should not the rich try to emulate the poor by living in what Richard Meier called "resource-conserving cities" (Meier 1970)?' In order to consider what this might imply we can study the metabolism of a city as it interacts with its hinterland to obtain the supply of materials and energy, and to dispose of its wastes.

Abel Wolman's concept of urban metabolism

Total population, number of households, areal extent, and employment breakdown are the statistics most commonly used to indicate the size of cities; but these are just aggregates which give little or no immediate indication of the impact of a city on the environment. Nonetheless, Abel Wolman used population alone to postulate the impact of a hypothetical American city, when he focused on three 'metabolic problems that have become more acute as cities have become larger and whose solution rests almost entirely in the hands of the local administrator' (Wolman

1965: 179). The main problems were water supply, disposal of sewage, and control of air pollution.The estimates were not based on field measurements for a particular city; they were derived from national totals, divided on a *per capita* basis (Figure 3.1). He did not analyse those metabolic inputs which are 'handled routinely, in part through local initiative and in part through large

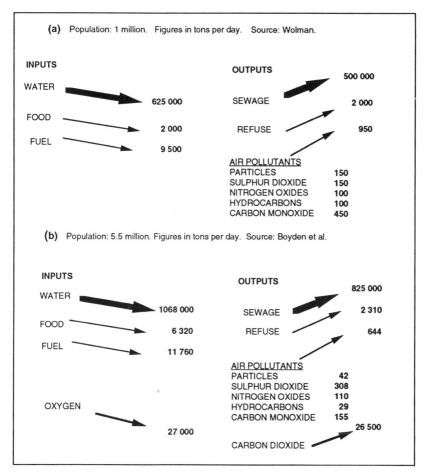

(a) Population: 1 million. Figures in tons per day. Source: Wolman.

INPUTS

WATER

625 000

FOOD

2 000

FUEL

9 500

OUTPUTS

500 000

SEWAGE   2 000

REFUSE   950

AIR POLLUTANTS
PARTICLES   150
SULPHUR DIOXIDE   150
NITROGEN OXIDES   100
HYDROCARBONS   100
CARBON MONOXIDE   450

(b) Population: 5.5 million. Figures in tons per day. Source: Boyden et al.

INPUTS

WATER

1068 000

FOOD

6 320

FUEL

11 760

OXYGEN

27 000

OUTPUTS

825 000

SEWAGE   2 310

REFUSE   644

AIR POLLUTANTS
PARTICLES   42
SULPHUR DIOXIDE   308
NITROGEN OXIDES   110
HYDROCARBONS   29
CARBON MONOXIDE   155

26 500

CARBON DIOXIDE

(In terms of quantity note the overwhelming preponderance of the water-sewage inflow-outflow. In the Figure 3 . 2 this quantity has been divided by 100 to make it more comparable to the other flows.)

Figure 3.1(a)   Wolman's Hypothetical American City; (b) The Metabolism of Hong Kong

organisations (public and private)'—inputs such as 'food, fuel, clothing, durable goods, construction materials and electric energy'.

At the time Wolman wrote his article a major public concern in the United States was air pollution, as it was highly visible, persistent, and increasing as car ownership continued to grow. People were also concerned about the provision of water. New York State was suffering from water shortages resulting from inadequate long-term planning and exacerbated by five dry years. Wolman noted:

> 'it is ironic that New York City ... should be running short of water while billions of gallons of fresh water flow past it to the sea. It is not easy for people in arid countries, or even for those living in the southwestern part of the U.S., to have much sympathy with New York's plight' (1965: 179).

A third major problem was becoming apparent—the inadequate treatment of sewage. The problem was most evident in shallow Lake Erie, where beaches were being closed and the fishery was suffering from oxygen depletion and toxic pollution.

Part of the value of Wolman's article was that it focused people's attention on those aspects of urban systems that could be quantified. By simply multiplying the *per capita* use of resources and production of residuals by population projections he showed that you could roughly predict those system-wide impacts that could be managed by local authorities, or, if they lay outside local jurisdiction, would be handled by state or national legislation. The concept of metabolism underlined the fact that people—by the very act of using resources—also create wastes. Although the goods have been 'consumed' in an economic sense, in an ecosystem sense the materials and energy *have simply been transformed into residuals*, both materials and energy. What form do these residuals take? Blair Bower offers the following classification of residuals, or non-product outputs:

- materials:
  —liquid
  —gaseous
  —solid

- energy:
  —heat
  —noise
  —radioactivity
(Bower, no date).

Obviously these highly varied residuals could be managed separately, but the organic analogy of metabolism allows the planner and the citizen to think in systems-wide terms over time, rather than just focus on the narrow concerns of one type of residual in the immediate present. Although such organic analogies have their dangers, Wolman's use of the term refers purely to the physical interaction of the city with some aspects of its environment; it does not imply any commitment to organic analogies about the way in which a city might grow and then decline.

His analysis, although intended only to be illustrative of the metabolism concept and not intended as a comprehensive balance of all material and energy inputs and outputs, did produce some preliminary conclusions. He found that water quality was a more critical factor than air quality, at least in terms of meeting health objectives. He also noted that discharges to the air were much more difficult to manage than the water cycle because of their multiple and mobile sources, especially from the transportation sector. (A few years later a study in the Delaware Valley found that the US federal air quality regulations were between six to eight times more expensive to meet than were water standards (Spofford et al. 1977: 101).) Wolman suggested that water was wastefully used in cities because the visible cost to the user reflected, at best, only the costs of delivery, and excluded the costs of production and restoration. He also drew attention to what has since become widely recognised as the lag time between water supply and the provision of water treatment. Even now there are large cities in Canada (including Victoria and Halifax) that discharge all their sewage to the ocean in untreated form (Environment Canada 1990: 21). This truly is a waste of water, as, with adequate treatment, urban water can almost always be restored and re-used. What Wolman's metabolism approach demonstrated was the need to see urban water as part of the hydrological cycle, not just a commodity that was produced, used, and discarded. Thus we can apply the metabolism concept to a new view of cities which sees them not as simply 'throughput', or a linear metabolism, but a circular metabolism in which the waste products must be re-used as far as possible (Girardet 1992: 22–25; Goodland et al. 1992). This view dovetails with Herman Daly's concept of the steady-state economy, in which 'throughput' is reduced, whereby throughput is defined as the 'entropic physical flow of matter-energy from nature's sources, through the human economy and back to nature's sinks' (Daly and Townsend 1993: 326). In the next section the concept of 'metabolic intensity' will be introduced as a measure of some aspects of Daly's throughput concept.

The Hong Kong human ecology programme

The relevance of Wolman's approach becomes daily more apparent, as the urban impact on the biosphere undermines ecological systems on land, in the ocean, and in the atmosphere. Yet, surprisingly, his contribution had a fairly limited impact on urban research at the time. The main cluster of urban ecological research, which used the metabolism approach, was developed within Project Area 11, An Ecological Approach to Human Settlements, of UNESCO's Man and the Biosphere Programme (MAB). Examples of the work carried out, under Project 11, include contributions from Stephen Boyden and colleagues at Australian National University (ANU), Project Ecoville at the University of Toronto, and MAB research groups in Germany and Italy (Boyden 1979; Federal Republic of Germany MAB National Committee 1980; Italia MAB 1981; White and Burton 1983). The ANU research team carried out the most comprehensive study in Hong Kong, paying tribute to the seminal work by Wolman:

'The expression "metabolism", as applied to a city, was coined by A. Wolman and it refers to the total flow of materials into and out of the system. The description of the metabolism of Hong Kong thus provides an overall picture of the rate of consumption of gaseous, liquid and solid resources, both renewable and non-renewable, and of the production of wastes by this settlement of 4 million people' (Boyden et al. 1981: 115).

Boyden and his colleagues undertook 'a comprehensive ecological description of Hong Kong' in order 'to improve knowledge and understanding of the ecology of human settlements, so that communities and their decision-makers will be in a better position to make wise decisions in the future' (Boyden et al. 1981: xv). They added the production of carbon dioxide to Wolman's list of gaseous outputs because, in their words:

'this gas reflects back to earth some of the infrared radiation from the earth's surface, and its accumulation in the atmosphere is therefore likely to result in the warming-up of the earth's surface' (Boyden et al. 1981: 117). (See Figure 3.1.)

Furthermore the team drew attention to the threat posed by the release of nitrous oxide and chlorofluoro-methanes to the potential depletion of the stratospheric ozone shield which protects the earth from ultra-violet radiation. The study also included the use of sea-water for cooling purposes in its analysis of the water balance. Particular attention was paid to food supply and its contribution to nutrients for somatic energy and to the health of the population. The results of a parallel 'biosocial' survey were published separately (Millar 1979).

At the time that the work was being carried out in Hong Kong the territory was undergoing very rapid economic growth, and for many of the people the pattern of resource use was moving quickly towards the pattern established in the industrialised West. The number of pigs and poultry sharply increased, reflecting increased purchasing power. The number of employees in manufacturing rose from 600 000 in 1974 to 900 000 by 1984 (Hills 1988: 47–9). Direct physical changes to the metabolism of the city included land reclamation and the building of causeways to protect the shore from the impact of typhoons. These changes to the shoreline also reduced circulation in the harbour and thereby reduced the scouring strength of the tides and currents; meanwhile untreated sewage continued to be dumped in the harbour.

However, the impact of Hong Kong had not yet reached the proportions of America's suburbanised and car-based cities

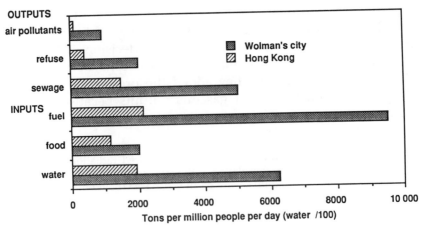

Figure 3.2 Inputs and Outputs from Wolman's City and Hong Kong

described by Wolman. Figure 3.2 shows a rough comparison of the *per capita* impact of individuals in Wolman's typical American city and in Hong Kong (bearing in mind the problems entailed in estimating wastes on this scale). The American city-dweller has a much heavier impact on the environment, especially in terms of the throughput of water and fuel. Figure 3.2 gives an indication of the 'metabolic intensity' of a city—a concept akin to Daly's concept of 'throughput', mentioned above.

Between the publication of Wolman's article (1965) and the Hong Kong research (begun in 1974, published in 1981), the metabolism approach to understanding systems had been extended in scope from one focused on problems of local pollution to a broader concern about the impact of our urban-industrial civilisation on ecosystems at the global scale. Furthermore, in the Hong Kong study the social variables that affected the human population (employment, health, mortality, and satisfaction), received as much attention as the physical indicators of the flows into and out of the city. Perhaps the most important extension to the metabolism concept provided in this study was the dynamic illustration of the principal flows of energy (both somatic and extra-somatic), nutrients, and water supply (Boyden et al. 1981: 162, 128, 165, 187 and 194). See, for example, the flows of water use summarised in Figure 3.3.

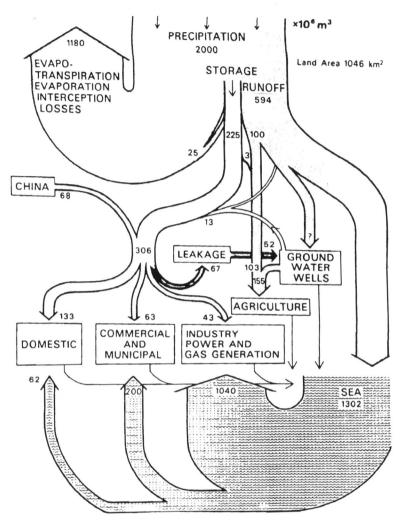

Figure 3.3 Hong Kong Water Use. *Source*: Boyden et al. 1981: 194

Energetics

The metabolism concept, especially as operationalised by Boyden and his colleagues in Hong Kong, is a great step forward towards a more holistic understanding of the physical basis and implications of urbanisation. Certainly it provides the framework for an integrated view of the challenge of contemporary urban environmental management. However, as long as we are listing inputs (water, fuel, food, etc.) and outputs (sewage, solid and gaseous wastes) we remain in the shadow of the input–output table, counting up our apples and oranges.

Although it would be premature to suggest that a methodology had already been operationalised for the purposes of urban environmental management, the study of energetics provides us with the possibility of integrating all these flows. Energetics, in its modern phase, has its origins in the middle of the last century when measurements were made to determine the mechanical equivalent of heat (Martinez-Alier 1990: 51). All forms of energy can be measured by 'the heat that is formed when energy in other forms is transferred into heat'. Thus 'a small calorie is the heat that raises one cubic centimetre of water one degree. A kilocalorie is 1000 small calories' (Odum 1983: 6). The basic assumption behind energetics is that any analysis of the environmental implications of human activities should begin with the observation (first attributed to Boltzmann, quoted in Odum 1983: 6) that the outcome of competition between members of all species was based on 'access to available energy'. Thus the gradual extension of human beings over the surface of the globe was first facilitated by their omnivorous diet, their hunting and organising skills, their tool-making, and their mastery of fire which made a greater variety of foodstuffs edible (and later made some foods storable, after curing). The agricultural revolution enormously increased human access to somatic energy, as did the harnessing of draught animals to plough the land and transport goods (Hillel 1991). All of these innovations assured people of a more reliable supply of calories and proteins which enabled them to do increasingly specialised work, and hence continually increase productivity— in terms both of output per hectare and output per hour worked by farmers and their animals. All of this can be analysed by looking at the kilocalories of inputs to people and their animals and the mechanical work that they could do as a result of those inputs. According to T. P. Bayliss-Smith the average male needs 2500 kilocalories or 10.5 megajoules each day to 'maintain the metabolism and tissue replacement of his body' (1982: 7).

Obviously we should not view society simply as a means of accessing energy and augmenting the human species; as such a view would exclude the myriad of other activities and ambitions that drive human endeavours. However, the increasing complexity of society since the industrial revolution has tended to obscure the physical basis for its survival, namely the ability to access the energy on which all human life depends. This process of losing touch with the energy basis of society stemmed from the growing dominance of fossil fuels which provided seemingly endless supplies of additional energy for doing work and producing goods. The industrialisation of agriculture began with mechanisation and then turned increasingly to chemical additives to increase output (Smil et al. 1983). However, from the beginning of this process, some observers questioned whether or not more energy was being put into this new industrial agriculture than was being produced by it, if you counted all the fossil fuel used in producing chemical fertilisers, farm machinery, and delivering irrigation water (Martinez-Alier 1990). Although, from a financial viewpoint, this system might be profitable, and from an output per hour, or per hectare, it might be productive, in energy terms it might be less efficient than traditional methods which relied more heavily on human and animal labour.

Such speculation might appear to be purely academic were it not for recent concerns about the human tenancy of the planet, especially with regard to the earth's ability to support a growing population at a decent standard of living, and the ability of the atmospheric and oceanic sinks to absorb carbon dioxide and other gaseous by-products of our chemical society. In particular our urban-industrial technology—like our industrialised agricultural technology—makes profligate use of energy, especially with regard to manufacturing, heating and cooling buildings, and transportation. Energetics allows us to add up the energy derived from food and the energy derived from (fossil) fuel. Some addition can also be made for the amount of energy used to produce, transport and recycle water, and the energy used to remove solid, liquid, and gaseous wastes. In this way we can begin to assess the degree of efficiency associated with various urban metabolisms.

Very quickly we should be able to identify the most wasteful energy transformations. Societies which consume large amounts of intensively raised animals, especially beef, would appear very wasteful, as would those that throw away expensively produced (in energy terms), containers such as metal and plastic bottles and packaging. Once people become aware of how many litres of water and kilocalories of energy are required to produce one aluminium can or one pound of prime beef then they may begin to re-evaluate the efficiency of modern urban society, especially if the cost to the consumer begins to reflect the cost of recovering the resources that have been used to produce the product. In the case of Brazil's decision to grow sugar cane to produce ethanol to power motor vehicles we could make a direct comparison of how much food production has been forgone in order to keep those vehicles running. Other significant quantities of Brazilian farmland are devoted to growing soybeans to export to Europe, partly to be used as animal feed, which in turn augments Europe's mountains of unwanted butter and beef. There is a certain symmetry in the more curious side-roads of international trade: the European Union eventually draws off parts of its surplus wine lake and turns it into alcohol for export to Brazil to help keep those motor vehicles running.

Within the urban environment, and directly within the realm of urban planners and managers, we can measure the energy balance for extra-somatic energy, which in the case of the Municipality of Toronto is based on hydro-electrical power and nuclear power, as well as fossil fuels. Figure 3.4 is a fascinating diagram which demonstrates that just less than half of the raw energy input becomes 'usable energy'—that is energy that heats buildings, powers electrical equipment, and drives our motor vehicles forward. It is difficult to imagine a diagram that paints the picture of the metabolic inefficiency of our cities more clearly. Half the energy is currently being wasted, and the most wasteful fraction of all is 'motion'—cars for the most part. Plans are now underway to harness the waste heat from power generation and other processes to provide district heating and cooling for the downtown core (Metropolitan Toronto Government 1992a; 1992b).

It is noteworthy that the decision to reduce energy consumption in Toronto did not spring from a desire to reduce energy consumption as a primary objective—the search for efficiency is the direct result of the government's goal to reduce the production of the greenhouse gases, carbon dioxide and methane. This concern

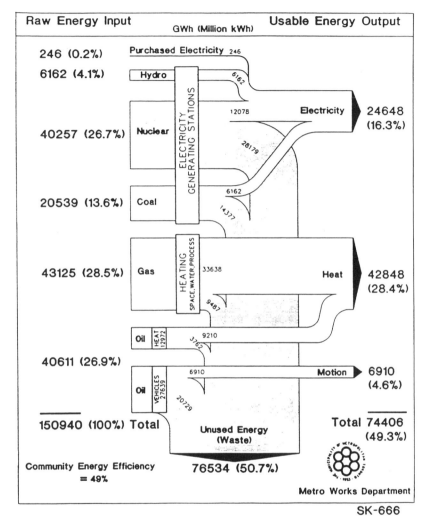

Figure 3.4 Energy Balance for Metro Toronto in 1988

is very closely intertwined with the need to reduce the consumption of CFCs (for cooling purposes) to meet federal requirements. Thus the decisions to be taken by the urban government are a direct response to concern about atmospheric change.

The study of energetics is broader than the study of extra-somatic energy as derived by cities from hydro, nuclear, and fossil-fuel power, as it also encompasses the biological energy that people derive from food and water. However, even this broad view of urban systems and their human populations, as part of the global ecosystem, does not give us an entirely integrated view of urban metabolism simply because so many of the city's functions (such as administration, communication, and innovation) cannot be quantified in simple energy terms. However, if we think back to the primitive methods used to produce the first agricultural surpluses to make the process of urbanisation and specialisation possible, it might appear that somewhere along the road human society took a wrong turn. This can be seen just by looking at any large city today. Optimists argue that this is all progress, and, though it may be materially rather wasteful, humanity as a whole if better off than it was before. Yet this attitude ignores the true *global* cost of how these cities have been built up. Since the industrial revolution took hold, cities have sustained themselves at the exp. nse of increasingly distant ecosystems which have been irreversibly modified to meet their needs.

Carrying capacity

Like 'metabolism' and 'energetics' the use of the term 'carrying capacity' has been controversial, and the recent reintroduction of the term into the environmental debate promises to be no less so. This is not surprising because 'carrying capacity' was first used by ecologists to refer to the size of the optimum population of a certain species which could be supported indefinitely in a given habitat (Jones et al. 1992: 63). When the term is applied to humans, critics have no difficulty in pointing out that humans—unlike rabbits and frogs—are renowned for their ability to innovate in order to survive and increase their numbers, albeit often at the expense of less innovative species. The assumption is that people will continue to innovate and hence constantly expand the ability of the earth to carry them.

This assumption is under clear challenge from two observations. One is that only *some* of the human population is prospering under this innovative process. The plight of the rest—some would say the majority—is increasingly desperate. The other is that the assimilative capacity of the major environmental sinks has now been reached, and this means that society will have to change direction. If any belt-tightening is called for it has some difficult implications for the first observation—the inequality between people. As Martinez-Alier trenchantly observes:

'Thus the "adjustment" programs to be recommended by the "IMF of Ecology" are, for some, reducing CO_2 emissions by increasing car mileage; for some, by burning less wood in the kitchen through improved stoves; for some, the very poor, presumably by exhaling less CO_2 through breathing slowly or not all' (Martinez-Alier 1991: 124).

Behind the bitterness of this comment lies the inescapable fact that although innovation has allowed some people to prosper materially it has signally failed, in this century, to extend that process to all of humanity. Indeed the twentieth century has seen the rapid growth of disparities between people in the North and the South, as well as within countries in both areas. Thus, if we are to talk about the carrying capacity of the earth we should do so for the whole of humanity, if we are to make realistic adjustments that might ensure some kind of planetary human habitat for our children and grandchildren.

How did this illusion about an endless stream of innovations and an ever-expanding carrying capacity persist for so long? The answer is empire. From the beginning of the European empires of the sixteenth century to the industrial empires of the present, the richer people in the richer countries have appropriated *global* hinterlands to meet the needs of their increasingly urban citizens (Crosby 1986; White and Whitney 1992). This has been widely acknowledged for some time, from the self-glorification of the early empire-builders to the 'global-sourcers' of today. And all has been cloaked under the impeccable credentials of free trade and international competition for markets. Eventually, however, whatever the stock exchanges tell us, underlying everything there is an energy basis for all life, including human life. That is what metabolism and the concept of carrying capacity attempt to capture. William Rees has coined the term 'ecological footprint' to emphasise the size of the boots that are required to establish global hinterlands to maintain our wasteful, energy-profligate societies (Rees 1992). In Chapter Seven of this book alternatives to this form of spatial organisation, such as the bio-region, will be considered.

Resources–activities–residuals

A simple concept is offered at this stage to summarise current thinking of the physical realities of the urban environmental dilemma. It is clearly an amalgam of the early work on input–output tables and the later concepts of urban metabolism, the steady-state economy, and residuals environmental quality management (REQM). 'Resources' and 'activities' sound like terms that come from the resource economics of the 50s and 60s, while the term 'residuals' did not become fashionable until the 70s. The concept is simple and less demanding than the total energetics approach proposed in the nineteenth century and operationalised in the field of systems ecology (Odum E. P. 1989; Odum H. T. 1983). It also simplifies the historical evolution of the impact of urban systems on the environment from the local, to the regional to the global, as illustrated by Figure 3.5. The R–A–R concept is summarised as Figure 3.6, and will be used throughout the rest of this book.

The top part of Figure 3.6 represents conventional thinking until the 1970s when people as producers and consumers simply acquired resources, used them to support human activities, and then discarded the residual materials. This was the hey-day of the 'throw-away' society when people in the richer countries were encouraged by advertising to buy bigger cars, bigger houses, bigger refrigerators, bigger televisions, and generally to use as many resources as possible. Governments encouraged this trend because an economy which supported an ever-increasing scale of resource-use appeared to offer the promise of more jobs and more tax revenue. The greater the use of resources—however destructive the impact on the environment—the bigger Gross National Product became. Only very small groups of people (in relation to the total number of consumers) worried about such things as resource-depletion or nature conservation.

The bottom half of the diagram sketches in some of the things that we have learned in the past twenty years. Essentially we have

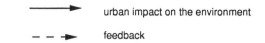

urban impact on the environment

feedback

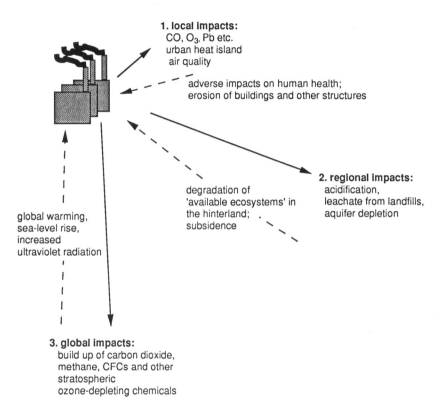

1. local impacts:
CO, O_3, Pb etc.
urban heat island
air quality

adverse impacts on human health;
erosion of buildings and other structures

2. regional impacts:
acidification,
leachate from landfills,
aquifer depletion

degradation of
'available ecosystems' in
the hinterland;
subsidence

global warming,
sea-level rise,
increased
ultraviolet radiation

3. global impacts:
build up of carbon dioxide,
methane, CFCs and other
stratospheric
ozone-depleting chemicals

Figure 3.5 Evolution of the Relationship between the City and the Environment

learned that the world is a closed system, from the perspective of the human use of resources. As the system is closed, it should be expected that *at a certain scale of resource use*, feedbacks will appear. The purpose of the book *Limits to Growth* (Meadows et al. 1972) was to show that that moment was upon us already. Unfortunately, most policy-makers did not want to hear the message. They were still thinking in terms of resource-depletion, and their major fears on this score—the availability of petroleum—were

The original input - output concept was developed to measure the effect of the economy <u>on</u> <u>itself</u>, on the basis of fixed, linear technical coefficients. The analysis produced quantities of pollution, whose first order impacts were added up as costs and benefits.

The resources - activities - residuals approach allows us to study the critical interactions, between residuals, between sinks and between urban systems and the totality of the environment in which they are situated. It can be applied at all scales from the impact of a car's exhaust pipe to the city system itself.

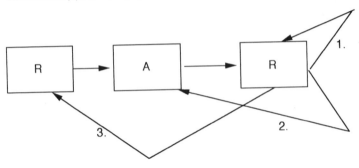

KEY
1. Interaction between residuals, e.g. volatile organic compounds and ozone.
2. Impacts of residuals on human activities, e.g. human health and sea-level rise.
3. residuals attack resources, e.g. the effect of ultra - violet radiation on phytoplankton.

Figure 3.6 The Resources–Activities–Residuals Approach

set aside by the OPEC oil price hikes to which the world economy responded swiftly by adopting conservation measures and finding new sources of supply. Resource-scarcity, is however, only the simplest type of feedback with which we are faced. The additional arrows (numbers 1, 2 and 3) in the bottom diagram illustrate feedbacks which relate to the exhaustion of some of the sinks. The first arrow notes that residuals may become so dense in our urban air-sheds as to interact with one another, in this case, to produce photo-chemical smog. The second arrow reminds us that residuals may affect human activities directly by attacking human health or by large-scale planetary modifications such as sea-level rise. The third arrow illustrates the impact of residuals directly on the availability of resources; the vulnerability of phytoplankton—the basis of the marine food chain—is chosen as an illustration of the probable impact of increased ultra-violet radiation, following the weakening of the stratospheric ozone shield.

It is important to come to terms with the fact that these kinds of feedbacks will be much more difficult to deal with than the resource-scarcity problems which preoccupied decision-makers until the end of the 1970s. Three relatively simple reactions could be developed for these: reduce use through greater efficiency, increase supply, switch to a substitute resource. The problems with sinks are far more dynamic and include unknown degrees of inertia. For example, the duration of the CFC-depleted ozone shield is a function of the long residence time of the CFCs in the stratosphere; while impacts of poor air quality on human health may be lifelong.

Thus Figure 3.6 is designed to remind us of the inescapable fact of the underlying physical basis of our urbanising society, however technically inventive we become and however tightly we seal ourselves away from nature. The metabolism concept places cities firmly in their natural setting, however much that may have been transformed by the fact of the urbanisation process itself. The REQM approach brings a management perspective to this situation which, usually, has not been managed at all. Residuals—or non-product outputs—are as much a part of our production processes as the marketable goods and services themselves. And the residuals have now accumulated in nature's sinks to such a concentration that these sinks are changing their means of processing these residuals. In the case of carbon dioxide —the most problematic residual—this change is expected to include higher air temperatures and higher sea-levels. The recent preoccupation with the problems developing in the global sinks should not, however, distract us from the problems of over-extraction which became apparent many years ago—problems such as soil erosion, deforestation, depletion of fisheries, and the non-sustainable use of water and energy sources. One means to keep both problems—overburdening sinks and depleting resources—in view would be to link the concept of resources–activities–residuals to the emerging field of environmental accounting (Elkin et al. 1991; Pearce et al. 1989: 62–7, 92–118). Environmental accounting adjusts the conventional measures of the Gross National Product by including both the depletion of natural capital stocks (such as fossil fuels and forests), and the cost of reducing the negative impacts of our conventional economic activities. These impacts include impaired human health, degraded landscapes and damaged production systems. It is remarkable that it has taken us so long to begin this task considering that the distinction between capital and recurrent accounts is fundamental to the modern way of running a business. Yet, on the scale of the planet—the largest system with which the human race is involved—the matter was hardly discussed, except in the limited case of non-renewable resources, until very recently. So the easier parts of natural resource accounting are now being brought into our accounting systems, beginning with the most visible stocks such as forests and soils. But the truth is that we simply do not know enough about our ecological niche to determine the capacity of some of our stocks or any of our sinks. We do not know how large a particular fishery stock might be until we have so overfished it that yields begin to fall very rapidly. Until that point is reached any reduction in catch could simply be a natural perturbation due to local climatic conditions or an oscillation in the breeding pattern.

Although our scientific knowledge is incomplete there are nonetheless very obvious steps that need to be taken quickly both to improve the quality of human life and to reduce the adverse impacts of humanity on the planet and other species. And nowhere is it more obvious what some of these steps should be than in our cities—both the rich cities in the North with their global hinterlands and growing population of cars, and the poor cities of the South with their highly adverse living standards and their growing population of human beings.

None of these observations should obscure the fact that even without the negative environmental repercussions of cities, the urbanisation process itself has developed several defects that have even more immediate consequences for the future of human society. These defects include the welfare concerns that are often bundled together as 'equity' or distributional issues. They include the visible features of the urban landscape such as derelict land, slums and homeless people, as well as the less visible but omnipresent problems of unemployment and impaired human health. In extreme situations some of these consequences threaten the viability of the urban systems itself and thus might be termed 'pathological'. These issues are the subject of the next chapter.

Further reading:

Bayliss-Smith, T. P. (1982). *The Ecology of Agricultural Systems.* Cambridge, Cambridge University Press.

Bower, B. T., Ed. (1977). *Regional Residuals Environmental Quality Management Modeling.* Washington DC, Resources for the Future.

Boyden, S., Millar, S. et al. (1981). *The Ecology of a City and its People: the case of Hong Kong.* Canberra, Australian National University Press.

Douglas, I. (1983). *The Urban Environment.* London, Edward Arnold.

Girardet, H. (1992). *The Gaia Atlas of Cities. New Directions for Sustainable Urban Living.* New York, Anchor Books published by Doubleday.

Goodland, R., Daly, H. E. and El Serafy, S., Eds. (1992). *Population, Technology and Lifestyle. The Transition to Sustainability.* Washington DC, Island Press.

Odum, E. P. (1989). *Ecology and Our Endangered Life-Support Systems.* Sunderland, Sinauer Associates.

Odum, H. T. (1983). *Systems Ecology. An Introduction.* New York, John Wiley and Sons.

Wolman, A. (1965). The metabolism of cities. *Scientific American* (September): 179–88.

4

Urban Pathology

As the quotations from Peter Hall and David Harvey suggest, the nature of the city has long been a subject of controversy and internal contradiction, a place of promise and of disappointment, a place of wealth and poverty, a place of power and powerlessness. This was never more so than today when we stand poised on the brink of widespread climate change to which cities are a major contributor and of which they are potentially a major victim.

Cities are first and foremost dense concentrations of people, and these concentrations are spreading rapidly in most parts of the world. In the poorest countries the age-old urban problems of poor air quality and poor water quality are major sources of morbidity and mortality. Although people are prey to diseases, natural disasters and old age, it is undeniable that mankind is his own most serious predator in that the great majority of diseases and deaths in the world today are preventable given the existing levels of technology and resource use. The problems persist because of the decisions that people take. The largest single group of preventable deaths are those of infant mortality in the South, where death rates are still more than ten times the comparable rates in the North.

For many people the large cities they inhabit are dysfunctional. This is particularly true for the poor, many of whom are homeless, unemployed, dispirited, or in poor health. For many their lives remain unfulfilled and the prospects are no better for their children. Even for the rich, the urban environment may be inefficient and a threat to their health—from poor air quality, accidents, and violence. In cities such as Rio de Janeiro—where some members of the police have recently been arrested for murdering street children—it appears that urban society is at war with itself in a fratricidal struggle in which people are not fighting for lofty principles, but simply for survival. All these conditions exist independently of the growing threats of climate change and water scarcity, and the increasing costs of disposing of solid and liquid wastes—all of which can only add to the problem mix. It seems frighteningly obvious that the world needs cities that function better, both in an ecological sense and by providing meaningful employment and justice for all their inhabitants.

The early advantages of urban life were that they brought people together for commercial, religious, and administrative purposes. At times of civil unrest they were places of relative security. They continued to provide these attractions even though health conditions were usually worse than the surrounding countryside, due to the contamination of food and water by human and animal wastes, and the increased exposure to contagious diseases. Their high mortality rates were made up by a continual stream of rural migrants. Some cities experienced prolonged decline and others were depopulated completely, due to commercial failure, plague, or warfare. Nevertheless the global process of urbanisation has continued virtually unabated since the dawn of the agricultural revolution. Sometime in the next 10 to 20 years human society will pass the 50% threshold and we will be a predominantly urban society for the first time (HABITAT 1987: 23). Unquestionably, the urban revolution stands with the agricultural and industrial revolutions as a major transformation of human society, yet the controversy concerning the relative advantages and disadvantages of urban living—and living in cities of various sizes—continues unabated.

In the previous chapter the city was examined from a metabolic viewpoint, as the physical transformer of materials and energy to produce growth—growth of the physical form of the city and the number of its inhabitants. If we can be permitted a further analogy we might also say that urban systems sometimes produce a pathological condition, in that the built form and/or the inhabitants experience decline, which may be fatal. Cities have always included this potentially destructive feature simply from the fact of concentration. People living at different levels of comfort, or discomfort, in close proximity to one another, clearly carry the potential for violent conflict, more so than in rural societies where the rich may be physically distanced (and protected) from the poor. On a purely physiological level, proximity carries the potential for the spread of contagious diseases, which may show little respect for differences in wealth. Peter Hall suggests that it was the rapid growth of cities in the industrial revolution that made an increasing number of the relatively well-off aware of the desperate condition of the urban poor and of the potential for danger this carried. The basis for speculation, prejudice, and fear on the part of the richer inhabitants was partly clarified by Charles Booth's survey of the East End of London in 1887. He was able to reassure members of the Royal Statistical Society that:

'The hordes of barbarians of whom we have heard, who, coming from their slums will some day overwhelm modern civilisation, do not exist. The barbarians are a very small and decreasing percentage. However (he continued), they render no useful service and create no wealth; indeed they often destroy it. They degrade whatever they touch and as individuals are almost incapable of improvement … It is much to be hoped that this class may become less hereditary in character' (Quoted in Hall 1988: 28).

As we see today, this problem of the highly marginalised is present to some extent in nearly every city of the world, and in some of them the number is certainly higher than the 1.25% of the total recorded by Booth in his survey. The fundamental problem, then as now, is that urban systems offer no guarantee, in themselves, of an improved material existence. Indeed, it is often said that the condition of the urban poor is worse than that of the rural poor, for, in addition to the problems of poverty, they live in a highly degraded environment without fresh water and without fresh air. In the discussion of these and similar drawbacks of urban life there is always the tendency to reify the city; yet the city is essentially a dense concentration of *people* who have erected buildings and infrastructure of a given size and capacity. This must be borne in mind—especially when we discuss problems of the physical blight of the built environment—otherwise when the problem is defined physically the proposed 'solution' is usually physical too. This is what critics deride as 'instrumentalism'—the fixing up of appearances without dealing with the underlying politics of the urban condition.

Physical blight

The physical symptoms of a pathological condition within an urban system are the easiest part of the problem to identify, and they are the easiest part to fix, at least superficially. Physical blight may arise when buildings and infrastructure are not maintained, either through insufficient finances or, through a shift in use, or outright abandonment. Two processes accelerate this condition. The first is a supply of new, very low-income immigrants who will inhabit buildings shunned by the existing populace. They create what E. W. Burgess called 'zones of transition' in his 1920s' study of Chicago (Hall 1988: 370). If the immigration cycle is active the new arrivals will later be replaced by the next wave of immigrants and the first group will move to improved housing and employment opportunities. The second process which produces blight is one of technological change which removes the demand for certain manufacturing, warehousing and transportation facilities as well as closing down jobs. In this situation, when the old industries are shut down and the air clears, the derelict buildings, the contaminated soil, and the unemployed remain.

Confronted with a physical problem city counsellors and planners have all too often conspired to treat the problem with a physical solution, such as redeveloping old dockside warehouses into high-income apartments and marinas. In one of the more bizarre responses to Liverpool's long decline through the 1980s the central government of the day embarked on a massive garden festival to revive part of the derelict waterfront. A more irrelevant response to the deep problems of unemployment and poor housing is difficult to imagine. Slightly nearer the mark is the declaration of 'enterprise zones', popular in Britain and the United States, because at least this approach recognises that a large part of the problem is employment. Even so, the declaration of an enterprise *zone*, as the target, rather than a group of people, somewhat misses the point. The point is that physical blight is a function of a social blight, which is usually a long-term problem not amenable to quick fixes in time for the next election.

Clearly these physical, social, and political problems are multi-faceted and even a general understanding of the interplay of the principal causal factors would require a book in itself even for a single case study. In this book, focused on an ecosystem approach to understanding urban systems, two European examples of pathological conditions will be presented briefly. One is from the West, the other from the East. Both examples relate simultaneously to local and global impacts; the local impact concerns human health, the global impact is climate change. These examples are followed by an overview of urban environmental conditions in the South.

Social blight

In his 1887 survey of the East End of London, Charles Booth was careful to distinguish between different types of poverty. For example, apart from the barbarian hordes who frightened the Victorian wealthy, there were single heads of families without the time to look after a young family and keep a job; there were people who were cyclically unemployed because of the kind of technological change mentioned above; and there were those who were simply trapped in very low paid work, which kept them alive but did little more. A similar survey today would add a category for new immigrants with an inadequate education and faced with discrimination in the workplace. It would also add many of the elderly, living on small, fixed incomes.

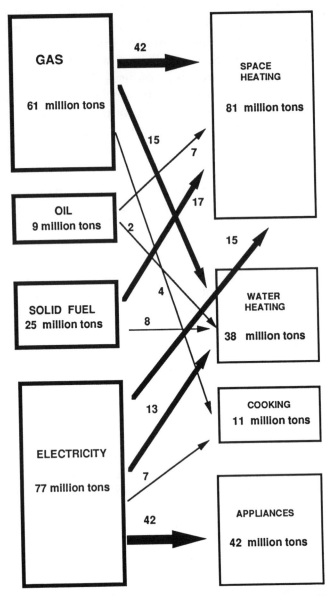

Figure 4.1 UK Household Carbon Dioxide Emissions (1987) by End-use and Source of Fuel (in million tons CO_2). *Source: Warm Homes—Cool Planet*, Friends of the Earth, 1990

In countries like Britain where the home heating bill is a significant part of the household budget and hypothermia is a cause of early deaths, the choice for the elderly poor can be summarised as simply 'heat or eat' (Boardman 1991: 17). Fortunately the upgrading of the housing stock—especially one so energy-inefficient as Britain's—should offer great hope for the fuel-poor, as well as for combating global warming (Boardman 1991: 7–8; Friends of the Earth 1990). The sources of carbon dioxide, by type of fuel and end-use, within the housing stock are well-known (Figure 4.1). Here, at least, is a problem for which the solution might appear to be fairly obvious—fuel-switching, insulation, and the installation of more efficient appliances. Such a solution is in the mutual interest of the landlord, the tenant, the owner–occupier, and the manufacturer. Furthermore, it involves incremental, rather than abrupt, changes in human behaviour. Unfortunately, as Brenda Boardman explains in her illuminating book, *Fuel Poverty*, little progress has been made on this persistent problem.

Figures 4.2, 4.3 and 4.4 offer further detail on the scope for improvement of the home heating problem. In those homes where electricity is still used as a household fuel, savings can be made by moving from electricity to gas to reduce emissions, and from peak period usage to off-peak to reduce costs, although, this is only a medium-term solution as gas is a fossil fuel which emits carbon dioxide and is a non-renewable resource.

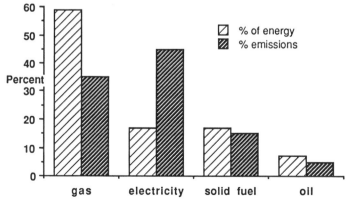

Figure 4.2 Carbon Dioxide Emissions and Energy from UK Households

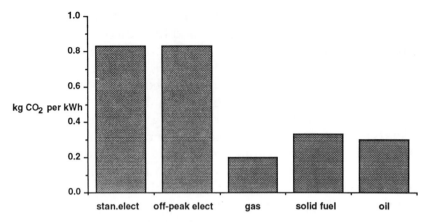

Figure 4.3 Carbon Dioxide Emissions per Unit of Energy in UK Households

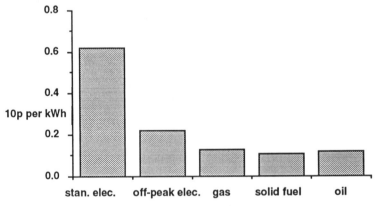

Figure 4.4 Cost of UK Household Energy. *Source*: Friends of the Earth, 1990

Note that this problem presents an opportunity to meet three important goals simultaneously. Its solution will reduce carbon dioxide emissions to the air, and thereby help the government meet its obligations to limit greenhouse gas emissions, as agreed under the UN Framework Convention on Climate Change (Grubb 1993). It will also reduce the financial burden on poor families and help those at risk within those families—the old and the very young. This is no small matter in Britain which records excess winter deaths that can be correlated with cold weather. In response to this problem the British government in 1989 set up an extraordinarily complex system of rebates that can be claimed by those in need. The system:

' ... enables "income support" claimants with anyone under 5, or over 60 or chronically sick or disabled in the household, to claim, if the average temperature for seven consecutive days is less than 0°C. Only claimants with savings less than £1,000 are entitled to apply and there is a standard payment (irrespective of actual use) of £5 per week of "exceptionally severe weather". It is estimated that 1.4m claimants are eligible on this basis ... Each £1 of benefit cost 50p to pay out' (Boardman 1991: 147).

The problem of excess winter deaths originates in the persistence of poverty in a rich country and the great inefficiency of its building standards, which lag far behind those of the rest of northern Europe. Yet the government's response is not to improve the standards but to set up an unbelievably inefficient system of rebates which are paid out after the time of greatest need has passed. As the author of the study added:

'If seasonal mortality in Britain could be reduced to the level of Scandinavian countries, excess winter deaths would be halved to bring the total down to 15,000–30,000: three to six times the number of road deaths could be saved through warmer homes' (Boardman 1991: 149).

This must be a case of instrumentalism at its worst. If Britain simply adopted the building standards of its neighbours (backed by a government-sponsored retrofit programme), it could reduce greenhouse gas emissions from households by 6%, down to about 6 tons per annum for poorer households (Boardman 1991: 164, 209). At the same time it would reduce financial hardship and reduce the number of excess deaths from which they suffer. The fact that Britain, one of the richest countries in the world, has been unable to deal with this relatively small and well-understood deficiency should be borne in mind when we look at the much larger and less tractable problems in the burgeoning cities of the South and the severely polluted industrial regions of Eastern Europe.

The objective of this book began as an attempt to operationalise a holistic approach to urban environmental management, rather than to propose solutions to the general problem of poverty, either in the North or in the South. To meet this objective the discussion will focus on physical variables like litres of water and tons of carbon dioxide. However, at no time do I wish to suggest that we can simply, physically plan our way out of the present crisis. The causes of human marginalisation are social and political and no number of garden festivals or enterprise zones can change that. What this book is designed to do is identify the physical instruments that are available to implement a politically conscious social policy with respect to resource use and residuals management.

Conditions in Central and Eastern Europe

The determination of communist governments to maximise industrial and agricultural output at any cost meant that the environment was given an even lower priority than it received under capitalism in the West. If anyone doubted that there is a connection between environmental quality and the quality of human life then Eastern Europe provided the proof that this connection is strong (Girardet 1992: 114–5; World Resources Institute 1992: 57). There used to be some justification for scepticism about the pollution–health link because, until recently, the dose–response sort of data were very sketchy for the impact of environmental quality on human morbidity and mortality, in the outdoors, or ambient, environment. Indeed the data were limited to a handful of extreme events like the intense smogs experienced in highly industrialised coal-mining valleys and in major cities like London, in the immediate post World War Two period. These gross abuses of air quality became much less common with the introduction of legislation which controlled emissions, specifically the Clean Air Acts of the 1950s and 1960s (Mansfield 1990). And so the connection became hypothetical once more, at least in the West. Everyone was for economic growth, and from this stemmed a general reluctance to introduce further legislation unless a health impact could be *proved*. However, the recent uncovering of conditions on Eastern Europe has now provided proof in abundance.

Life expectancy in Eastern Europe, in the immediate post World War Two period, benefited from the availability of free health services and an improved diet, and began to close up on life expectancy in the West. Since the 1960s however the rates have begun to widen again (Sylvan 1992: 85). Even though the temporal data do not provide conclusive proof that there is a correlation between environmental quality (especially air and water) and life expectancy, the spatial data from heavily industrialised regions like the Voivodeship (province) of Katowice, Poland, are quite clear:

'The 1989 infant mortality rate was 25.5 per 1,000 live births in Katowice City, with an average of 18.5 in the Voivodeship; this compares unfavorably with the national average of 16.1 per 1,000. The results of a six-year study in the 1980s in sub-regions of the Voivodeship conclude that infant mortality is correlated with dust fall, ambient levels of lead, tar, phenols, formaldehyde and benzo(a)pyrene ... The Voivodeship also suffers from the highest incidence of premature births (8.5%), genetic birth defects (10.1% of all live births), and spontaneous miscarriages in Poland' (Borkiewicz et al. 1991: 19).

Katowice is the centre of Poland's iron and steel and metallurgical industry which is fuelled by coal. The surrounding region is heavily acidified. Juraj Sylvan reports that in Eastern Europe, as a whole, it is estimated that harvests suffer a 30% decline due to air pollution (Sylvan 1992: 91). Forest decline is also widespread. Insofar as the adult human health connection is concerned one can still argue that other factors, such as lack of exercise, diet, alcohol, and smoking, must be taken into account. However, the general picture is clear—heavy industrialisation, fuelled by coal and without environmental safeguards is very dangerous for many aspects of human health, especially pulmonary, cardiac, reproductive, and skin problems (French 1990: 10). It is no exaggeration to describe this type of urban-industrial development as pathological when all sections of the population from workers to schoolchildren and the newborn are suffering heavily. It is probably redundant to add that this is bad for the economy too, but perhaps the point should be added to silence the last claims for the freedom to pollute as the necessary 'price of progress'.

The fall of communism was due in some measure to the revolt of the people against the environmental conditions in which they were forced to live; however, the problems do not end with the return of democracy. Much of Poland's industry, as well as its export earnings, depend on coal—or else on oil, which is

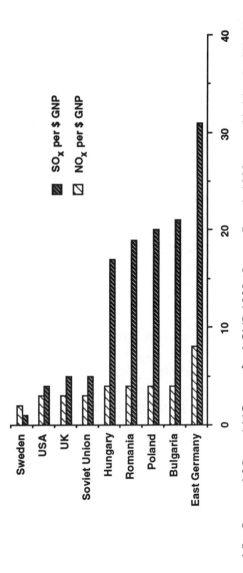

Figure 4.5 Grams of SO$_x$ and NO$_x$ per $ of GNP 1988. *Source:* French 1990, assembled by the Worldwatch Institute

imported from the former Soviet Union. The same is true of the other economies of the region such as Slovakia, the Czech Republic, Hungary, and Bulgaria. The former German Democratic Republic burns lignite, which is even more polluting than coal. The total restructuring of the economies of Eastern Europe is being greatly complicated by the environmental consequences of industrialisation under communism. There is no alternative, however, to reconstruction because the old ways are very harmful to human health and economically highly inefficient in terms of the volume of emissions compared with the value of the goods produced (Figure 4.5). However, new ways (if patterned on the West) will bring new problems, especially in the form of the private car (French 1990: 42–3). More fuel-efficient and less polluting cars on the Western model are all very well, but they will *add* to environmental breakdown if there are *more* of them and if they are driven over *greater distances*. As Figure 4.6 indicates, the former communist countries of Central and Eastern Europe currently enjoy the environmental advantage of making substantial use of public transport. It would be a great loss to the drive for environmental quality if this advantage were abandoned. The answer certainly does not lie in emulating the West, but in developing a better approach, for East and West, together. This has been stated repeatedly by many experts, but the advice so far has gone unheeded. One of the most visible signs of Poland's new freedom is the rapid proliferation of garages to sell petrol to the suddenly expanded population of motor vehicles.

Conditions in the South

The revelations from Central and Eastern Europe, while not completely unexpected, came as a shock for those people in the West who had not visited the region. Even in the region itself it is unlikely that many people were aware of the extent of the environmental damage. The same cannot be said for conditions in the cities of the South, where the decline from marginality to desperation has been charted in great detail. (See, for example, Deelstra et al. 1990; HABITAT 1987; Hardoy and Satterthwaite 1989; Hardoy et al. 1992; Hills and Whitney 1988; Linn 1983; McAuslan 1985; Stren and White 1989; Stren, White and Whitney 1992.) Of

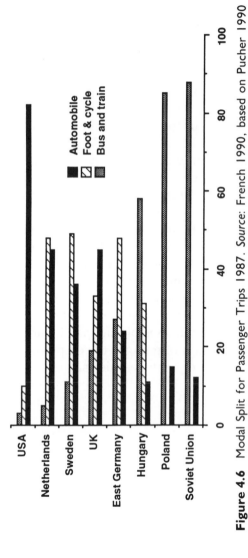

Figure 4.6 Modal Split for Passenger Trips 1987. *Source:* French 1990, based on Pucher 1990

course conditions do vary greatly, as the term 'South' becomes more and more heterogeneous. This brief discussion has no bearing on Singapore, which has become a world model for urban traffic management, or on Curitiba, Brazil, where, despite high car-ownership, the public transport system has been steadily enhanced over the past 20 years, persuading two thirds of commuters to take the bus (Gilbert 1993: 19; Rabinovitch 1992: 66). At the other end of the scale, though, the term 'pathological' does apply, as the adverse impact on human health has become demonstrable. Here, Mexico City provides the most telling example of the impact of air quality on human health, due to industrial and car pollution, especially in the latter's contribution to ambient lead. It is now believed by epidemiologists that lead levels can be correlated with an increase in learning disabilities in primary schools, across the urban system. Luis Manuel Guerra reports that in Mexico City 70% of the newborn have elevated lead levels in their blood (Guerra 1991). Such a development has enormous consequences for the population, whether they are looked upon as human beings, or merely as 'human resources' to be fed into the economy. The city is, literally, poisoning its own people, or—to avoid the problem of reifying the city—the citizens are poisoning themselves and their children.

Mexico City, like Sao Paulo and other car-choked cities, is in a sense suffering from its affluence, if it can be called that. Other megacities of the South are suffering from poverty pure and simple. This is nowhere clearer than in the recent (1991–2) outbreaks of cholera in Peru and Zambia, which spread rapidly due to the poor quality of the water supply. What was particularly alarming about these incidents was that the disease spread so far and so quickly, whereas, in the past, cholera often remained confined to clusters of cases in towns and villages with infected water supplies.

A new strain of cholera, known as Bengal cholera, has appeared in India and is expected to produce another worldwide epidemic which will strike with greatest force in the giant cities of the South with the most inadequate supply of water and the most inadequate level of water treatment. The giant cities with the poorest level of water management are bound to become more dangerous to human health, and less conducive to economic development, as the population continues to grow and water supplies and treatment capacity remain fixed, or begin to decline due to lack of maintenance. This has been an inescapable fact of urbanisation since it first appeared in the cities of Sumer more than 5000 years ago. People produce pathological wastes, and etiologies dependent on contagion intensify, as the density of inhabitants increases—unless adequate means for handling the wastes can be put in place. In tropical cities like Lagos and Kinshasa, with several million inhabitants and a water table that remains very near the surface all year, water-borne diseases will increase.

This is not simply some natural occurrence, as contemporary social Darwinists might have us believe. It is partly the result of the system of international trade which has encouraged the first-industrialised countries to export their already-deficient urban technology to the South without sufficient safeguards (White 1992b). Two slightly contradictory assumptions have operated to fuel this process. First, it has been generally assumed that the evolution of the South would follow that of the North, with a variable time lag depending on the stage of development reached by a particular country in the South. Thus, in the transportation sector, if the North was building ever-longer runways and ever-wider highways, then that is what the South needed too. For the wealthier cities in the South subway systems and hovercraft ferries would also be in order. For waste management, the solution was obviously incineration; it got rid of the waste and could provide a source of energy. When incineration came under criticism and stringent regulation in the West, the South became an even more important outlet for the older, obsolete versions of the technology. This latter procedure could be justified by the second assumption—the South could not afford the best technology, so the second-rate would be quite appropriate, or perhaps even more appropriate. Only very recently have these attitudes begun to change. It has now become clear that the planet cannot absorb even the present 5.5 billion people living on a Western scale of resource use, even if the South had the financial means to follow this path. So the South will follow a different, as yet unspecified, route to development. It is now also being appreciated that the best technology does not have to be the most expensive—the best technology, in the environmental context, may turn out to be cheaper, both for the purchaser and for the planet.

It would be easy to stand back now and say that the plight of urban areas (and rural areas too) in the South, is the result of rapid population growth at a time of prolonged economic stagnation. But this is only part of a problem which has been intensified by the policy vacillations of the development agencies which serve as the main official channels for North–South relations in the development arena. In the post-war period these urban policies passed through two phases and are now (I hope) entering a third.

Until the mid-1970s, urbanisation was regarded by the development agencies as an indispensable component of the process of economic development. Cities were viewed as 'engines of growth' which brought together the various factors of production and, simultaneously, created a local market for urban goods and services. It was shown that cities produced 'agglomeration economies' both in terms of one productive sector serving another and in terms of the economies of scale with which services (such as water supply, education, etcetera) could be delivered. Cities were indispensable for progress, even if the living conditions of some of their poorer inhabitants did sometimes leave something to be desired.

This optimistic (complacent?) view of the city in the Third World shifted dramatically in the early 1970s when it became clear that most governments in the South had fixed prices which discriminated against the rural dweller in favour of the urban dweller (Lipton 1977). The assumption was that most members of the government were (or had become) urban dwellers and therefore favoured their own group. Another explanation for policies with an urban bias was that, if people who were concentrated in urban settlements were dissatisfied with their lot, they would constitute a more immediate (and possibly violent), threat to the government and therefore they must be placated. Whatever the rationale, which must have varied from place to place, the outcome was usually the same—fixed prices for commodities, services, and foreign exchange which favoured the consuming, importing urban dweller over the rural producer. This produced a serious distortion of the rural–urban terms of trade, accelerated urban growth, and discouraged rural production. Once the bilateral and multilateral development agencies recognised this problem, with one exception (the World Bank) they withdrew all support for anything identifiable as an 'urban project'. (I think the Bank's reaction was less categorical because, although the Bank's officers were as critical of Third World governments' urban bias as anyone else, they accepted that, if properly handled, cities must still play a vital role as engines of growth, as originally formulated.)

With very rapid population growth, rapid urbanisation and economic stagnation, or slow growth, in the South, the cities simply became the residual problem of the process, whatever domestic or agency policies were adopted. The domestic policy of the urban bias accentuated the attractiveness of the cities and undermined the rural economy. The agency response—withdrawal from urban projects from the mid-1970s to the present—deepened the urban crisis. Today we have very large cities on a shaky economic base which have become extremely unhealthy for all their citizens, even the rich. I think that one viewpoint that might guide us out of the mess is not ideological or even technical, it is ecological. This is the third phase referred to above. However, I do not think the return of urban settlements to the development agencies' agenda necessarily implies an appreciation of the need for an ecosystem approach to urban management. On the contrary cities are back on the agenda because the impossibility of excluding them from an analysis of the current economic problems has become very apparent. If the cities are dysfunctional, so is the national economy. We still have a long way to go before the environmental consequences of urbanisation are fully factored into the picture.

Ecosystems, not instrumentalism

Throughout history, cities have been a source of conflict and a cauldron of ideas. In a sense the intensification of human contact within the city brings out the worst and the best of human society. As the density of human occupancy of the planet goes up, as cities become very large, this contradictory aspect of urbanisation becomes more acute. In the managerial jargon fashionable at this time, no-one knows how the urbanisation process will 'net out' in its impact on the human species and other parts of the global ecosystem.

In ideological terms, opinion is deeply divided between those who see competition as the lifeblood of the human species (variously appearing as social Darwinists between the World Wars, and latterly as free marketeers, with the export version prepared as 'structural adjustment') and those who see cooperation between all members of the human species (and other species), as the only road to survival. I do not intend to enmesh myself in this aspect of the debate, as my task is a preliminary one—to present a view of the city as one ecosystem, in which the relations between various members of the human species play a very important, indeed critical, part. It is clear that these relations produce conditions that are already pathological in some cases, from hypothermia among the elderly in the UK, to multiple types of morbidity and mortality from air pollution in Central and Eastern Europe, to a fatally impure water supply in many cities of the South.

In conclusion:

● cities always present certain problems in their very concentration of human occupancy of space—for example, contamination of the environment with implications for health, and concentration of competitive political interests which challenge the central government;
● as cities are a source of a great many problems (human health, over-consumption, and pollution, etcetera), they must also be a part of the solution (Gilbert 1991);
● although it is tempting to deal separately with the physical problems of water supply and treatment, energy, transportation, and so on, these are only symptoms of the basic problems which are social and political, and therefore deeply rooted in the human condition.

The last point underlines the fact that although this book is focused on the physical urban environment, it rejects an instrumentalist approach to planning. On the contrary, the current environmental crisis has exposed some of the deepest problems of contemporary society, which arise from the favouring of a short-term, competitive basis for human relations. Annual measurements of GNP and inflation are virtually the only indicators that guide political decision-making in most countries today. Even unemployment is now regarded as a by-product of political decisions, rather than as a target in itself. An assessment of the physical condition of our cities—even the most privileged among them—brings us almost back, as Peter Hall observed, 'to where we started ... the city itself is seen as a place of decay, poverty, social malaise, civil unrest and possibly even insurrection'.

Further reading:

Boardman, B. (1991). *Fuel Poverty. From Cold Homes to Affordable Warmth*. London, Belhaven Press.

French, H. F. (1990). *Green Revolutions: Environmental Reconstruction in Eastern Europe and the Soviet Union*. Washington DC, Worldwatch Institute.

Hall, P. (1988). *Cities of Tomorrow*. Oxford, Basil Blackwell.

Hardoy, J. and Satterthwaite, D. (1989). *Squatter Citizen. Life in the Urban Third World*. London, Earthscan Publications.

Hardoy, J. E., Mitlin, D. and Satterthwaite, D. (1992). *Environmental Problems in Third World Cities*. London, Earthscan Publications Ltd.

Harvey, D. (1989). *The Urban Experience*. Oxford, Basil Blackwell.

Hills, P. and Whitney, J. Eds. (1988). *Environmental Quality Issues in Asian Cities*. Project Ecoville Working Paper. Hong Kong and Toronto, University of Hong Kong, University of Toronto, IFIAS.

Short, J. R. (1989). *The Humane City. Cities as if People Matter*. Oxford, Basil Blackwell.

Stren, R. and White, R. Eds. (1989). *African Cities in Crisis. Managing Rapid Urban Growth*. African Modernization and Development Series. Boulder, Westview Press.

Sylvan, J. (1992). Eastern Europe. *Sustainable Cities*. Eds. R. Stren, R. White and J. Whitney. Boulder, Westview Press. 83–104.

5

Urban Impacts on the Air

'The buildup of carbon dioxide and other greenhouse gases will raise average temperatures on earth ... Low-lying nations are at risk, and forests and ecosystems may not adapt easily to shifts in climatic zones' (The World Bank 1992: 7).

'Lead poisons many systems in the body and is particularly dangerous to children's developing brains and nervous systems. Airborne lead concentrations are high in polluted urban environments, where lead comes mainly from the exhaust of vehicles burning leaded petrol. Elevated lead levels in children have been associated with impaired neuropsychologic development as measured by loss of IQ, poor school performance, and behavioral difficulties' (The World Bank 1993: 96).

It would be easier to arrange the subsequent chapters of this book in the traditional, sectoral way—housing, transportation, waste management, and so on—the various aspects of the urban system as usually classified by the human beings who built them. However, the ecosystem approach, and the metabolism metaphor, suggest that we look at the ways an urban system, as a whole, modifies the surrounding environment—the atmosphere, the lithosphere, and the hydrosphere. The ecosystem approach is based on the components of the biosphere itself—air, ground and water—rather than the superimposed creations of human beings, such as houses, cars and human wastes. Even with this approach, in the context of urban systems, air, ground and water may not be treated as three separate realms because they interpenetrate one another. In terms of the impacts of the residuals from urban systems on the biosphere the major division is between those gaseous residuals that are discharged from vehicles, buildings and industrial premises into the air, and those solid and liquid wastes that are discharged into water bodies and directly into the ground. Clearly this is still an arbitrary distinction as the gaseous residuals eventually fall on water bodies or on the ground, while moisture vaporises to the air; other elements (such as nitrogen and carbon) oxidise, and so on. Thus the distinction on which Chapters Five and Six are based is an imperfect one.

In terms of impacts both the authorities and the individuals are most concerned with the immediate health implications of uncontrolled, or poorly controlled, discharges to the air, although the inter-related nature of the problem is becoming more widely appreciated:

> 'Of foremost concern is the health and well-being of urban residents. The concentrations of ambient air pollutants which prevail in many urban areas are sufficiently high to cause increased mortality, morbidity, deficits in pulmonary function and cardiovascular and neurobehavioural effects ... Air pollution is seriously damaging material resources in cities, such as buildings and various works of art. Its impact on vegetation is also of concern. Finally urban agglomerations are also the major sources of regional and global atmospheric pollution and emissions of greenhouse gases' (WHO and UNEP 1992: 1).

Until quite recently air quality legislation was considered a luxury that only the richer countries could afford. The health impacts of polluted air—except in the exceptionally severe, but short-lived incidents—were of far less concern that the health impacts of polluted water. There was no pulmonary disease to act as a spur to action as cholera and typhoid had done for water quality in the nineteenth century. There was even a tendency to celebrate the smokestack as a symbol of modernity and industrial progress, whereas no-one ever celebrated the virtues of dirty water.

One reason for heightened concern, as noted in the previous chapter, is the revelation of the disastrous impact of industrialisation on air quality and health in Eastern Europe. Simultaneously the results of the first decade of systematic monitoring of air quality, around the world, paint a very clear picture of what the impacts will be if current trends towards population growth, urbanisation, industrialisation, and increased vehicular traffic continue. As noted by the World Bank:

> 'If the projected growth in demand for vehicular transport and electricity were to be met with the technologies currently in use, emissions of the

main pollutants deriving from these sources would increase five-fold and eleven-fold, respectively, by about 2030 ... In those developing countries now in the throws of industrialization, city air pollution is far worse than in today's industrial countries ... The gap widened marginally over the past decade; high income countries took measures to manage emissions, while pollution levels deteriorated in low-income countries' (World Bank 1992: 90–91).

Unlike the knowledge gaps that hold people back from the development of cheap, non-polluting energy or a cheap means of desalinising salt-water, the provision of decent air quality is one of the situations where humankind is not restrained by lack of knowledge. It is several years since the World Health Organisation laid down guidelines for air quality, as indicated by levels of sulphur dioxide, carbon monoxide, nitrogen dioxide, ozone, lead, and suspended particulate matter (WHO and UNEP 1992: 12). Although, only recently, has the World Bank quantified the 'global burden of disease' by estimating 'disability-adjusted-life-years', as a combination of losses from premature death and losses from disabilities (World Bank 1993: 24). The Bank's report went on to add that acute respiratory infections (largely attributable to poor air quality in developing countries) amounted to 10% of their burden of disease (1993: 91). Faced with the tangible costs of inaction one must estimate the costs of preventative actions. Sadly the WHO-UNEP study notes, 'modern combustion technology is relatively expensive and therefore beyond the scope of many developing countries' (1992: 13).

However, this type of conclusion reflects the traditional approach to reducing harmful discharges to the air by end-of-pipe (or post-combustion) control technologies such as scrubbers on chimneys and catalytic converters on cars, whereas 'Pre-combustion control techniques are often the simplest and most cost-effective method of reducing emissions' (WHO and UNEP 1992: 12). Unfortunately they also tend to be more expensive in terms of capital costs.

Probably there is no economically-feasible technological solution to our worldwide air quality problem, under the present method of accounting costs and benefits, and looking at the urban system as a set of separate emitters of a variety of residuals to the air. If a solution is to be found it will begin with looking at the urban system as an organic whole, and considering the quality of life it

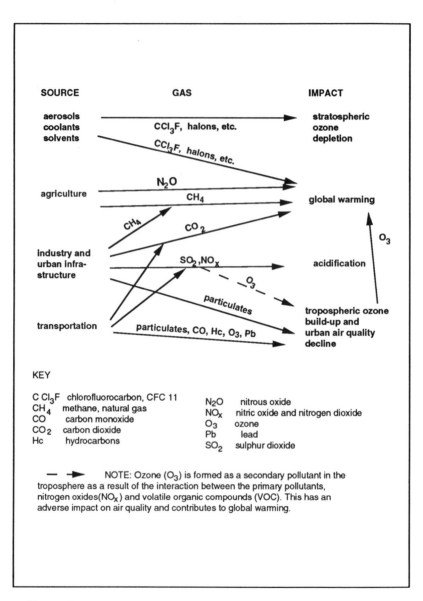

Figure 5.1 Sources and Impacts of Trace Gases in the Atmosphere

provides for all its inhabitants. The rest of this chapter is an attempt to develop such a perspective.

The various impacts of an urban system (and industrialised agriculture) on the air were introduced in Figure 1.3. This figure is redrawn as Figure 5.1, in which the various gases are identified. To these discharge problems should be added the problem of the urban heat island, the phenomenon whereby urban activities and infrastructure raise the air temperature in a city above that of the surrounding countryside. The effect is especially marked in the summertime, and then more especially in the evening and night-time when the dense mass of buildings in the city core slowly releases the heat it has absorbed during the day. The summertime air temperature differential in urban areas in the United States has typically been recorded at about 5°C at night and 2°C during the day (Garbesi et al. 1989: 4).

The interlinked nature of the various problems of urban impacts on the atmosphere is nowhere better illustrated than in the study of this heat island phenomenon which has been underway since early 1970s (Oke 1973). As the heat island effect causes personal discomfort, increases the demand for energy to cool buildings and cars, and increases the rate of smog formation, it is the sub-ject of great interest to urban planners. However, the advent of global warming has further heightened interest in the topic for two reasons. First, the increase in urban temperatures that is predicted for global warming will be *added* to the increase already caused by the heat island effect. Second, mitigation of one effect could lead to mitigation of the other, whether the response comes from reduced car emissions, reduced need for energy for cooling buildings or from the expansion of urban tree-planting pro-grammes (Akbari et al. 1992).

Other elements of the urban impact on the air through emissions of trace gases have already been introduced in the first half of this book. Table 5.1 provides a summary of when the problems were first recognised and when urban planners and city governments began to respond. The dates, of course, are somewhat arbitrary and approximate as problems might be recognised by one sector of the community and yet be ignored, or even denied by another sector. Also responses have varied greatly from country to

Table 5.1 Urban Impacts on the Air: Recognition and Response

	Date Recognised	Date of Response
1. The urban heat island	early 1970s	partial, pending
2. Urban air quality	since antiquity	partial, since 1950s
3. Regional acidification	1950s	early 1970s
4. Greenhouse gas emissions	1896, 1960s	proposals only
5. Stratospheric ozone depletion	1974	1987, Montreal Protocol signed

country. The two widely-separated recognition dates for the problem of greenhouse gas emissions arise from the date of Svante Arrhenius' paper which predicted the global warming impact in 1896 (Arrhenius 1896). However, it was not until the middle of the 1980s that serious attention was paid to the phenomenon, although several scientists repeated his warning in the intervening century (Firor 1990: 44–52). Three points might be made to summarise the response to all of these impacts.

First, they have, so far, been treated as separate issues by the various levels of government, despite scientists' attempts to link them (White 1989). Second, they arise from a common set of causes, namely the increase in the size of the human population, the continuing trend towards urbanisation, the increasing rate of the use of resources, and the production of residuals by the world's richer countries, now joined by the major industrial producers of the South, such as China, India, Brazil, and Mexico. Third, their elimination, or reduction, must be tackled in an integrated fashion, partly because the solution to one may be the solution to another, and partly because the solution of one may increase the impact of another.

An example of the reduction of one problem leading to the reduction of another has already been mentioned above—the reduction in car traffic would improve local air quality and would reduce the production of greenhouse gases. The contrary case— where the reduction of one leads to a deterioration of another— is provided by the reduction of acidifying compounds, like sulphur dioxide and nitrogen dioxide. As they have a cooling effect on air temperature, their reduction is expected to enhance the warming impact of greenhouse gases. More generally, many forms of waste treatment concentrate the wastes into even more problematic forms. For example, scrubbers on power stations concentrate the particles that they prevent from escaping to the atmosphere. Similarly, treated sewage sludge concentrates the heavy metals in the liquid waste stream, as do waste incinerators in their fly ash. Some resources may be recovered from these concentrates but what is left in the scrubbers, the sludge, and the ash must finally be discharged to the ground or the water. Logically the only way to reduce discharges *in toto* is to reduce the generation of residuals through a reduction in the use of resources.

Thus, the impact of our urban, industrial society on the atmosphere may be summarised quite briefly. The technological base of our society has come increasingly to rely on the burning of fossil fuels and the development of synthetic chemicals. We discover the negative side-effects of these innovations only after they have been in use for many years, by which time some of us have become dependent on their continued availability. The reversal of these impacts is always costly and sets one segment of society against another, generally along the lines of the impact*er* and the impact*ee*. The impacts of different technologies are imperfectly known, but linkages between the problematic technologies, both in origin and in impact, are daily becoming more evident (Moroz 1989: 476–81). Rather than attempting to disentangle such impacts at this stage, it might be more useful to examine the technologies themselves. These are divided into buildings, industry, and transportation.

The buildings we live and work in

In Chapter One it was shown how countries pass through a 'pollution transition' as they become richer, increase the intensity of their resource use, and adopt modern technology (See Figure 1.2). For the poorer countries the first hurdle is to reduce the quantity of particulate matter suspended in the air. It is this form of air pollution that has the most direct consequences for human health, both in the outdoor (ambient) environment and in the indoor environment (home and workplace). The WHO 24-hour guideline for total suspended particulates (TSP) is a maximum of

150 to 230 micrograms per cubic metre, yet 'air in such cities as Delhi, India and Xian, China contains daily averages of 500 micrograms' and 'smoky houses in Nepal and Papua New Guinea have peak levels of 10,000 or more' (World Bank 1993: 91). Of course, for the poorest people, the indoor/outdoor comparisons are meaningless, because they live and work outdoors, as hawkers selling in the street, and, as pavement dwellers, sleeping there at night.

For the countries of the South it is the perhaps the impact of buildings on their inhabitants that is of most critical concern, whether it be from smoky cooking fires in the home or from particulates in cement factories or heavy metals in paint factories. In contrast, indoor air quality has been a target for building designers in the North for many years, although sometimes this has produced paradoxical results as people have insulated themselves more and more from the outside world. In doing so they contribute significantly to the heat indoors from the warmth of their own bodies and this requires energy intensive air conditioning, sometimes even in winter in cold countries. This development has taken place in a piecemeal fashion, however, and not as part of an overall design for urban living. We are now facing some difficult consequences of this blind evolution of the modern, energy-intensive city.

We can readily trace the stages by which human society has become more urbanised, and consequently people have progressively removed themselves from the natural environment. Humans first flourished in forests and along the sea-shore, where both tools and food were most readily available. In cities today, we grow very little of our own food, and for much of the day we may live in offices and factories where the air is breathable only because energy is brought in to clean and cool the air and circulate it around the buildings. In Toronto, if you live in a high-rise apartment building over a subway station, and you work in a similarly situated office downtown, it is possible to go from bedroom to office without setting foot outside. There is now a very extensive and interconnected underground mall system throughout the downtown core which connects with the subway system, so, if you go 'out' to shop or eat at lunchtime you need not go outside then either. Although this arrangement might be very convenient on a cold day in winter, as well as on a hot day in summer, it has been achieved by creating a totally artificial environment, and one that is heavily dependent on the consumption of cheap energy. The implications of the development of an artificial environment can be divided into the indoor impacts on people and the outdoor impacts on the air.

The risks of the indoor environment in the rich countries of the North have become better known over the last 15 years, especially since the recognition of 'sick building syndrome'—a condition in which the indoor air quality is so poor that it can be correlated with the ill health of the regular inhabitants (Deelstra 1992: 77). The potentially lethal aspects of indoor air quality were dramatically illustrated by the outbreak of Legionnaire's disease (a pulmonary infection spread by bacteria living in contaminated water in air conditioners) which resulted in fatalities in Philadelphia in 1976 (Rowland and Cooper 1983: 40). Since that time the issue of indoor air quality has received a great deal of attention, especially once it was linked to patterns of absenteeism which had implications for profitability. The change in attitude can also be seen by the speed with which legislation to curtail smoking indoors has been enacted in many cities. What was once considered an inalienable right to pollute one's lungs and the atmosphere has now become a punishable offence. The reason for the speed of the response was probably not so much the evidence for the carcinogenic properties of secondary smoke, nor the death toll that could be attributed to smokers, but the evident cost to the company owning or renting the buildings. These financial costs included the health impacts on the employees (smokers and non-smokers alike), the cleaning bill for curtains, carpets, and paintwork, the fire insurance premiums and the malfunctioning of computer disks affected by deposits of nicotine and particulates. In the end, the company accountants achieved what the non-smoking lobbies could not; they calculated a new bottom line and smoking in the workplace is being abolished. Ironically, the very measures that had been taken to draught-proof and insulate buildings to reduce energy consumption, have also reduced air circulation and hence increased the pressure to stop smoking indoors (Rowland and Cooper 1983:125). Because the drive to make buildings more efficient will continue, the indoor issues are now linked to the wider, outdoor environmental changes. The better insulated buildings will be warmer, and this may require year-round air conditioning to counteract the effect of body heat. In the absence of other technological changes this would, in turn, boost the energy requirement for the building and thereby increase the production of troublesome residuals such as sulphur dioxide and carbon dioxide.

Meanwhile, global atmospheric changes have also increased the pressure to change the design of buildings, both residential and commercial. A recent proposal for district cooling in downtown Toronto using cold water drawn from Lake Ontario stated:

> 'The primary motivation was the growing public concern to reduce the contribution made by Toronto to global environmental problems, notably potential global warming from emission of carbon dioxide during the burning of fossil fuels and also depletion of the ozone layer in the upper atmosphere from the release of chlorofluorocarbons (CFCs) used in conventional air-conditioning and other equipment' (Canadian Urban Institute 1993:11).

The proposal recommended drawing water at $4°C$, from 80m deep, 6 km from the shore, to cool office buildings in the downtown core. This would reduce electric power use in the buildings by 90%, reduce recurrent costs to the user by 50% and eliminate the use of 450 tons of CFCs presently employed in the chiller plants run by the individual buildings. The original proposal for the scheme dubbed it 'Freecool', but this label has since been dropped as there is an estimated capital cost of Cnd.$ 611 million (Gilbert 1993b). The concerns that were raised during a preliminary appraisal of the project included the environmental impact of returning warmer water to the lake, the possible weakening of the first priority for reducing demand for power (mainly by retrofitting buildings), and the uncertainties surrounding the availability of cold water at that depth under scenarios predicting global warming (Canadian Urban Institute 1993). Perhaps the main problem, however, is not financial, technical or environmental, but bureaucratic. It is a radical proposal; it requires close cooperation among a variety of interests (including four levels of government and the private sector), and timing is crucial. In order to comply with federal legislation to phase out the use of CFCs in Canada, building owners and operators have to make decisions regarding new technology in the next two or three years. Without a clear signal on the project from the governments involved, the operators will go ahead independently to implement other cooling techniques, which may be simpler and cheaper to install but less energy-efficient for the urban system as a whole.

Complicated as such decisions are there is some hope that they will be made in a fairly rational manner because the costs and benefits are visible, the CFC problem now has a legal basis, and the global warming issue is firmly on the urban agenda (City of Toronto 1991; Metropolitan Toronto Government 1991). Faced with these developments, owners and operators of large buildings will have to formulate a strategy. However, there is less pressure to adjust for the individual homeowner and tenant. Despite the emergence of household energy audits the housing market will be slow to respond to the issues of environmental change, even when the benefits of improved practice can clearly be shown. In North American suburbs there are demonstrable capital savings and recurrent savings (especially from reduced energy demand), for new, semi-detached, two-storey houses on a 21 foot wide lot compared with ranch-style, detached houses on a 'traditional suburban 45 foot lot' (Vojnovic 1992: 42). New houses are also being built in clusters and rows; in North America they are sold as 'townhouses' in an effort to recall the elegance of the eighteenth century upper classes, and to avoid the image of the working class 'terrace' that housed the workers of the industrial revolution. However, the very efficiency of the more compact type of housing development will make it more afford-able, and hence accessible to lower income groups, and this factor may make the concept unattractive to people living in adjacent, higher income neighbourhoods (Vojnovic 1992: 52), where space is widely valued as a visible sign of social status. In Europe, espe-cially in the Netherlands, this is less of a problem. There, at least, the government and many of the people accept that land is a very scarce resource and must be treated accordingly.

Because the housing stock is replaced very slowly it is even more important to encourage the retrofitting of older houses to reduce CO_2 emissions and simultaneously reduce the recurrent costs for the occupant. For electrical appliances, alone, in the UK, the saving represented by the best that are available and the average

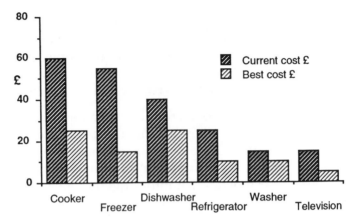

Figure 5.2   Annual Cost of Energy for Household Appliances. *Source*: UK Department of Energy 1991a: 14

appliances currently in use is about 50%, both in annual cost to the user and annual emissions of CO_2. (See Figures 5.2 and 5.3.) Even greater reductions in running costs and emissions can be gained by installing double glazing and fully insulating the building envelope and hot water pipes. Even if all the work were done by a contractor, the Department of Energy (UK) estimates a payback period of five to six years for comprehensive insulation,

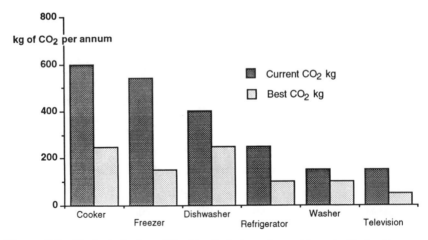

Figure 5.3   Typical Carbon Dioxide Emissions from Household Appliances. *Source*: UK Department of Energy 1991a: 14

and a further reduction of 3500 kg of CO_2 annually per house. Thus, despite the imperfections of the housing market, and the capital costs involved, there are major gains to be made in the reduction of CO_2 discharges alone if the housing stock were upgraded and more efficient appliances installed. The savings to be gained will vary from place to place, of course, according to the source of energy currently in use.

In the United States, in 1989, buildings used $200 billion worth of energy just for basic lighting, space heating and air conditioning, which is more than was used by the industrial processes and transportation. Of this total, residences used $120 billion and the balance was attributed to commercial buildings, including offices, shops, schools and hospitals (Rosenfeld and Ward 1992: 223). Despite the fact that many people in the North have been aware of an energy crisis for some time, improvements are painfully slow.

'Many studies have quantified the vast "reserves" of energy being squan-dered by outmoded building technologies and processes in the United States. These studies show that improving the efficiency of U.S. energy end uses—refrigerators, lights and HVAC systems (for heating, ventilation and air conditioning)—could make as much energy available as would be supplied by a major new oil or natural gas field. Energy-efficient retrofits (improvements in existing buildings) can affordably reduce demand in U.S. buildings by as much as 50% ... As replacing conventional sources of energy with alternatives (wind, biomass, solar and others) could take as long as 20 years, energy-efficient improvements can bridge this time gap' (Rosenfeld and Ward 1992: 223–4).

One reason why progress has been slow in reducing the energy demands and the environmental impacts of our buildings is that improvement is a function of the many thousands of decisions of householders and building owners, many of whom lack capital or else have a very short-term perspective on the problem. These constraints are less evident in the industrial sector, and, in some countries, significant progress has been made.

The industrial processes we use

A 1988 estimate of carbon dioxide emissions from the City of Toronto attributed 46% to commercial and residential buildings,

37% to transport and 17% to industry. Hence the significance of the Deep Lake Water Cooling Proposal. However, in the broader context of the whole of the Province of Ontario, even this ambitious project would reduce current carbon dioxide emissions by 'only' 146 000 tons per year, compared with the total emissions of all coal-fired generating plants of 28 million tons, or half a per-cent (Canadian Urban Institute 1993: 43). Outside the downtown cores of modern cities, with their clusters of energy-voracious skyscrapers, transportation and industry contribute much more to the total. Furthermore, the transportation sector is increasing its absolute, and percentage, contribution worldwide, as cars pro-liferate and road haulage captures the freight market from the railways (International Energy Agency 1991: 33). Indeed one can easily see an evolution in the importance of discharges to the air that is correlated with *per capita* income. (See Figure 1.2 in Chapter One.) Thus, under present trends, the countries of the South that do grow economically will bring their particulate emissions under control, then go through a phase of emitting more sulphur oxides and nitrogen oxides (SO_2 and NO_x), before they too are controlled, but, inexorably, it presently seems, their economic growth will add to the global carbon dioxide overload, because no country yet has done better than hold these emissions steady. (See Figures 5.4, 5.5 and 5.6.) CO_2 emissions, in the OECD, are roughly

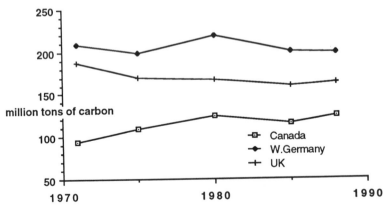

Figure 5.4   Carbon Dioxide Emissions from Energy Use. *Source*: OECD 1991b: 17

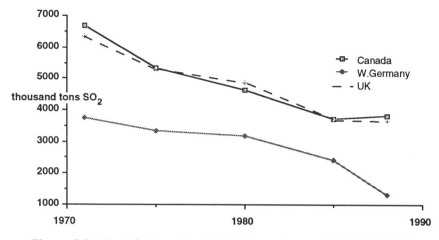

Figure 5.5 Total Sulphur Dioxide Emissions. *Source*: OECD 1991: 21

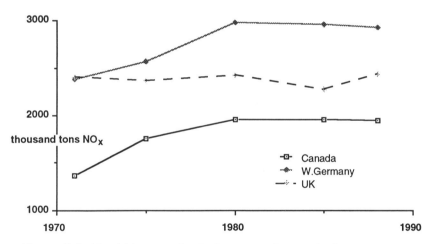

Figure 5.6 Total Nitrogen Oxide Emissions. *Source*: OECD 1991b: 23

apportioned one third each to transportation, industry and 'other' activities, where 93% of the last category comes from residential and commercial buildings (International Energy Agency 1991: 27–8). Industry makes the heaviest contribution to SO_2 emissions, and transport the most to NO_x. From industry, half of the CO_2 emissions come from iron and steel, and chemicals. (See Figures 5.7 and 5.8.) The calculations 'include emissions related to the end-use of electricity in each sector' (International Energy

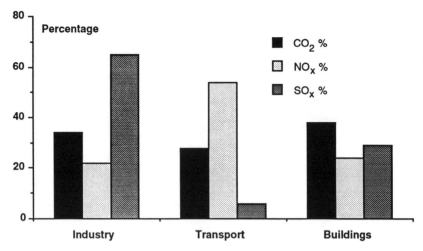

Figure 5.7   OECD Emissions by Economic Sector. *Source*: International Energy Agency 1991: 27–32

Agency 1991: 26–7), as well as the primary contribution from each sector.

It is in the industrial sector that the most encouraging progress has been made in reducing discharges to the air, primarily by using energy more efficiently (through in-plant energy recovery, for example), and by installing scrubbers and introducing other emission-reduction processes to thermal generating stations, smelters, and other industrial plants. Partly this can be attributed to the greater ease with which bureaucracy can legislate for, and then enforce, emission controls on point sources of pollution— as opposed to area sources of pollution, such as masses of buildings and vehicles—and thus provide an incentive for industry to respond. This has happened because the damage done by the impact of SO_2 and NO_x on urban infrastructure, buildings (including world-famous sites like the Acropolis and the Taj Mahal), crops, forests and lakes is very visible and has been monitored for over 30 years. Because the acidification problems have been studied and partly rectified (at least in some countries of the North), attitudes have also changed. Some industrialists have learned that low waste technology is more efficient, and that some waste products can be sold (Campbell and Glenn 1982; Kanté 1986). There is growing interest in examining the

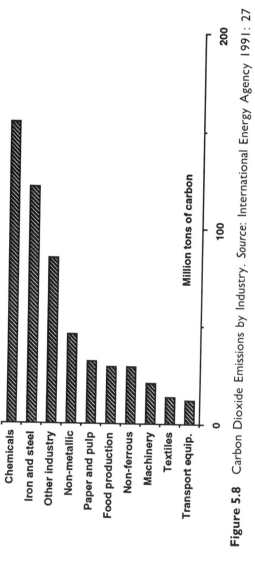

Figure 5.8 Carbon Dioxide Emissions by Industry. *Source*: International Energy Agency 1991: 27

whole product life cycle of goods like cars, and then planning—from the time the product is designed—for the eventual recovery of materials. Products such as refrigerators and office equipment are now being designed with the eventual costs of dismantling them, and recovering the materials, in mind. Thus there is increasing acceptance of the idea that manufacturing produces residuals as well as products, and that someone must accept responsibility for the residuals.

The foregoing should not suggest that the battle is won and that industry henceforth will not be a problem for air quality, acidification, or climate change. Only a few governments, and a few industrialists in a few countries are committed to this new way of thinking. Many governments (including the United States and the United Kingdom) hope that the sale of (annual) pollution rights will keep the problem in check, without worrying about the cumulative impact over many years, or the transboundary effects of airborne residuals arriving from neighbouring, and even distant, countries. Hardly anyone has yet seriously addressed the problem of the transfer of the best and cleanest technology to the newly-industrialising countries of the South (White 1992b). However, many ecosystems are already severely degraded, as we have seen in Central and Eastern Europe, and it is far from clear how such regions can be rehabilitated without significant international cooperation.

The vehicles we travel in

Perhaps within the next 20 or 30 years social historians will look back at the car age and search for factors that will explain the sudden explosion of what can only be considered as humankind's greatest peacetime aberration. The car evolved from being the luxury conveyance of the rich to a means of mass transportation in a scant 30 years, interrupted by the Second World War. In so doing it ceased to be a personal convenience and, instead, became an article of mass misery. The journey to and from work by car, in most cities, is the urban scale equivalent of hundreds of people trying to force their way through a revolving door at the same time. Logistically, financially, and environmentally it makes no sense at all. Despite all this, the car continues to proliferate inexorably; between 1970 and 1987 the number of cars worldwide doubled from 200 million to 400 million. Figure 5.9 tells the story only so far, and the bottom of the figure shows the small number of cars in the East and the South, areas where—under the present trajectory—some measure of prosperity threatens to produce huge numbers of additional cars, as mentioned in the previous

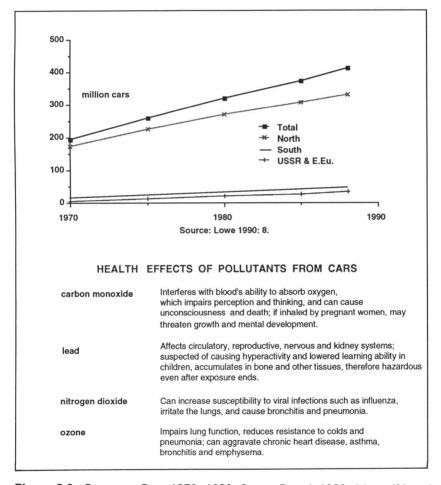

Figure 5.9 Passenger Cars, 1970–1988. *Source*: French 1990: 14, itself based mainly on *The Clean Air Act: A Briefing Book for Members of Congress*, National Clean Air Coalition, Washington DC 1985. *Note*: Cars are a primary source, but not the only source, of these pollutants

chapter. In Mexico City—the most polluted air-shed in the world —'only' 20% of the city's families own cars. There is a considerable 'latent demand' for more, meaning that the market is far from saturated, and, if incomes increase, so will sales of cars. Nor can this process be ascribed solely to individual selfishness or shortsightedness. The vision which abets the process is eagerly supported by most governments in the world, either because they cannot imagine an alternative or because they fear the unemployment that might result from a decline in the manufacture of private cars. In a few cities of the South, like Singapore and Curitiba, and a few in the North, like Vienna, Zurich, and Delft, a stand has been made to bring some sanity back to urban transportation, using public transport, cycling, and walking.

It is ironic that, even before the current concern over global warming, the petrol engine, and the car in particular (through sheer numbers), has long been a very deficient technology from the perspective of the health of the urban ecosystem and its human inhabitants. Emission figures from the UK attribute 90% of carbon monoxide, 90% of lead, 25% of nitrogen oxides and 30% of hydrocarbons to motor vehicles (Rowland and Cooper 1983: 121). Figures from Los Angeles in the 1970s confirmed the predominant role of the motor vehicles as a source of hydrocarbons and carbon monoxide—the major contributors to poor air quality in the urban environment (Figure 5.10). Since then increasingly stringent legislation for California has reduced the problem in Los Angeles, mostly through requiring the fitting of catalytic converters on all new cars. The effect has been fairly rapid because of the frequent turnover of the car population. However, the 1973 picture for Los Angeles remains the norm for most countries of the South, where legislation is much weaker, enforcement more difficult, and the car population much older and poorly maintained.

Until recently the local air quality issues dominated the debate over emission control and thus the use of catalytic converters has been made mandatory, at national level, in most countries of the North, beginning with the United States in 1975. However, the converters do nothing for the emission of carbon dioxide. The solution of this problem will require fundamental changes in human behaviour in the car-owning portion of the world's

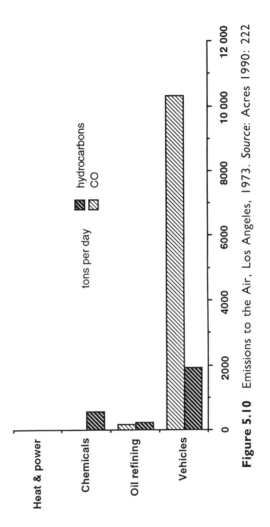

Figure 5.10 Emissions to the Air, Los Angeles, 1973. *Source: Acres 1990: 222*

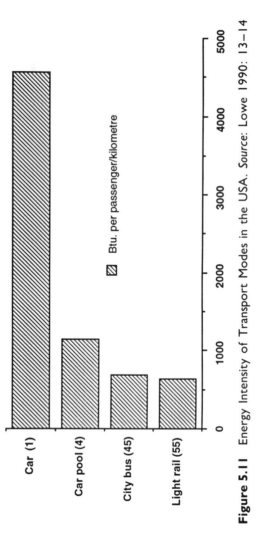

Figure 5.11 Energy Intensity of Transport Modes in the USA. *Source*: Lowe 1990: 13–14

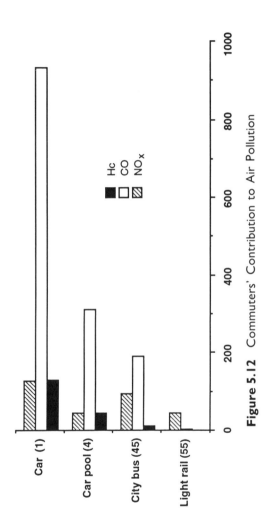

Figure 5.12 Commuters' Contribution to Air Pollution

population, not just a technological fix. Typically, in North America, 80% of commuters travel alone. This is a group that Wilfred Bach categorises as 'motorised individual traffic' (Bach et al. 1993). Some of the implications of this fact, in terms of energy intensity and air pollution, are indicated in Figures 5.11 and 5.12. For urban planners it is becoming increasingly obvious that car use is inversely correlated with density of settlement, specifically the sprawl of the suburbs in the North (Figures 5.13 and 5.14). That is one of the principal reasons why many planners are now advocating the intensification of suburbs, whereby the higher density would make public transport viable and private transport less necessary, while shortening journeys to work, shopping, and recreation (Canadian Urban Institute 1993).

Undoubtedly, the transportation sector has the greatest potential for reducing harmful discharges to the air because it is so extraordinarily inefficient; indeed our old technologies, like the bicycle and the trolley bus (not to mention feet), are far more efficient when all the environmental implications are taken into account (Lowe 1989). However, the urban planner's dilemma is that this is the sector where the greatest resistance to improvements will probably come. Because the car has come to epitomise material progress (meaning accumulation), individuals will resist limitations on their use if it. This is true for the car-based cities of North

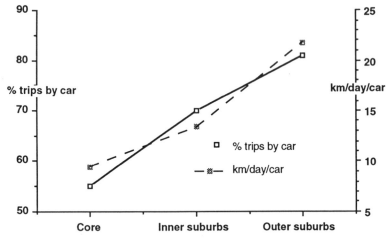

Figure 5.13 Car Use and Distance Travelled. *Source:* Gilbert 1991: 184

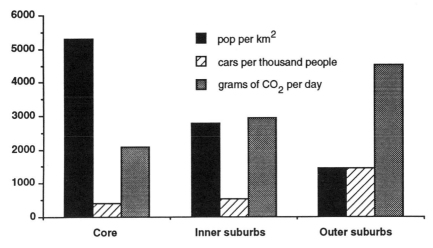

Figure 5.14 Toronto: Population, Car Ownership, Carbon Dioxide Impact. *Source*: Gilbert 1991: 184

America, the dispersed suburbs of post-war Europe and the emerging urban consumers of the South and the East. It is especially true in the American West where low densities of population appear to require the car for the continuation of the local culture. This regional predicament makes it difficult for any American government, whether federal or state, to raise the price of petrol through taxation, even though prices in America are less than half the prices in Europe.

A comparison between the three sectors—housing, industry and transportation

The advantage that the industrial sector enjoys over the household sector and the transportation sector is that the decisions are concentrated in fewer hands and they are made by people who are accustomed to comparing capital costs with recurrent costs. They can fairly readily estimate the pay-back period on a piece of equipment that will reduce energy use, as well as the production of residuals. And they are being progressively obliged to internalise the cost of those residuals by government legislation. However, the processes available for achieving the same result in the transportation and housing sectors are more cumbersome, in terms of legislation, and also both must work against rising trends in terms of demand. Industry, throughout the North at least, is learning to produce more value of output with fewer inputs, and thus could meet increased demands without using more energy or producing more residuals. The unmet demand for both housing and transportation is so large, however, that huge increases in efficiency will be required to counter-balance rising demand, especially if the South continues to imitate the North's inefficient urban systems.

In terms of discharges to the air it would appear that several changes in direction are required. First, a denser urban form than that of the Northern suburb (especially the North American suburb), will help to reduce the energy demand for housing, while at the same time reducing dependence on motorised individual transport for commuting and for other trips. It is unlikely that such changes will occur by following the present piecemeal approach to change in the North, while simultaneously ignoring the deep problems posed by poverty and rapid population growth in the South. It is likely, however, that an integrated approach to the problem will produce better results.

An integrated energy and ecosystem approach

As we will see in the next chapter, water is probably the most critical limiting factor in the maintenance of our urban culture. However, as far as discharges to the air are concerned, energy is the heart of the issue (Hollander 1992). This is especially true for carbon dioxide and sulphur dioxide, the principal contributors to global warming and acidification respectively. (See Table 5.2.) Within this field there is every possibility for the agencies responsible for urban environmental management to work at cross purposes. As was clear in the example regarding cooling buildings in downtown Toronto, one group might advocate the switch to a less polluting source of energy—deep lake water. While another would emphasise that the key is to reduce demand, which retrofitting the buildings in the Toronto core could do by 75% (Canadian Urban Institute 1993: 45). If such alternatives are considered from the ecosystem vantage point they can readily

Table 5.2   Examples of Environmental Impacts of the Energy Sector

Type of impact on the atmosphere	Human impact compared to natural processes	Energy's share of the human impact
Greenhouse gases		
Build-up of CO_2	27%	80%
Emission of CH_4 (methane)	100%	25%
Acidification		
Emission of SO_2	140%	85%
Local air quality		
Emission of Pb (lead)	1500%	65%
Emission of particulates	25%	45%

Source: Holdren 1992: 167.

be reconciled—retrofit is an essential step, and deep lake water cooling should be made available for the remaining demand.

It has been known for 30 years that, so long as private travel demand remains unsaturated, any increase in car infrastructure, such as roads and parking spaces, will soon become congested. Thus, the traffic conundrum is a deep problem, although reality is beginning to seep through into the argument. Philip Goodwin reports an interesting example of this process at work in the British Government:

'In April 1989 the Department of Transport issued some revised traffic forecasts (the earlier forecasts having underestimated traffic growth). These forecasts suggested that economic growth and existing trends would result in traffic levels by the year 2025 that would be between 83% and 143% higher than in 1988—i.e. broadly double the current levels ... The single most important conclusion of the resulting discussion was the proposition that there is no possibility of increasing road supply at a level which matches the growth in demand ... Demand management would therefore become the centre of transport policy; if supply cannot be matched to demand, demand has to be matched to supply' (Goodwin 1991: 9–10).

Systems engineers and ecologists would both paraphrase this realisation as meaning that you cannot outfeed a positive feed-back. Roads encourage cars; more cars produce congestion; congestion requires more roads; roads encourage ... Note that this is a universal rule. It even applies in a small densely populated country like Britain, which still has good inter-city trains, public transport in the cities, and a high degree of public support for the preservation of green space and urban amenities. Yet, despite all these factors, and despite the fact that the Department of Transport knows that the traditional responses cannot work, the road construction programme in Britain continues unabated.

Discussion of demand management is the starting point on a saner path, although one can remain at the discussion stage for a long time without anything being done. Some progress has been made in beginning to apply demand management to the water and energy sectors, but it will be more difficult to apply to transportation, especially in countries where car ownership is already widespread. Moreover, demand management implies that people can still manage the system using traditional planning concepts, making policy choices between managing supply or managing demand, as if the process were flexible and reversible. Environmental impacts that we have been measuring for more than 30 years (in the case of acid deposition and carbon dioxide build-up) insist that reality is otherwise. Large scale system changes in the atmosphere have been indicating for some time that the air is not an inexhaustible sink that need concern us only when it becomes difficult to breathe. This same principle applies to the capacity of forests and fisheries to produce a sustainable yield, and to the capacity of the ground and water to assimilate human wastes. Some of these problems are introduced in the next chapter.

Further reading:

Acres, G. J. K. (1990). Catalyst systems for emission control from motor vehicles. *Pollution. Causes, Effects and Controls*. Ed. R. M. Harrison. Cambridge, The Royal Society of Chemistry. 221–236.

Davison, A. and Barnes, J. (1992). Patterns of air pollution: critical loads and abatement strategies. *Managing the Human Impact on the Natural Environment*. Ed. M. Newson. London, Belhaven Press. 109–29.

Douglas, I. (1983). *The Urban Environment*. London, Edward Arnold. See Chapter 4, The energy balance of the city.

Firor, J. (1990). *The Changing Atmosphere. A Global Challenge*. New Haven, Yale University Press.

Goudie, A. (1986). *The Human Impact on the Natural Environment.* Cambridge, MIT Press. See Chapter 7, The human impact on climate and the atmosphere.

Harrison, R. M., Ed. (1990). *Pollution: Causes, Effects and Control.* Cambridge, Royal Society of Chemistry. See Chapters 7–12, including Acres, cited above.

International Energy Agency (1991). *Energy Efficiency and the Environment.* Paris, OECD.

Lowe, M. D. (1990). *Alternatives to the Automobile: Transport for Livable Cities.* Washington, DC, Worldwatch Institute.

Moroz, W. J. (1989). Air pollution. *Environmental Science and Engineering.* Eds. J. G. Henry and G. W. Heinke. Englewood Cliffs, Prentice-Hall.

White, J. C., Ed. (1989). *Global Climate Change Linkages. Acid Rain, Air Quality, and Stratospheric Ozone.* New York, Elsevier.

6

Urban Impacts on Ground and Water

'When waste from a dump at Love Canal, near Niagara, USA started bubbling into people's cellars and gardens the government declared a national emergency. The subsequent lawsuits over the deformities and cancers the chemicals may have caused lasted for many years' (Douglas 1983: 158).

As they contemplate multistorey buildings, flyovers, and factory chimneys, humans may be impressed by the three-dimensional nature of the city, but from a more lofty perspective the city is an almost flat, two-dimensional structure, spread thinly over the earth's surface. It is exactly this kind of large, multicellular structure that James Lovelock predicted would have difficulty developing adequate circulatory systems to bring in nutrients and extrude wastes. (See Chapter Three.) This remains a serious physical problem. Whatever planners may say about the agglomeration economies of large settlements, it remains an inescapable physical fact that larger and larger quantities of energy are required to maintain the circulatory system as a city grows in size. It may be financially cheaper, per unit, for larger settlements to educate one child, deliver 1000 litres of water and provide 1000 kilowatt hours of electricity, but more energy is required to perform the task, simply because of the movement required to carry it out. In most large cities of the North fewer and fewer children walk or cycle to school; they need a bus or a parent's car. Human wastes can no longer be carried out to the fields to be used as fertiliser; they must be flushed through a sewer system. Householders no longer collect their own firewood; they must be hooked to the grid which may bring electricity from hundreds of kilometres away. Indeed, if you asked an average group of citizens of a large city where their power or water came from, or where their wastes ended up (especially their sewage), very few would know, and even fewer would care.

From time to time these provision and disposal problems reach crisis proportions and they rise swiftly on the political agenda; although, as soon as the problem appears to be fixed, the issue disappears totally from view. However, we are now approaching a whole set of interlinked urban provision and disposal problems because human numbers are rising, urbanisation continues, and the process of economic development in many countries in the South has stalled. Urban dwellers can no longer take the physical environment for granted, as an endless supplier of needs and as a receptacle for wastes. This is visibly evident in most cities of the South where many of the inhabitants live in shantytowns that are completely without infrastructure of any kind. As Hardoy and Satterthwaite bluntly put it: 'Most cities in Africa, and many in Asia have no sewers at all' (Hardoy and Satterthwaite 1992: iv).

Meanwhile, in those cities of the North that went through the nineteenth century industrial revolution much of the infrastructure in the core of the city is over a hundred years old and urgently needs replacement. In some cases simple replacement will not suffice because the increasing size of cities has overwhelmed the old technology, as is seen frequently in combined sewer and stormwater discharge systems. Some of these problems are chronic in the sense that they may impede the daily life of the city and affect the health of the poorer members of society. Sometimes they become acute, as in the case of the underground Chicago flood in April 1992 which is estimated to have cost businesses US $ 1 billion in lost sales and clean-up operations, before facing the public costs of infrastructure repairs to the subway and drainage systems (Durr 1992). Only a few days after the Chicago accident, the explosion of underground gas pipelines, in the Mexican city of Guadalajara, killed over 200 people, injured 1200 and left thousands more homeless (Grant 1992). Both accidents were caused by the failure of infrastructure which had already been signalled as unsafe. Fire, floods and diseases have been persistent threats to urban life, but for a time—

in some cities, at least—they appeared to be under control. Now, in many parts of the world they are returning.

However much control people seemed to exert over their physical surroundings, cities have remained inescapably part of the global hydrological cycle and have remained dependent on the produce of the soil. It is true that they have put these components of the environment to their use, but they have never ceased to be totally dependent on them in the deepest sense. Few people in modern cities collect rainwater (except perhaps for the garden), and thus they are dependent on water being brought in, either from surface sources or pumped from groundwater. The presence of water in those locations is dependent on recharge from rainfall and hence the crucial importance of the rainfall changes associated with the greenhouse effect. Although it is known that the warming effect will increase the evaporation of water from the soil, there is much uncertainty concerning changes in patterns of precipitation. Thus, it is not yet possible to predict, regionally, whether the increase in evaporation will be compensated for by increased precipitation. Increased evaporation will also tend to reduce the availability of water stored on the surface in reservoirs. In England there is real concern that clay soils will shrink as a result of evaporation and thus destabilise the foundations of buildings as well as affect the suitability of soils for agriculture, especially in the drier south-east half of the country (Parry and contributors 1991: 15–27). However, climate change would simply exacerbate environmental trends that were already well underway due to the non-sustainable use of resources by human beings. For example, cities themselves have had a dramatic effect on the availability of water through overpumping the groundwater. Andrew Goudie cites the case of London, which between 1850 and the Second World War, reduced the groundwater levels in the local basin by 60m (Goudie 1986: 168). Similar falls in groundwater levels are still taking place in the fast-growing cities of the South, with Mexico City and Bangkok providing the most dramatic examples. The adverse impacts of falls in the water table, other than the decreasing availability of water, are numerous. Subsidence is an obvious danger to buildings and underground infrastructure, such as sewage pipes, water pipes, and gas lines.

For coastal cities the overpumping problem may be compounded by saline intrusion into aquifers. Reduced elevation also makes the city more prone to flooding both from the sea and from the rivers upstream. Not only the city suffers from overpumping; so does the surrounding countryside, especially in areas where agriculture is dependent on irrigation. Apart from overpumping groundwater, cities have altered the local hydrological cycle by replacing vegetation with the impermeable surfaces of cement and bitumen, thereby increasing rainfall runoff, especially for peak flows, and thereby increasing the likelihood of floods in the city and increasing the erosion of channels downstream.

One of the difficulties in treating sewage in the richer countries of the North is the great quantity of waste water that flows with it in those cities where combined evacuation systems mix sewage and stormwater. The problem becomes acute when heavy storms overload the sewage treatment capacity and thus both rainwater and sewage are discharged, untreated, to the environment. The problem is exacerbated by the fact that the very process of Western urbanisation, by cementing over much of the land surface and canalising river channels through cement causeways and tunnels, has greatly increased the rate of runoff that follows a storm (Goudie 1986: 158–62).

In addition to direct urban impacts on the hydrological cycle through abstracting water from the surface and from the ground, urban dwellers affect the quality of the soil and the water by their methods of waste disposal, both for liquid and solid wastes. Until recently solid waste disposal has been seen as less problematic than water supply because the negative health impacts of inadequate waste management systems are less immediate than the impacts of having too little water or water of poor quality. However, the recent, large scale outbreaks of cholera in Latin America and Africa have served as a reminder that our methods of waste disposal are inextricably linked to the provision of an adequate water supply.

Surface discharges to streams and beaches

Overall, the human use of water can be grouped into six sets of operations—water supply, treatment, and distribution, followed by wastewater collection, treatment and discharge. However, these operations should not be managed in isolation. Whereas water supply has been an urban preoccupation since antiquity, the disposal of wastes, especially liquid wastes, has usually been treated as a much lower priority. Even today, when the folly of providing water, using it, and then disposing of it without treatment is well understood, waste treatment capacity frequently lags several years behind the provision of water. Partly this is due simply to the inertia in the system—logically more water must be provided before more water needs to be treated, or perhaps it is assumed that the existing treatment facilities will be adequate.

All too often, if there is a nearby waterbody to absorb the wastes, used water is discharged into that waterbody, untreated. Even in the rich countries of the OECD some 330 million people are not served with wastewater treatment plants (OECD 1991a: 29). In all these countries there has been improvement in the last 20 years but there is still some way to go. Surprisingly, countries with a strong environmental movement (like Norway), and countries with a good record on curbing emissions to the air (like Japan), provide wastewater treatment for less than half their people. Even so, progress in the North, on this issue anyway, may be characterised as 'slow, but steady'. In most regions of the South, however, not only is the starting situation much worse, progress is imperceptible compared with the growth of population. Figure 6.1 shows how far we still have to go even in water supply and

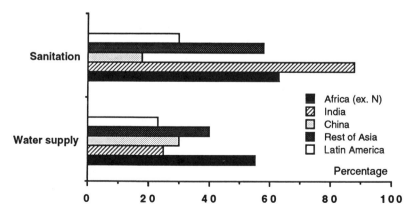

Figure 6.1   Population Without Water Supply and Sanitation. *Source*: Based on World Bank 1993: 91

sanitation, where 'sanitation' refers only to the collection and disposal of wastes, not to treatment.

As the human population has increased, the practice of discharging raw sewage to rivers and shorelines is having increasingly serious impacts. In 1990 a UN advisory group stated:

> 'the principal problem for human health of a world-wide scale is the existence of pathogenic organisms discharged with domestic sewage to coastal waters, estuaries or rivers and drainage canals that carry these organisms to the sea' (quoted in World Resources Institute 1992: 177).

The availability of water of adequate quality and quantity is the most fundamental problem of urban environmental management, for without it mortality rates cannot be brought down. Thus, until we resort to desalinising water or melting glaciers and polar ice-caps on a significant scale, the renewable stock of water should be considered as finite, and it must be managed in a way that will maintain its quality for re-use, as far as possible. This is a difficult objective to accept not only in the poorer countries, but also in the richer ones where there is still a tendency to seek the cheapest water management technique, which is to dump the used water in the nearest waterbody, unless this is prohibited by national legislation. Even when sewage is treated, the disposal of sewage sludge remains a problem. It is argued that land disposal of treated sewage is the most effective means of maintaining nutrient cycles and preventing harmful concentrations of heavy metals and pathogens. The viability of land disposal has been proved, using long term experiments, but the public is generally distrustful of such methods (Sopper 1990: 145; Henry 1989: 438). The alternatives (to recycling sewage within a natural cycle) for disposing of treated sewage sludge are to dump it at sea, to incinerate it (either on land or sea), or to landfill it.

Clean water supply is the number one problem for urban systems, and the presence of sewage is the number one contributor to that problem. However, the supply and treatment of water cannot be considered independently of the energy implications of each process. For example, desalinisation, the incineration of sewage sludge, and the pumping of water from distant sources are all energy-intensive operations. Today, in the North at least, we tend to take the availability of a regular, safe supply of water for granted, but it is not so long ago, in the nineteenth century, that the cities of North America were acutely aware of the critical importance of a reliable water supply to combat the major threats of fire and disease. Yet, even then, there was a reluctance to face up to the problem. Ironically, in Philadelphia, the decision to bring in a public water supply was made in response to an outbreak of yellow fever in 1801—ironic because yellow fever is not a water-borne disease (Blake 1991). The reasoning was that yellow fever was related to the heaps of rubbish and sewage in the streets, and those could best be cleaned by flushing them with water. In New York the spur to action was an outbreak of cholera (which *is* water-borne), in 1832, which killed 3500 people and forced 100 000 to flee the city. Three years later the core of the city was destroyed by fire, and the insurance companies were bankrupted by the ensuing claims (Blake 1991). Eventually, the authorities accepted the need to ensure an adequate supply of water, but always reluctantly and usually (as seen from Wolman's comments quoted in Chapter Three) it was a matter of 'too little, too late'. Yet these towns were little more than large villages at the beginning of the nineteenth century and the early engineers calculated daily demand on a basis of 20 gallons per person (approximately 75 litres)—barely a tenth of what their successors allow for today (Blake 1991).

The tragedy is that in many of the megacities of the South, municipal and national governments need to deal with much larger problems than the early industrial cities of North America, and they have much smaller financial resources *per capita*. The scale of the cholera outbreaks in Peru and Zambia, in 1991–92, demonstrates how the problem has changed in the last 150 years. The cholera outbreaks that afflicted New York and Philadelphia (and the towns of Europe too) were fairly local, being confined to areas of contaminated urban water supply (Douglas 1983: 161). The recent outbreaks, in Latin America and Africa, swept rural and urban areas alike, and spread rapidly into neighbouring countries:

'By the end of April 1991, cholera had reached epidemic proportions in Peru: more than 166,000 cases had been reported and 1,075 people were dead. The epidemic began in the shanty towns along the coastal plain, then spread to the rest of the country—and across the continent. Cholera has now been identified in Ecuador, Colombia, Chile and Brazil, although it has been absent from these countries for decades' (Davidson et al. 1992: 112).

Cholera is transmitted by bacteria living in contaminated water. It causes intense diarrhoea and most fatalities result from extreme dehydration. Unfortunately, the treatment requires a clean supply of water to rehydrate the patient. The return of cholera to Latin America, and Africa, symbolises the *impasse* that has been reached in the processes of Westernisation and urbanisation that are the hallmarks of the development process. Their problem is intensified by the continued rapid growth of the population which constantly worsens the population/resource ratio, especially in those countries where water is already in short supply.

When the scale of the problems of the poorest countries of the South is set alongside the resource use of the North, it seems that the human population is living on two quite different planets. Nothing illustrates this more clearly than the differing rates of water use. Figure 6.2 illustrates the pattern of use in the typical Canadian household of four people averaged over the year. The data are taken from a booklet on water conservation which carries

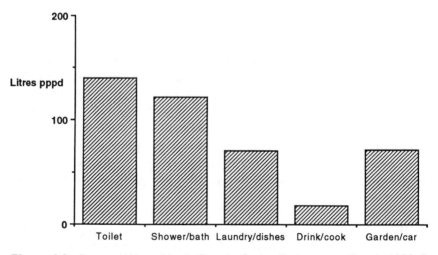

Figure 6.2   Personal Water Use in Canada. *Source:* Environment Canada 1990: 5

such well-meant admonitions as:

> 'Using a running hose to wash your car can waste about 400 litres of water. Using a bucket with a sponge plus a trigger nozzle on the hose will save you about 300 of those litres. And, never clean the driveway or sidewalk with the hose. Use a rake and broom and save about 200 litres of water every time you sweep. If you own a pool, be sure to use a pool cover when it's not in use' (Environment Canada 1990: 15).

It might be thought that water use was one aspect of resource use in the North that had no bearing on resource availability in the South. After all there is no global market for water as a good. However, water needs energy for delivery and treatment; in the household, water used for washing is heated, thereby using more energy (forty times as much as cold water). And, as shown in the previous chapter, energy use is the key to reducing discharges to the air, including greenhouse gases, which is quite certainly a global issue. It has been suggested by Richard Gilbert that, globally, we need to reduce the emission of greenhouse gases by 60% to stabilise the composition of the atmosphere, and, in order to allow for increased energy use for the economic growth of the South, the North should set a 90% reduction in emissions as its share of the target (Gilbert 1992: 2). Under these circumstances the wastage of water is not simply a local issue, but a global one.

Extracting groundwater

The great advantage of extracting water from the ground, compared with using, or creating, a surface storage area, was that it was often of better quality, as many impurities would be filtered as it flowed underground. (This was not always the case, of course, as some groundwater sources were found to be highly mineralised or contained various impurities.) As drilling and pumping techniques improved in the nineteenth century (and as knowledge of the links between water supply and disease became apparent), these advantages of underground sources were greatly prized (Goubert 1989: 197). Only in this century, as human withdrawal of water from the natural cycle has increased so dramatically, have the dangers of misusing groundwater become apparent. First, unconfined groundwater can become contaminated by pesticides, industrial wastes, and household wastes, although not as readily as surface water. Even confined sources can become contaminated through abandoned wells. However, being underground, the contamination is less visible. The other danger of invisibility is that the drawing down of the water table (which occurs as soon as withdrawal exceeds the recharge rate) is not visible to the urban consumer at all, only to engineers who monitor the system. As noted above, in extreme cases the fall in the level of the water table can lead to problems of subsidence and flooding from surface water. A more widespread problem arising from draw-down is the increase in energy required for pumping and the increased flow of contaminants into the wells. Among the major industrial countries it is the United States that has become most dependent on groundwater sources which supply 'about one half of the drinking water and 40% of the irrigation water' (World Resources Institute 1992: 166). In the western part of the country some of the major aquifers have been drawn down for many decades, principally to irrigate crops (Postel 1992: 33; Reisner 1986: 452–4).

Overpumping the aquifer on which a city stands has had dramatic impacts in the South, as is seen nowhere more clearly than in the case of Bangkok. Just as Mexico City's topographical situation aggravates its air quality problem, so Bangkok's situation increases its susceptibility to flooding. Much of the city was only about 2 m above sea level; subsidence in the last 50 years has reduced this by about 60 cm. This is a very significant fall, as the tidal level in November can exceed the norm by 2m. As a consequence:

'flooding ... occurs almost every year, in the months of October and November, and has resulted in great misery for residents and enormous economic costs in terms of damaged roads, telephones, cars etc., and the additional time taken to get to work and school. During the 1975 flood, which lasted three months, total private and public damage was estimated at over ... US$50 million at current prices' (Xoomsai 1988: 10–11).

Although Bangkok is probably the world's most threatened major city due to the rate of depletion and coastal location at the mouth of a major river, many other cities of the South are in a similar predicament, especially other coastal cities such as Manila and Jakarta. For example, 'in Jakarta excessive pumping has resulted in significant salinity intrusion in the unconfined aquifer and in at least one of the confined aquifers' (Bower 1993).

Discharges to the ground

So far attention has focused on the urban impact on water, particularly on the way that engineers have harnessed flowing water to remove the major urban contaminant—wastewater. As shown in Figure 3.1 this water–sewage inflow–outflow is the largest metabolic feature of the urban system, being 60 to 100 times the size of the flow of fuel. If this sanitation technology had not been developed in the nineteenth century cities in the North could not have grown to their present size. Yet, for a long time the way forward was not at all clear, as urban populations made do with open sewers in the streets and household collection services by cart. Eventually urban governments were persuaded that the investment in the rudiments of a circulatory system were worthwhile, at least to evacuate the wastes, if not to treat them. Smaller settlements continued to make do with septic tanks. Unfortunately, as the South urbanises, even that hundred-year old technology is not being applied. Only a small percentage of the houses are attached to a sewer or septic tank system, and virtually none of the sewage is treated (World Resources Institute 1992: 168).

It is mostly sewage that is discharged directly to waterbodies, but a great variety of materials are discharged which go directly to the ground, such as pathogens, excess nutrients, heavy metals, and synthetic organic compounds, toxic industrial wastes, and nuclear wastes, as well as 'normal' municipal wastes. Over the years many of these have come to pose a serious hazard to human health and the integrity of the biosphere. (See Figure 6.3, which shows that, among the OECD countries, Japan produces the most industrial waste per dollar of Gross Domestic Product; the USA produces the most municipal waste per head; while Canada produces the most nuclear waste in relation to the total amount of energy produced.) Only in the last 20 years have even the

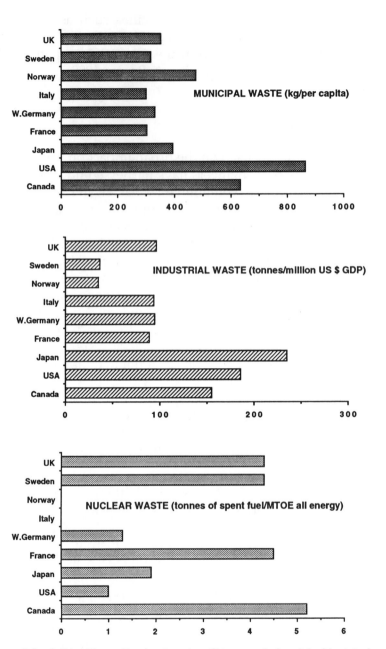

Figure 6.3 Solid Waste Production by Country: Industrial, Municipal and Nuclear. *Source*: OECD 1991a: 45

richest countries taken notice of these various threats, and now attempts are being made to at least identify the more dangerous sites, and priorities are being assigned for cleaning up. However, as the dangers of an improperly managed landfill are being recognised, potential rural sites for landfills are disappearing as local residents adopt the Not In My Backyard Syndrome, even for so-called 'normal' municipal wastes, untainted by the 'special wastes' label that goes with sewage sludge, toxic, medical, and nuclear wastes. Objection is partly a reaction to the daily nuisance of trucks, odour and dust, and the immediate impact of the landfill on land values, but there is a growing fear that harmful substances, known as leachate, may drain from the landfill and contaminate the local groundwater. Those rural areas that are subject to intensive agriculture have already come to the limit of the land's ability to absorb locally produced wastes, especially from agricultural chemicals and from animal manure which produces unabsorbable concentrations of ammonia (Netherlands Ministry of Housing, Physical Planning and Environment 1985: 33).

The richer cities of the North have responded in a variety of ways to these new difficulties. Some have deliberately exported their wastes out of the region, away from their fussy rural neighbours and into lower income regions of the country, and (for toxic wastes) around the world (White 1993a: 154–9). Once this development came to light, steps were taken to eliminate the trade, or at least limit it to appropriate waste disposal facilities. Under the Basel Convention the exporting country is expected to fully inform the recipient of the composition of the waste and make sure that adequate facilities are available to receive it. But in practice it is very difficult for either the shipping or the receiving government to regulate the trade.

Before waste-exporting became popular some cities had turned to incineration as the obvious solution to the disappearance of new landfill sites. But this 1970s solution has also come into disrepute because of the problematic emissions from the stack and the difficulty of landfilling the fly ash which could contain dangerous concentrations of heavy metals. Finally in some cities they have accepted that the best approach to the problem is to reduce, re-use and recycle, in order to minimise the demand for landfill

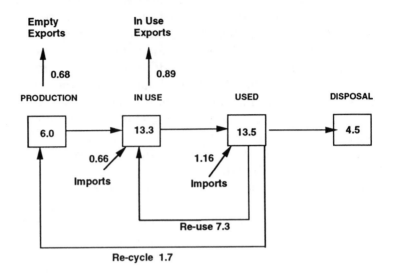

DISPOSITION OF PACKAGING BY MATERIAL

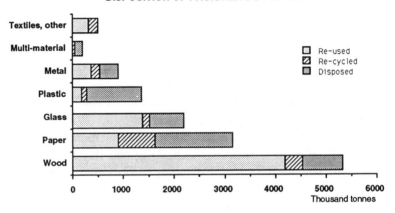

The materials include the following types of packaging:

Wood	pallets, boxes, crates
Paper	corrugated cartons, boxes, labels
Glass	carboys, bottles, containers
Plastic	containers, foam egg trays, wrap, liners
Metal	aluminum cans, caps, steel strapping
Multi-material	milk and juice cartons
Textiles, other	jute sacks, bags, wrappings

Figure 6.4 Packaging Flows in Canada, 1990. *Source*: Based on Statistics Canada 1993: 63–4

facilities. Burning, burying and exporting are not sustainable strategies. In Canada, the goal for discarded packaging is at least a 50% reduction of the 1988 total of 5.3 million tons (Statistics Canada 1993: 63). (See Figure 6.4.)

Although cities of the South do have very serious waste management problems they also have one advantage, which Christine Furedy calls 'resource recognition' (Furedy 1992: 42). The very poverty of the South means that many of the poorer members of society can re-use what the richer ones throw away—thus providing building materials for their own shelters, and recyclable materials to sell to dealers or to re-use themselves.

> 'Nevertheless, waste pickers and waste buyers usually feel insecure in their work. Downturns in the economy are reflected in more people resorting to waste-picking as a "survival strategy". It is a typical activity of street children. While poor and inaccessible areas are plagued by pollution from uncollected wastes, many of the inhabitants of these areas depend upon waste recovery and recycling to meet some of their basic needs—for shelter, food and employment. They want access to good wastes as close as possible to the sources in better-off residential and commercial areas' (Furedy 1992: 44).

The informal approach to waste management has the dual advantage of providing a living for the poorer members of society and reducing the amount of waste that has to be buried. The disadvantage is the health risk to the pickers and traders. For example, an old municipal dump in Dakar, Senegal, is now being excavated and the contents are sold for compost. This too reduces waste, recycles nutrient-rich biomass, and provides employment; but there is no analysis of the compost to test for harmful concentrations of hydrocarbons or heavy metals, for example. The people who sort the materials and transfer the compost to trucks actually live directly on the dump.

Discharges to the ground have many close links and complementarities to discharges to the air. For example, one frequently proposed solution to the emissions of acidifying compounds and greenhouse gases is nuclear power. Unfortunately—apart from the danger of malfunctioning power stations—the nuclear industry produces wastes for which no disposal solution has yet been generally accepted, not even for the low-level wastes. In

Britain and the United States, for example, the first generation of nuclear power plants are coming to the end of their productive life; in Britain the decommissioning costs are being calculated in the billions of pounds, even assuming that an acceptable means of waste disposal can be found. Even when inflation is taken into account, it seems likely that it will cost more to fully decommission a nuclear plant than it did to build it. The average service life of those plants that have already been retired, so far, is only 17 years (Brown et al. 1993: 50). In Hanford, in the northwestern United States, the nuclear waste material, produced from its old plutonium factory, was deposited in old mine shafts. These have now been declared unsafe, because even the low-level waste is leaking into the groundwater from the drums in which it was placed, and all the material is now being excavated. More people are now being employed on the clean-up operations than were employed at the peak of plutonium production in the 1960s.

If the richer countries fail to reduce energy use significantly, it is inevitable that the nuclear option for electricity production will remain on the table. Because the nuclear industry evolved as a by-product of the Cold War demand for nuclear weapons, it was protected from public enquiry, from public criticism regarding safety, and from realistic estimates of the cost of power production with the full costs of waste treatment and plant decommissioning being taken into account. The lessons of Three Mile Island and Chernobyl are still fresh in people's minds. That memory, coupled with the upward revision of the true cost of nuclear power, has made the nuclear option unpopular even in governments like those of France and Ontario where the energy strategy, developed in the 1960s and 1970s, was based on a significant (more than 30%) contribution from nuclear power.

Pathways and accumulation

As the human population increases, under present trends, the number of people exposed to contaminated food and water will increase. Even if waste-water treatment becomes the norm and if solid wastes are buried only in properly managed, sanitary landfills, the potential for exposure remains. Thus, the ultimate 'chemical fate' of a great variety of potentially harmful substances is a matter of increasing concern (Mackay 1991). For organic substances, at least, scientists can develop models which predict the time a substance is likely to spend in the various environmental media—air, water, soils, sediments, and biota (Mackay 1991: 2). Often the critical determinants of the chemical fate of substances are their reaction to the media itself and the transportation pathways that are available. For example, we may know the average residence time for water in a large lake is five years and that, in that time, some chemicals, or a portion of them, will volatilise to the air, some may sink, and some may remain in suspension and eventually leave the lake at the point of outlet and be transported downstream. On the basis of such models we can then estimate the rate at which a chemical may accumulate on the shore or within biota, such as shellfish, which may be ingested by humans. The more we know about the movement of the various residuals of human activities, in the urban context, the more accurately we will be able to devise legislation and incentives to minimise the risk to humans and to other species. As Don Mackay has warned us:

> 'If we are to discharge chemicals into the environment, it must be with a full appreciation of their ultimate fate, how they will be transported and transformed, and where and to what extent they may accumulate. We must ensure the mistakes of the past with PCBs, mercury, and DDT are not repeated' (Mackay 1991: preface).

However, as we saw with the problem of discharges to the air in the previous chapter, point sources, such as factories, are easier to regulate than dispersed sources such as buildings and transportation. In the urban environment the institutional capacity to track the environmental fate of the chemical stream that humanity uses, and, in an increasing number of cases, has created, is generally lacking.

Because insufficient is known about these environmental pathways, or their implications for human health, we usually have little recourse except to react only when an event is so damaging that the critical agent can be identified. In the industrial countries of the North we have accepted that we can re-use waste-water many times over as it passes along rivers on its route to the sea. Except in cases of accidental spills of industrial residuals, transportation accidents, or improper operation of water treatment plants, we would expect there to be no adverse effect on human health. So far, studies in the Britain and the United States, for example, have justified this assumption (Harrison 1990: 92–3). But some effects may be long term, or their impact may be masked by other factors such as an individual's age, occupation, and lifestyle, or other sources of pollution.

Despite the unknown long-term effects of material re-use (including the re-use of water) it is already clear that the scope for re-use is immense, whether dependent on hand sorting and the informal sector in the South, or through higher landfill costs and product life-cycle design in the North. Recently a composting company in Newfoundland, mixing wood bark, fish offal and chicken manure, has found an export market in Saudi Arabia, where the product mixes well with sand. Plastic drinks bottles are being ground up and extruded into fibre to make T-shirts, while used computer paper is fetching $200 per ton for recycling, much more per ton than many raw materials (*Globe and Mail*, Report on Recycling, 14/12/93). In this sort of situation it seems likely that a change in perspective, driven by a change in legislation, is capable of making a significant difference.

However, the intermixture of new environmental standards and a market-driven economy can produce unexpected results. In its attempts to internalise the real costs of the landfill disposal of waste the government of Metropolitan Toronto (referred to by the Canadian Environmental Industries Association Chairman as the 'OPEC of rubbish'), raised the price of disposal to $152 per tonne in 1990. The immediate result was the diversion of waste to the United States of about 1.6 million tons annually and a negative impact on the balance of trade amounting to $224 million over two years.

An integrated approach

It is a matter of everyday observation that urban systems, in both rich and poor countries, are having major impacts on the hydro-logical cycle and on soils from which our food is produced. For most of our urban history, water was taken from the nearest clean source, when possible, and returned untreated to the stream. As cities became larger the accidents of fire and disease became more costly and water demands steadily increased. In 1800, the 600 000 inhabitants of Paris used 1.33 litres per head, per day, including industrial and commercial use. One hundred years later the 2 700 000 inhabitants used, on an average, 249 litres per head (Goubert 1989: 196–7). Today the average use for the whole of France is 320 litres per day (World Bank 1992: 283). Similar increases have occurred throughout the industrialised world, although use increased faster in North America, for example, than in France. Each increase in use raises the metabolic intensity of the impact of a city on its surrounding environment (Chapter Three). This can be sustained only so long as these impacts are mitigated. In the case of water use this means treatment so that the water can be continually re-used, excepting, of course, the portion that is actually consumed through evaporation or incorporated into products, such as foodstuffs. Some cities of the North are only just moving through this phase now, while hardly any cities in the South have begun.

Although the water management systems of the South are dangerously unsafe, the cities do produce much less waste than cities in the North. That is because they possess what Joe Whitney calls a 'waste economy' which encourages one person to recover what another has discarded (White and Whitney 1992: 23). It is true that this informal, largely invisible, economy is being displaced by the modern, Western-style economy of higher wages, higher resource use, and more wasted materials. This is most regrettable, because it is the North that needs to emulate the more frugal South in this regard—not the other way round. The environmental benefits from recycling are considerable, once the true, environmental costs of our present wasteful modes of production and use are taken into account. Thus, there is an important warning here, as there was in the previous chapter on the impact of cities on the air. In that context it is clear that a shift in the South and East toward Western levels of car usage is enormously threatening from the global point of view. From the present chapter we may similarly conclude that a move in the South towards Northern levels of material wastage, especially water wastage, has very serious implications for the global hydrological cycle, especially concerning the availability of potable water for humans.

The reduction of demand for energy, water, and industrial materials is the most promising way to reduce urban impacts on the ground and on the hydrological cycle, just as it is to reduce impacts on the atmosphere. These impacts are already a serious threat to the future of urban systems, even without the further complications heralded by global warming and sea-level rise. The four principle problems already evident in the present global urban systems are the very size of the largest cities, the proliferation of the car as a means of mass transportation, the rapid rate of population growth, and the persistence of widespread poverty, the latter two problems being especially marked in the cities of the South. In a sense the car symbolises the wasteful lifestyle of the North which is based on the non-sustainable use of resources. This a lifestyle in which the creation and distribution of products has been, until recently, the only measure of a successful economy. The costs—to the biosphere—of this single-minded pursuit of material accumulation are now becoming apparent on every front—the land, the oceans and, most recently, the atmosphere.

Where can humanity go from here? We certainly cannot go much further along the present trajectory without large-scale failure in the social and physical fabric. The problems are serious enough to warrant a close examination of the concept of an ecological city—that being a city that minimises the depletion of the resources that constitute the biosphere on which it depends.

Further reading:

Douglas, I. (1983). *The Urban Environment*. London, Edward Arnold.
Goubert, J.-P. (1989). *The Conquest of Water. The Advent of Health in the Industrial Age*. Cambridge, Polity Press.
Goudie, A. (1986). *The Human Impact on the Natural Environment*. Cambridge, MIT Press.
Harrison, R. M., Ed. (1990). *Pollution: Causes, Effects and Control*. Cambridge, Royal Society of Chemistry.

Newson, M., Ed. (1992). *Managing the Human Impact on the Natural Environment*. London, Belhaven Press. See Chapters 7, 8 and 9.
Nisbet, E. G. (1991). *Leaving Eden. To Protect and Manage the Earth*. Cambridge, Cambridge University Press.
Parry, M. L. and other contributors (1991). *The Potential Effects of Climate Change in the United Kingdom*. London, HMSO.
World Bank (1992). *World Development Report 1992*. Oxford, Oxford University Press. See Chapter 5.

7

The Ecological City

'There are in reality not only, as is so constantly assumed, two alternatives—town life and country life—but a third alternative, in which all the advantages of the most energetic and active town life, with all the beauty and delight of the country, may be secured in perfect combination; and the certainty of being able to live this life will be the magnet which will produce the effect for which we are all striving—the spontaneous movement of the people from our crowded cities to the bosom of our kindly mother earth, at once the source of life, of happiness, of wealth, and of power' (Howard 1898: 8–9).

Much of this book has been devoted to a *diagnosis* of the environmental problems associated with urban systems. Little has been offered in the way of *prognosis* because the future is highly uncertain due to the limitations of our knowledge about the impact of our society on the climate and other aspects of the environment. Another source of uncertainty is the human response to the knowledge that we *do* have concerning our environmental predicament. For example, whereas the climate modellers have produced estimates of surface temperatures once the quantity of carbon dioxide in the atmosphere is doubled through human actions, neither they nor anyone else has any idea when (or even, if) this will occur. The best predictions we have are simply what is known as the 'business-as-usual scenario' which is a straight extrapolation from current trends. It is just as likely that the trend will be dampened by vigorous preventative action as it is that the trend will accelerate due, primarily, to economic expansion in Asia and central and eastern Europe.

Despite this highly uncertain state of affairs this chapter will present a set of *prescriptions* for at least reducing the impacts and the uncertainties associated with the current situation. The emphasis will be on survival and resilience—the latter being interpreted as 'a system's ability to recover from the damage inflicted' (Burton 1983: 112). The hope is that this will increase the probability of society evolving in a way which is good for each individual's physical and mental health, and includes the provision of meaningful labour for all. Such goals are embodied in the 'healthy cities' concept which links the health of the urban system with the health of its inhabitants (Ashton 1992).

'Increasingly, people are making the connection between the urban condition and the eco-crisis confronting the planet ... A recent workshop of environmental and public health professionals, meeting under the auspices of the World Health Organization in Liverpool, concluded that there is a need for a shared vision of the ecological city, and that such a vision should incorporate four principles:
—minimum intrusion into the natural state ...
—maximum variety (regarding land uses and activities) ...
—as closed a system as possible ...
—an optimum balance between population and resources'
(Ashton 1992: 6–8).

It is worth adding an important link-up here between the health of the urban dweller and the health of the urban system, as well as the health of the human population, as a whole, with the health of the global biosphere. It is an ancient belief that all these elements—people, their creations, and the globe (as the deity's creation)—should exist in harmony. Some have taken this principle further and stated that humanity's main purpose in life is to identify and replicate that natural harmony that existed before humanity exploded on the scene. For anyone who adheres to this line of reasoning the net impact of human beings, so far, would appear to be the very antithesis of what it was supposed to be.

All these ideas may seem hopelessly idealistic and not very helpful to a planner struggling with the everyday reality of diminished budgets and jurisdictional gridlock, the chief characteristics of many urban planning situations at this time. And the sense of unreality may be deepened by a discussion of the Utopian city, because that term is misused today to mean 'unrealistic'. In contrast to this common usage, I will argue (alongside Adrian Atkinson) that the design of a Utopian city was never a more urgent and practical task for the urban planner (Atkinson 1991: 124).

Utopian cities

Utopianism is an important antidote to the siren of incremental environmentalism, or a step-by-step, fix-up approach to our environmental crisis which will ensure that much time is wasted while the most critical issues are postponed indefinitely. The obligation of the Utopian planner is to present an integrated and coherent plan of how society might organise itself to meet a specific goal or goals; in this context an important goal is to devise an urban system which has a fairly benign impact on its supportive environment or ecological niche. (I will not go so far as to say that any urban system will be 'sustainable' for all time, because I think such an objective is too difficult to envisage from the current vantage point.) Not only must the Utopian planner specify how this benign city would operate; he or she must also try to explain how we might get from here to there, what we might call 'managing the transition'.

Although I have used the word 'prescription' to describe the task, I am not proposing that only the changes suggested here will do the job. There are a multiplicity of approaches to the problem. Nor am I proposing that once Utopian cities exist they will remain static; I expect such cities will continue to evolve, even if they do not get any bigger, either in population or in areal extent. It is important to emphasise this point because I think that one reason why some people resent, and even fear, a radical re-evaluation of our relationship to the biosphere is that they assume that modern Western civilisation will lose its purpose if it ceases to expand in terms of gross national product and the throughput of resources. Hence the elevation of the economic growth as the supreme purpose of modern, Western society. The assumption seems to be that, if we do not grow, we will lose our momentum and society will become disoriented and perhaps collapse, like a cyclist who rides more and more slowly and eventually falls over. Such a viewpoint might explain the rejection of concepts like the 'steady-state economy' and *Limits to Growth* (Daly and Townsend 1993;

Meadows et al. 1992: xiii). I do not find that people cease to be interesting or purposive when they cease to grow physically; no more should we assume that the only imaginable kind of society is one that becomes more populous, and whose people devour ever more resources. Utopian cities will not be static; nor is there only one kind of Utopia; nor is there only one route to a particular Utopian vision.

Utopian visions have tended to focus on social relations more than environmental questions, although, as Adrian Atkinson has argued, there is no reason why this should be so today. Our social problems remain as strongly entrenched as ever, but today they have been joined by a startling array of large-scale environmental problems. It is on these physical, environmental problems that this book is focused, and, accordingly, the ideas for a Utopian vision presented in this chapter will continue to emphasise the physical variables.

This chapter is an attempt to begin that task, although it leaves many questions unanswered. Principal among them is the size of the urban hinterland, in William Rees' terms, the size of a city's 'ecological footprint' (Rees 1992). How should cities be organised in relation to the location of the resources they draw upon for their sustenance? Under the traditional assumptions of development economics, the theoretical argument in favour of unhindered international trade is difficult to refute, if the objective is specified as the provision of the cheapest and most abundant choice of goods. However, given the asymmetry in the trading capacity of North and South in the colonial and post-colonial era, this has not led to a wide distribution of the benefits of international trade. On the contrary, the cities of the North have, in a sense, appropriated additional 'carrying capacity' by imposing very uneven terms of trade on the poorer countries (White and Whitney 1992: 9–19). The conventional wisdom is that this uneven use of resources can be redressed by further global economic growth in which the South eventually 'catches up' to the Northern level of resource depletion. However, as the environmental crisis unfolds, there is very well-founded scepticism about this assumption (Goodland and Daly 1992).

In stark contrast to a truly global, international economy, it has been proposed that the only workable arrangement is for each city (or perhaps a system of cities) to confine its impact to (thus, draw its resources from) its own bioregion. (For a discussion of some of the implications of this see Atkinson 1992: 192–6.) But what does the term 'bioregion' mean in this context? It has been defined very loosely, in the context of planning in Toronto, as the biological region (Crombie 1992: 10), and then put directly into use as the basis for planning:

'The geographic area considered in this overview is defined on the basis of natural boundaries, rather than political jurisdictions. This biological region, or "bioregion", comprises the major basin formed by the Niagara Escarpment on the west, the Oak Ridges Moraine to the north and east, and the Lake Ontario shoreline to the south. It is described by its natural characteristics: landforms, the lake and the watersheds' (Crombie 1992: 21).

The purpose of the term in the above context of taking an ecosystem approach to planning the Toronto region seems quite clear: it is to place the problem in an environmental context first, and deal with the jurisdictional problems later. The purpose implied in the search for the ecological city, in the context of Adrian Atkinson's political ecology, is far more radical; indeed it seems not dissimilar from the anarchists' concept of regional autarky, where each region (however defined) would be completely self-sufficient. Clearly such a state of affairs is a *very* long way from our present world in which material wealth, in a Western context, depends on international trade for virtually every resource we use, without the slightest consideration of the environmental implications of such a trading system. In contrast, in a self-sufficient bioregion the environmental implications of urbanisation would be highly visible and citizens would have a very direct interest in maintaining their ecological niche. Indeed, environmental considerations would become paramount as a matter of survival, because society would have been thrust back into the condition that Murray Bookchin calls an 'organic society' where 'Nature generally imposes such restrictive conditions on human behaviour that the social limits encountered by the individual are almost congruent with those created by the natural world' (Bookchin 1982: 114–15).

At this point several major divergences in viewpoint appear. Spatially, we are confronted with two extreme forms of organisation, represented by global sourcing, global urban hinterlands, and complete freedom of international trade on the one hand, and the decentralised, self-sufficient bioregion on the other. Even a casual consideration of these possibilities underlines the conceptual gulf between those who feel that our best hope lies in nudging our society, using technological and economic instruments, away from our self-destructive path to something that we hope will turn out to be 'sustainable', and those that feel that we must examine the roots of our dilemma, which are essentially moral and philosophical. The latter point of view is put forward by Adrian Atkinson in the context of the carbon dioxide problem:

> 'Notwithstanding the possibility of displacing some of these emissions by a concerted programme to tap renewable energy resources, to take truly effective action implies radical reductions in transport movement, restructuring of industry and major modifications in personal consumption patterns relative to what the average middle class citizen is used to. This implies major reductions in international trade and hence truncation of the international division of labour; it also places a very large question mark over megacity regions as functioning socio-economic entities' (Atkinson 1992: 2–3).

From an environmental perspective, bioregional self-sufficiency is an appealing idea, although the political implications of it are mindboggling. The appeal lies partly in its justice. Why should the hillsides of the Philippines and Indonesia be stripped of their forests to provide hardwoods for the North? 'So that those two countries, and others like them in the South, can "develop" and become like the North', was the conventional answer until a few years ago; although perhaps many people can now see that this justification is nothing but a cruel hoax. Another part of the appeal lies in what Bookchin is referring to as the 'restrictions' of the natural world, or what Atkinson refers to as 'transparency'. If you can *see* where you draw your resources from and where your residuals end up you are far more likely to realistically address the roots of your physical existence and work out how to make it more sustainable, like a modern-day Robinson Crusoe. If you can see the outcome of your actions you are far more likely to pay heed to them than if you can simply externalise all your impacts away into some ever-provident open system. Cybernetically the idea is very sound—feedbacks that are visible provoke reactions. We can see some evidence of this happening in the prominent displays of air quality indicators in Vienna, the news announcements of daily ultra-violet readings, and the effect of water metering on household water use.

Morally and cybernetically then, as well as environmentally, the bioregion concept is very attractive. But it runs directly counter to very powerful currents, some of which people champion for very good reasons. The painful passage of the Uruguay Round of the General Agreement on Trade and Tariffs was a long-awaited signal that the world was not going to slide towards protectionism, and hence perhaps a global recession on the scale of the 1930s. It would certainly be dangerous to tinker with this momentum so painfully gained. Furthermore, under a bioregion form of spatial organisation there is no doubt that some cities would find themselves very cramped indeed.

Yet, the bioregion remains a very stimulating concept even if it is difficult to see it being operationally defined and implemented in our age, which has cloaked the international plundering of the planet under the sobriquet of 'global sourcing'. However, this may not necessarily be an 'either/or' choice for the global system as a whole, because some parts of the world may continue to trade over great distances, while other places may become more self-sufficient, in a bioregional sort of way. Certainly the impact of an internationally levied carbon tax would significantly increase the cost of transport, which, in itself, would work directly to shrink urban hinterlands. If the cost of petrol trebled would it still be profitable to truck fruits and vegetables from the southern United States to Canada? What would be the additional impact of internalising all the road transport costs (including infrastructure construction and maintenance) into the balance sheets of road-users? If such cost increases occur then market forces alone would shrink the cities' hinterlands, without any international debate on the merits of free trade versus protectionism.

It is currently difficult to imagine that a global authority is likely to emerge, and then work towards the imposition either of bioregions or of global hinterlands based on the continuation of cheap energy for transportation and completely free trade. Nevertheless, the question ranges over territory that is fundamental to the future of urban management in an environmental context, and the debate on the route we should take has already begun. At the moment it is difficult to see the many sides of this debate as it is often overshadowed by the forces of inertia. On the one hand there are calls to restructure 'our cities to achieve near-zero levels of fossil fuel use' (Gilbert 1992: 4), while, at the same time, the transportation juggernaut keeps on rolling with undiminished momentum, especially in countries like Britain, Germany, Canada, and the United States where there is a substantial body of public opinion, supported by some government (mostly local) commitment, in favour of reducing private car use and strengthening communal mass transit. So an agreement on a new direction is still far from resolved, but, at the very least, we must assume that the 'out of sight, out of mind' attitude to the spatially and temporally distant implications of our lifestyle is no longer useful or acceptable.

The next step, after admitting that the present societal trajectory is not sustainable is to begin to imagine one that is. Such is the role of the Utopian planner. Our Utopia is the ecological city—one that can endure and can provide its inhabitants with a meaningful existence without destroying the ecological base on which it stands. That definition implies respect for the maintenance for the ecological base of other cities and for the global sinks on which they too depend. How the international implications of such respect may be operationalised is far from clear, but that should not prevent us from starting with a bottom-up approach, beginning in every city, indeed in every human settlement. Thus we must return to the city itself to search for ways of reducing its impact on the environment, however broadly or locally that impact might be felt.

Various planning situations

Urban planning may take place in three or four very different land-use contexts, which are sketched in Figure 7.1, although, obviously, many combinations of these situations are possible:

- the regeneration of part (1a and 1b), or all, of an existing urban system,
- an extension of an existing urban system, on a greenfield site (1c),
- the development of a new town (1d).

The first type (1a and 1b)—regeneration of an existing system—will be the most commonly encountered, as all urban systems require major adjustments to meet the environmental challenge. Typically the project will begin with a part of the system that is seen to be in particular need, such as the downtown core or a surrounding 'zone of transition' (as discussed in Chapter Four). It

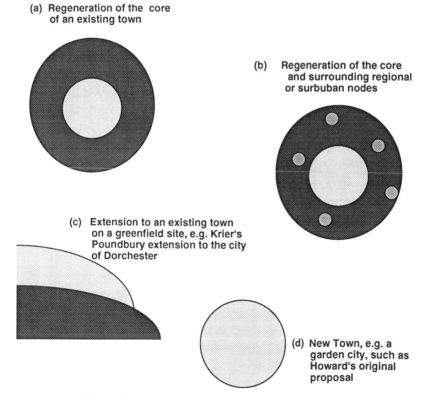

(a) Regeneration of the core of an existing town

(b) Regeneration of the core and surrounding regional or surbuban nodes

(c) Extension to an existing town on a greenfield site, e.g. Krier's Poundbury extension to the city of Dorchester

(d) New Town, e.g. a garden city, such as Howard's original proposal

Figure 7.1   Various Land-use Planning Situations

might be focused on the regeneration of the urban core at the same time as the upgrading of suburban and/or regional nuclei (1b). However, the process of regeneration will have to be extended from such a partial beginning to encompass the whole of the system under a particular administrative jurisdiction, and then to cooperative action with neighbouring jurisdictions. The need for this process is illustrated by the activities underway in Toronto, which began with a Royal Commission (referred to above), which was established to study the future of the waterfront (Crombie 1992). The study was framed in the context of the watersheds draining into the waterfront, and then, in ascending scale order, it encompassed the Greater Toronto Bioregion, the Great Lakes, and the global biosphere itself (Crombie 1992: 41). As is recognised in the Toronto study, environmental regeneration requires, most of all, a major reversal in attitudes:

'Healing a damaged watershed is a great challenge. First, it requires changing the attitude that nature is merely a resource to be used, and abused, by human beings. That kind of 'old think'—clear the woodlands, fill the marshes, pave over the countryside, and treat streams as storm sewers—is still pervasive. It is our most environmentally damaging inheritance' (Crombie 1992: 236).

The report goes on to propose seven principles for regeneration:

● protect natural and cultural features
● let topography and countryside define urban form
● ensure that development enhances environmental health
● intensify and diversify development
● maintain rural traditions
● work with nature
● encourage watershed consciousness (Crombie 1992: 239–42).

This concept of the city following, and coexisting with, nature has long been advocated, from the time of Thomas More in his *Utopia*:

'No city is anxious to extend its territory. For they think themselves farmers rather than masters of what they have' (More 1974 (1516): 44), to Ebenezer Howard in his *Garden Cities of Tomorrow*:

> 'But neither the Town magnet nor the Country magnet represents the full plan and purpose of nature. Human society and the beauty of nature are meant to be enjoyed together' (Howard 1985 (1898): 11).

More recently, Ian McHarg championed the cause in *Design with Nature* (1969); as did Michael Hough in *City Form and Natural Process* (1984) and Stephen Owen in *Planning Settlements Naturally* (1991). Our modern urban systems were created by variously taming, or even destroying, nature in the city. Rivers were straightened (Figure 7.2) and often forced underground; trees were removed and waterfronts became too polluted to support

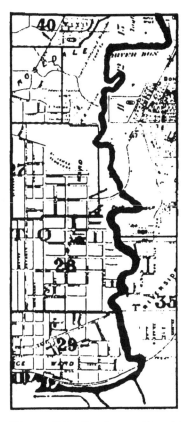 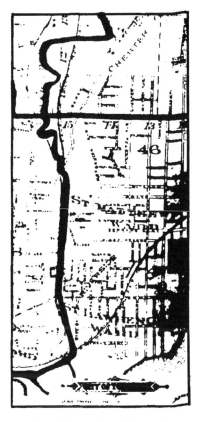

Figure 7.2 The Lower Don River before and after Channelling. *Source:* Based on C. E. Goad, *Mapping of Victorian Toronto (Paget Press, 1984)*

fish; urban systems even modified the local climate. Many of these moves have proved to be very costly mistakes, both in terms of the financial running costs of the city and in terms of the loss of the ecosystem integrity on which the city, like all human settlements, depends. However, whereas better planning can readily be attempted on greenfield sites, our major challenge is to regenerate our existing settlements. This will be a long-term exercise, for which some suggestions are made later in this chapter.

Just how much better we can do, on a greenfield site, is demonstrated by a plan for an extension to an existing settlement—the Poundbury extension to the English town of Dorchester, in the county of Dorset. (This is representative of type 1c in Figure 7.1.) It is a 450 acre addition to a town which currently covers 750 acres. The design is by the architect, Leon Krier, for whom the central problem:

'is that modernist urban planning works through mono-functional zoning. As a result, circulation of people between zones by way of artificial arteries becomes the central occupation of the planner, generating an urban pattern that is, in Krier's judgment, "anti-ecological" because it is wasteful of time, energy and land ... Krier contrasts this situation with the "good city" (by its nature ecological) in which the "totality of urban functions" are provided within "compatible and pleasant walking distances"' (Harvey 1989b: 67).

Krier's ecological alternative is illustrated by Figures 7.3, 7.4 and 7.5. Three very different land-use patterns are shown in Figure 7.3. The historic town centre of Dorchester remained virtually within the confines of the Roman walls (an area of 100 acres) until the beginning of the nineteenth century, when its population was 4000 people. In the twentieth century there was a (relatively) vast suburban expansion of the city based on transportation by private car and a bus network which radiated from the old city centre. The population is now about 15 000 people. The Poundbury extension, shown to the west of the city, is higher density, mixed land-use, with each district focused on its own shops and businesses, to which people could walk in a few minutes.

'Each of these districts is conceived of as a traditional Dorset town or village with a traditional street pattern and common, traditional building types and materials. Each section of development will be self-sufficient in

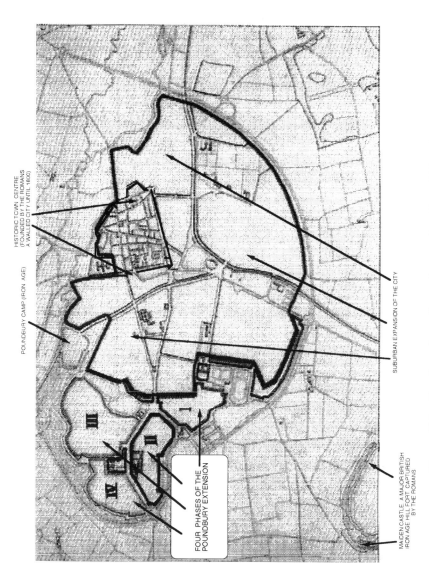

HISTORIC TOWN CENTRE
(FOUNDED BY THE ROMANS
A WALLED CITY UNTIL 1800)

POUNDBURY CAMP (IRON AGE)

SUBURBAN EXPANSION OF THE CITY

FOUR PHASES OF THE
POUNDBURY EXTENSION

MAIDEN CASTLE. A MAJOR BRITISH
IRON AGE HILL FORT CAPTURED
BY THE ROMANS

Figure 7.3 The Poundbury Extension to the City of Dorchester

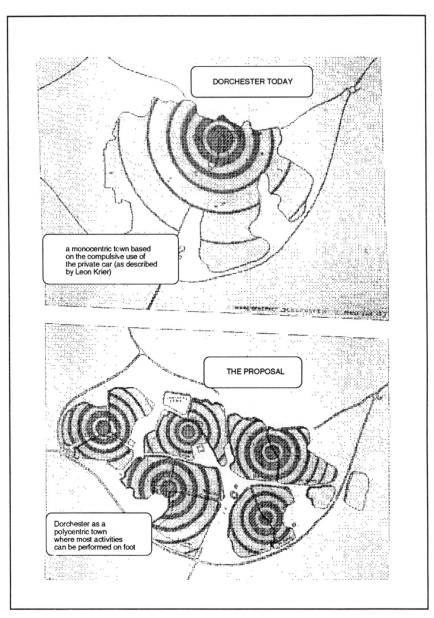

Figure 7.4 Transportation Patterns for Dorchester and Poundbury

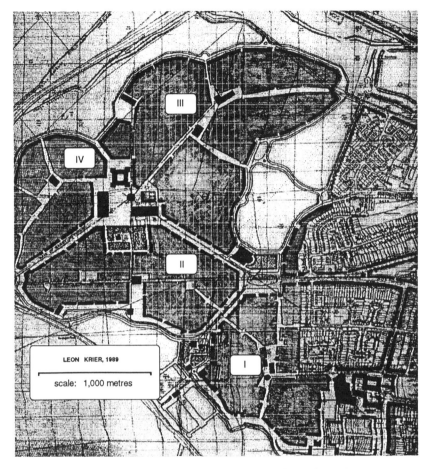

Figure 7.5 Phases of the Masterplan for the Poundbury Extension

education, employment, shopping, leisure. Those who seek employment
will be able to find residential accommodation within five to ten minutes
walking distance. Regular markets will be held within each district and
most shopping needs satisfied without using a car' (Krier 1989: 47).

Figure 7.4 contrasts the transportation implications for the two
concepts, the old and the new—the first depends on the unres-
trained use of the car and is focused on the city centre; the second
is based mainly on walking trips within each district. Each of the
four districts proposed for the Poundbury extension will include
housing for 500 to 800 households and none will be larger than
the original 100 acres enclosed by the old city walls. This is

important because it restores a pedestrian scale to the urban fabric, a scale which allows a 10 minute walk from one side of the district to the other. In his article Krier shows that this scale is consistent for many small market towns as well as the mediaeval cores of major regional centres, from Weymouth in England to Florence in Italy and Munich in Germany (Krier 1989: 52 and 55).

The present population of Dorchester is living at half the density enjoyed by their forbears at the beginning of the last century; while the proposed density for Poundbury is about half way between the two. The Poundbury proposal has an implicit agenda for re-orienting the existing, car-based suburbs by encouraging local shopping centres to which people could walk. Figure 7.5 shows how the building of Poundbury would be phased in over a period of 10 to 15 years. The contrasting pattern of mono-functional suburban land-use appears on the right, or eastern side of the map.

It might be thought that this project was a special case as it is an extension to a fairly small, European town of considerable historic interest and with a quite high average income per household. But the principles that it could establish are of major importance, if it is accepted by the planning authorities and if enough people are enthusiastic about living without being dependent on their cars. Just proving that such a thing were *possible*, as a matter of per-sonal choice, would change the nature of the debate concerning car-free living enormously (White 1993b). Of course, there is a long way to go from showing that something is possible to creating the conditions in which it is probable. Even in ideal cir-cumstances there is the fundamental problem of pedestrian living and employment mobility, voluntary and otherwise. You might only be able to walk (or bicycle) from home to job as long as you have the same job or another one in close proximity. Thus, to maintain the short commuting distance, either you need long-term job security or you need to be willing to relocate whenever your job location changes. Of course, this would not be a problem for the retired or the self-employed, and thus it could be that such groups will be the first (among those wealthy enough to have a car) to consider the transition to car-free living.

It should be added that Dorchester's 'suburban sprawl' still confined its 15 000 inhabitants to 750 acres, a density of 20 people per acre, which is approximately 5000 per square kilometre. This is still 'high density' by North American standards. For example, the core of Toronto has 5300 per sq km, the inner suburbs have 2780, and the outer suburbs, 1440 (Gilbert 1991: 184). At these lower densities it is unlikely that society will re-orient itself towards public transport and taking more journeys by foot and bicycle. Instead the planner's task has been defined as 'completing the suburbs, with a full array of retail, social, health and recreational services' and, implicitly raising population densities by intensification of land-use (Martin 1991: 178). In order to encourage this trend Metropolitan Toronto (comprised of the City and the surrounding boroughs) has reconsidered the establishment of a green belt which was originally part of the regional plan, but which was overrun in the development rush of the 1970s and early 1980s.

One of the first tasks in moving towards more sustainable urban forms is to reduce car dependency (Tolley 1990; Zuckerman 1991). Such a step entails far more than simply encouraging a more compact urban form by changing zoning by-laws, reducing the amount of space devoted to the car, improving public transport and so on. It involves reversing major economic and social trends. In fact David Harvey sees the encouragement of suburbanisation and car-dependency as major support for the evolution of capitalism in the post-war period:

> 'Suburbanization ... meant the mobilization of effective demand through the total restructuring of space so as to make the consumption of the products of the car, oil, rubber and construction industries a necessity rather than a luxury ... It is now hard to imagine that postwar capitalism could have survived, or what it would now have been like, without suburbanization and proliferating urban development' (Harvey 1989a: 39).

It is, indeed, a sobering experience to look back at what an ecological city might have looked like if that dependency had not been encouraged to grow. Fortunately we still have a good model to help us to do exactly that. (This is situation 'd' in Figure 7.1.) Ebenezer Howard proposed his concept of a 'garden city' before the current obsession with cars became established (Figure 7.6). Road traffic was often congested with a variety of traffic at the

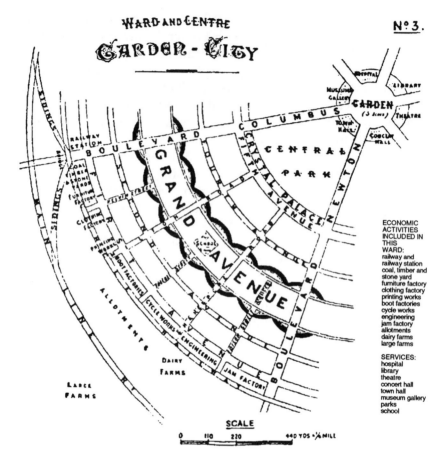

Figure 7.6   Ebenezer Howard's Garden City

turn of the century, but the personal car was a rarity. However, although Howard did not face the current preoccupation with trying to disentangle the city from the car, he did have to deal with the familiar problems of the lack of affordable housing, air pollution and waste management:

> 'On the outer ring of the town are factories, warehouses, dairies, markets, coal yards, timber yards etc ... This system (encourages) the reducing of traffic on the roads of the town, lessening to a very marked extent the cost of their maintenance. The smoke fiend is kept well within bounds in Garden City ... The refuse of the town is utilised on the agricultural portion of the estate' (Howard 1985 (1898): 18).

Howard's Garden City model was for 32 000 people on 1000 acres, each city to be surrounded by 5000 acres of farmland. The proposed urban density, at 32 per acre is close to the density Krier has proposed for Poundbury. The basis for transportation between cities was the railway system, and a new city could be added on a linked, greenfield site, as population rose. In this way the urban impact on the stock of agricultural land would be carefully controlled. Howard's plan called for cooperative ownership, public transportation, the juxtaposition of town and country, and an urban commitment to produce its own food from the surrounding countryside. All these components are remarkably similar to Thomas More's Utopia, and they also foreshadow aspects of the self-sufficient bioregion debate today.

Thus, it is one of the great ironies of planning history that Howard's layout design was most widely implemented by the private sector developers who built the twentieth century suburbs and satellite towns, which, in the second half of the century, became the favourite breeding ground of the car (Hall 1988: 108–12). Howard's plan for cooperative ownership was never adopted. Even when Britain began building new towns (on the Howard plan) after the Second World War these were managed by municipal corporations and the land was mostly privately owned, or else it was owned by the state. It would be fitting if Howard's concept could—100 years later—be used to solve today's problem by providing a working model of the pedestrian city. Admittedly, many conditions are more adverse now than they were 100 years ago: the world holds more than three times as many people, the car is a deeply entrenched part of Western culture, the waste streams from our towns (as described in Chapters Five and Six) are less organic than they were in Howard's day, and so on. But the challenge remains. Our cities are highly dysfunctional and likely to become more so. What alternative forms of urban organisation do we have?

The pedestrian city

By using the term 'pedestrian city', I do not mean that all journeys would be on foot, only that most trips could be made, as Krier suggested, without being dependent on cars. Other trips could be made by bicycle or on public transport. Vehicles powered by the combustion engine, or an electrical substitute, would then be needed only for deliveries, emergencies, people with special needs, and for journeys from rural areas to the urban periphery, from which they would walk or take public transport within the town. This would reduce gaseous discharges to the air, improve human health (better air and more exercise), and, as Howard observed, would significantly reduce the cost of road construction and maintenance. Many cities have already established 'park-and-ride' facilities to allow incoming drivers to leave their cars outside the city and travel—usually on a priority bus route or subway—quickly to their destination. It is true that the concept has not been highly developed yet and motorists sometimes worry about vandalism to the car, or their own personal safety, especially at night. But there is no reason why these peripheral car parks should be dangerous or unattractive because the problem would be greatly reduced if retail facilities and other services were put in the same location. The commuters, on the reverse trip, could get off the bus, or subway, do their shopping, load up the car and drive home (Rees 1992). One reason for the limited success of such park-and-ride schemes is that more emphasis has been put on the parking (simply to temporarily dispose of the car), and less of the riding—that is, integrating the system into a new approach to personal mobility in the town.

Within the city, the pedestrian-only zone could gradually be extended outwards, from the core, as the city is modified to give priority to pedestrians and cyclists. Again, in the last 10 or 15 years the pedestrian precinct has gained acceptance from Cardiff to Vienna, overcoming the fears of the shopkeepers and the police. The shopkeepers feared a decline in sales, whereas the reverse has been recorded. The police feared more petty crime, but that too has not happened. Indeed, after the April 1993 bomb blast in the City of London, the police have supported the proposal to make the whole of the City a pedestrian zone, on the grounds that it would be more difficult for terrorists to plant car bombs.

There is an infinite array of options between 'pedestrian-only' areas and the present chaotic mix of people and vehicles. For example, the practice of 'traffic calming' has been widely adopted, especially in Europe (Whitelegg 1990). The basic aim is to change the configuration of the roadway and the surface so as to slow traffic down, discourage traffic making through-trips, and provide a safer environment for cyclists and pedestrians. (See Figure 7.7.) The difficulty with this kind of compromise is that it can easily be reversed, if it does not retain political support. Furthermore, if the traffic does not slow down, it can be even more

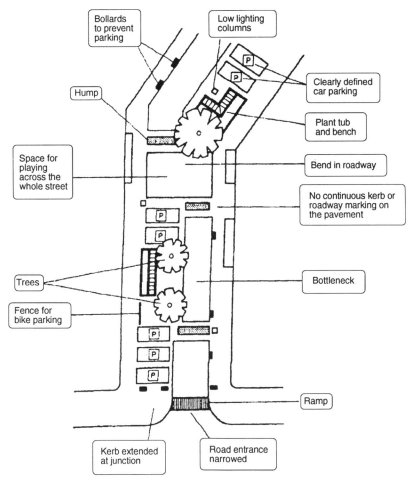

Figure 7.7 Traffic Calming in a Residential Street. *Source*: Elkin et al. 1991: 73, based on Royal Dutch Touring Club, *Woonerf*, Den Haag, 1980

dangerous than the present 'priority for vehicles' rule (which still dominates most urban traffic situations) because the pedestrians may assume a false sense of security. At least in most urban spaces today, people know that cars and their users are more important than anything else and they behave with appropriate caution.

The ecological city

On the other hand, if we make the city a safe place for pedestrians and cyclists, by excluding the motorist, then a great step will have been taken towards encouraging a more ecological city, meaning one that does less harm to its ecological niche. But many more steps will also need to be taken before any vision of a sustainable city comes into view. As Chapters Five and Six implied, the key targets are the water budget and the energy budget, which are the major elements in Wolman's concept of urban metabolism (Chapter Three).

Except for fairly small and isolated settlements, the new goal must be 100% treatment of used water—admittedly that still leaves the degree of treatment to be determined, and it still leaves the problem of disposal of the sludge. However, depleting aquifers and returning unusable water to the river or the lake is something we can no longer afford in *any* country. Each city and industry will have to internalise this concern. In practice, this should not mean taking the present level of use as a given and simply paying the cost of returning the used water to a potable state. As in the energy case, the cheapest part of the solution will be to reduce demand. Within homes this has been found to happen, without hardship, once the water is metered. Studies have usually recorded a fairly rapid decline of between 20% and 40% in the water bill following the installation of meters, compared with the flat rate previously charged. Households could progress from the first point—stop wasting water—to deciding how they could reduce use. Some households, of course, may no longer have cars that need to be washed because they now live in a pedestrian city. The laundry bill (in water and financial terms) should fall once the air is cleaner; gardeners might decide to grow

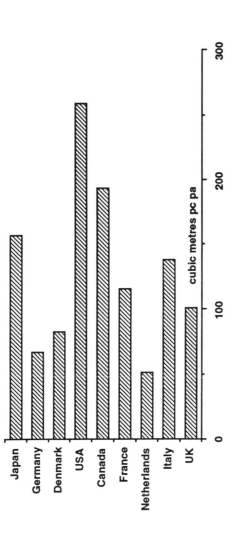

Figure 7.8 Domestic Water Used per capita per annum. The data are taken from Table 33 of the *World Development Report 1992*. Domestic use 'includes drinking water, municipal use or supply, and uses for public services, commercial establishments, and homes'. It does not include direct withdrawals by industry or agriculture (World Bank 1992: 303)

less thirsty plants. The huge difference in the level of household use in countries at the same high level of material prosperity suggests that in some countries much household water is used needlessly. (Figure 7.8.)

In the South the problems associated with the water budget are different. There is still much wastage, this time from poorly maintained distribution networks. Also, some low-income countries have invested heavily in tourism, which is a prodigious water consumer (White 1993a: 127). However, in the South, as in the North, the main culprit is irrigated agriculture. This might not be seen as an *urban* environmental issue, but, in a sense, it is an urban issue because most of the irrigated crops are destined either directly for the city, or for the export market to earn foreign exchange, much of which is needed to maintain urban consumption patterns and infrastructure, such as imported food and petroleum. Most irrigation is wastefully carried out, and the full price of the water is hidden in government subsidies and the abuse of nature's capital. As far as I know, no country is requiring the water user to pay the full, replacement cost of either irrigation water or potable water.

Many of the same approaches can be taken for the energy sector. Replacing the car with feet and bicycles will be a tremendous step forward in reducing energy consumption. Further savings can be gained from reducing the urban heat island effect by tree-shading and using light coloured surfaces (Akbari et al. 1992). More can also be gained by insulating buildings in order to reduce heating demands. In general we need to examine the energy implications of a building as thoroughly as we would the financial implications. Labelling will help, as will the introduction of carbon taxes. Retailers have found that customers respond to environmental labels on products, while producers in Germany and elsewhere have requested legislation for labelling because they believe they have a better product and thus labelling will strengthen their competitive position. Similarly carbon taxes will benefit those users and producers that are the more energy-efficient.

As global warming becomes more evident, and as carbon taxes become a significant part of the price of energy, householders, and city planners and managers will have little choice but to become more energy conscious. Indeed, for several years already, 'energy-conscious planning' has been advocated and proposals published (Owens 1986; 1991). However, the issue has yet to make much impact on public opinion or on the urban planning profession at large, although some utility companies are already committed to energy efficiency and demand management.

The intelligent city

The speed with which this situation might change will be a function of how much information people are given about their urban environment. For example, at the household level, the installation of water meters has reduced the quantity used. More frequent billing and more prominent displays of gas and electricity meters should have the same effect on fuel consumption. Currently these meters are anything but visible to the household, as they are either outside (as in Canada), or hidden in the below-stairs closet (as in Britain). A nice, bright, prominent panel, at head height, in the kitchen might also reduce quite a lot of intergenerational aggravation.

In the outdoor environment, concern about air quality led the City of Vienna to establish a large monitoring screen near Stephansplatz, in the heart of the city, to record levels of sulphur dioxide, particulates, and ozone. As the screen is right in the middle of a large pedestrian area it is very visible. There was a time when passers-by simply needed displays of the time and the temperature. Now, air pollution information is used in many cities to directly control emissions to the air by ordering the shutdown of factories when air quality is poor. In this way the city and its inhabitants are developing a capacity to regulate the metabolism of their urban systems. In effect, they have set up a negative feedback loop, through legislation, to control their excesses. The use of this type of regulation has so constrained the operation of power plants and industries in Mexico City, that there is now support for long-term reduction through relocation of the production facilities and the introduction of cleaner technology.

On a broader scale, city managers need to develop an intelligent, underground circulatory system, similar to the body's nervous system, which tells them the status of the various items that circulate beneath the city streets. This would include clean water, sewage, electricity, gas, and communications. (See Figure 7.9.) The communications in the trench would also include communications about the status of the circulatory system itself—routine information about pressure, volume, contaminants, if any, and the capacity for the instant signalling to the central processing unit of any malfunction. The system would have the capacity to make the immediate precautionary response to a malfunction, by

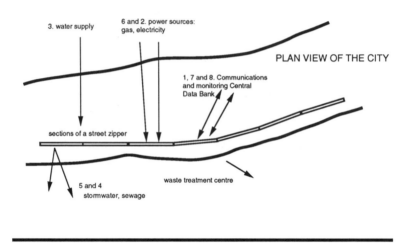

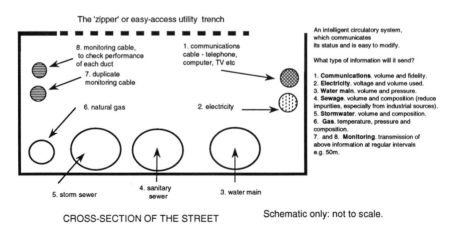

Figure 7.9 A Linear City with a Combined Utility Trench

isolating the troubled sector and circulating each of the flows by an alternative route until the repair was made. The juxtaposition of water, gas and electricity would obviously require adequate separation and insulation to meet safety requirements. Once in place, such a system would greatly reduce the chance of accidents such as the Guadalajara gas explosion or the Chicago underground flood (referred to in Chapter Six).

Some examples already exist of bundled water supply and sewage evacuation for small mining communities in the Canadian north where the pipes must be heated to ensure continued flow through the permafrost. As the heat would melt the permafrost the pipes must also be insulated. However, this is a special adaptation to unusual circumstances, and for a small number of people. The problem becomes more complex for larger communities and more services. Trunk sewers and water pipes need the continuous support provided by the soil; likewise there are restrictions on the angles which the larger pipes can turn. While some variables, like voltage and pressure, are relatively easy to monitor on a continual basis, the composition of liquids (for water quality) and flow rates are more difficult (Adams 1993). Nonetheless, despite these practical difficulties, the principle of a combined utility trench complements the proposal for visible monitoring of water and energy use in the home, and the public display of information on the contamination of the atmosphere. Currently most people live in total ignorance of the quantity of resources they use and the quantity and type of wastes they create. These proposals should go some way to remedy this omission. Indeed, it is one of the first principles of cybernetics that information is required to develop the feedbacks that a system needs in order to regulate itself.

A proposal for an intelligent circulatory system and constant air quality monitoring should not raise fears of a 'cybernetic city' in which the city is reified and people become merely its servitors. On the contrary, it provides a means for the people to take control of their lives, become aware of the costs of the decisions they take (or postpone), and then prepare to make more intelligent choices. There are opportunities here both for the cities of the North, that need to replace their crumbling nineteenth-century infrastructure, and the poorest cities of the South which need to start from scratch. The idea of an urban system that constantly monitors its status springs directly from an analogy with James Lovelock's description of the evolution of multicellular creatures:

> 'A spherical community of cells, larger than a few millimetres in diameter, would have difficulties in sustaining the supply of oxygen, and the removal of carbon dioxide, to and from its interior. This problem would be much greater if this communal organism used energy for motion, or to keep warm. The advantages of community living can be had, however, without paying the penalty of asphyxiation or starvation. The evolution of two-dimensional flat organisms or of open-mesh three dimensional sponges illustrated two of the possible strategies. A more sophisticated solution to this problem came with the development of circulatory systems, with a network of channels and a means to sustain the flow of blood or plasma through them' (Lovelock 1991: 105).

Ironically, our methods of constructing and maintaining these underground networks have changed little since Roman times, although new functions have been added. Now, the constant digging up of large parts of the city to lay and repair these various systems is an enormous waste of materials and energy, including such precious materials as water. Furthermore, it creates dust, noise, and waste heat. It may seem Utopian to propose a balanced budget for water and a reduced budget for energy, but that is what our ecological Utopia will need. In order to follow this path we will need new signposts, not the old ones which encouraged us to maximise our throughput of resources.

Seven principles

As a suggestion as to what these new signposts might be, the following principles have been selected from Adrian Atkinson's argument in favour of Utopia, in his book, *Principles of Political Ecology*.

- 'Utopia is above all the fulfilment of the desirable life for everyone in the here-and-now'
- 'Utopia must confront the material aspects of life in a coherent way'
- 'Utopia needs to develop strategies to get us from here to

there, in as serious a fashion as it attempts to formulate the structure of Utopia itself'
(This I have referred to as 'managing the transition'.)

- 'Utopia involves choices, but, must also present a consistent and workable set of ideas and proposals'
- 'Society is an integral part of the metabolism of natural systems'
- 'Utopian thought focuses on the arrangement of the physical environment. This includes the size and structure of urban areas and the arrangement and use of the land. It attempts to abolish the antithesis between town and country'
- 'Decentralisation as the key to what much of Utopian organisation is about, means the construction of a world which is of a scale that can be grasped by the majority of people and is controlled by them within manageable organisational systems' (Atkinson 1991: 116–24).

Note there is nothing here that promises that our society will be *sustainable*, even if reformed along the lines suggested by these principles. Indeed, I hope I have avoided making any promises about sustainable development in this book, because by setting such a thing as a goal I believe we would be aiming too high. We should instead concentrate on what is urgent and doable. That still leaves us with a very wide choice of actions. I think that is what Utopian planners have had in mind throughout the ages, not some mad dream that would cure all of humanity's problems at one blow. On the contrary, the key to designing and building an ecological city, as a Utopian project, is that it should be *practical*; and practical means that it should be designed to be in tune with nature, rather than designed to destroy the biosphere on which we all depend. We cannot guarantee that such a city would be sustainable for all time, but we can be fairly confident that it will greatly reduce the rate at which we use resources and create residuals. This is all that the resources–activities–residuals approach sets out to do.

Further reading:

Atkinson, A. (1991). *Principles of Political Ecology*. London, Belhaven Press.

Crombie, D. (1992). *Regeneration. Toronto's Waterfront and the Sustainable City: Final Report.* Ottawa, Ministry of Supply and Services.

Elkin, T., et al. (1991). *Reviving the City. Towards Sustainable Urban Development.* London, Friends of the Earth.

Hall, P. (1988). *Cities of Tomorrow.* Oxford, Basil Blackwell.

Hough, M. (1989). *City Form and Natural Process.* London, Routledge.

Howard, E. (1985 (1898)). *Garden Cities of Tomorrow.* Builth Wells, Attic Press.

Krier, L. (1989). Master Plan for Poundbury Development in Dorchester. *Architectural Design Profile*: 46–55.

McHarg, I. L. (1969). *Design with Nature.* Garden City, New York, Doubleday and Company.

Owens, S. (1986). *Energy, Planning and Urban Form.* London, Pion Limited.

8

Toronto Initiatives

'Action is needed to limit global warming and ozone depletion, to reduce solid wastes, and to protect the quality of water, soil, and air. The urban form of our cities determines to a great extent, how sustainable we will be and it is critical to our attempts to become a more environmentally sound society. By planning urban form and urban densities carefully, cities contribute to the efficient use of materials and energy. A concentrated urban form can decrease reliance on cars and, by doing so, lower harmful emissions and help protect natural habitats' (Metropolitan Toronto Government 1991: 16).

References have been made throughout this book to urban environmental management initiatives that have been undertaken in Toronto. Partly this is a reflection of the place of residence of the author, but more importantly, it is because the Toronto situation has special relevance to the global urban predicament. This relevance lies to some extent in the varied characteristics it exhibits, such as a well-populated downtown core (found in many European cities, but rare in North America). This core is surrounded by a vast extension of low density suburbs (typical of North America). Toronto has a large and rapidly growing immigrant population (nearly 50% of the population have neither English nor French as their mother tongue), and despite its prosperity and modernity, it has (like so many cities of the North) a growing population of homeless and destitute people. Another aspect that is relevant to the themes of this book is that Toronto has initiated several programmes and hosted several conferences, such as the Healthy Cities Movement, and the conferences on 'The Changing Atmosphere' and 'Cities and Global Change'. Add to this the fact that Canadians (on average) are among the world's most prodigious users of energy, materials, and water, and are among the most extravagant producers of waste. In Herman Daly's terms 'throughput' is high; in terms of Abel Woman's urban metabolism, Toronto's metabolic intensity is among the world's highest.

Partly this high level of resource use is due to the long distances between cities and the extreme temperatures in winter and summer. But the level is higher than in Scandinavia where the climate is just as extreme. Another part of the explanation lies in the fact that energy prices have always been lower than in Europe, and thus the payback period from investment in insulation and more efficient vehicles is longer (Richardson 1992: 155). Curiously, although the houses are much better insulated than those of Britain (described in Chapter Four), there is still a reluctance to adopt the energy standards current in the United States, where the winter is milder and the energy prices are even lower. Part of the problem lies in two features of the North American lifestyle which must entrain higher resource use where the climate is harsher and the distances between cities longer, these features being the detached single family dwelling and the private car. Nigel Richardson notes that '60 percent of all dwellings in Canada are single-family houses' (1992: 155); north of Toronto, in the new suburbs under construction, this proportion is as high as 80%. As Richardson goes on to observe:

'The private car is even more ubiquitous than the one-family house. In 1986, 77 percent of all households owned one or more cars. According to a 1983 survey, 73 percent of all journeys to work in Canada were made by private car (Rostrum 1987). An annual growth rate of 6 percent in motor traffic in the Toronto area is producing rapidly increasing peak-hour congestion, which adds to air pollution as well as energy consumption' (Richardson 1992:155).

On the subject of waste, Richardson also credits Canada with the world number 1 position at two kilograms per person per day. He concludes: 'No Canadian city has yet arrived at a satisfactory long-term solution to the problem of waste-disposal' (1992: 156).

It seems that by hosting international conferences on important aspects of the urban environmental management problem and launching the Healthy Cities Movement, Toronto—as the largest city in a resource-intensive country—set itself a considerable challenge.

Themes from this book seen in the Toronto context

The hosting, in Toronto, of the 1988 conference, 'The Changing Atmosphere', by the federal ministry, Environment Canada, was an important catalyst for future action in the city. Although the conference working group on urbanisation and settlement focused on the impacts of environmental change *on cities* (rather than the other way round), it was clearly incumbent upon urban managers in Toronto to develop responses to the other recommendations regarding responsibility for the problem (Environment Canada 1988: 9). This connection—urban responsibility for mitigating the impacts—was followed up by a conference in Toronto exactly one year later. It was called 'Cities and Global Change', organised under the auspices of the Climate Institute of Washington DC, and supported by all relevant levels of Canadian government and some members of the private sector.

Completely independent of these atmospheric concerns was the Healthy Cities Movement, which was an outgrowth of a 1970s Canadian federal government report. The report reminded health authorities that environmental factors were an important key to public health and had been so throughout history. The report recommended that more attention be paid to water quality, nutrition, community services, recreational facilities, and so on, rather than acting as if curative health facilities were the only important part of the equation. This marked a significant shift in the quest for better health in cities, not only in Canada, but also in the United States and in Europe. In 1984 the Toronto Board of Health hosted a workshop called 'Healthy Toronto 2000', and from that the World Health Organisation picked up the idea and encouraged a worldwide movement (Hancock 1992a: 44–5). As Trevor Hancock has pointed out this is a 'renaissance of the public health movement', which had started in the modern period in the 1830s and 1840s in Britain. There the wealthier classes in the cities decided that their health was not just a private concern, but a public one, and they began to take effective steps to create an adequate public infrastructure for the provision of water and the disposal of wastes, for the first time (in Britain, at least) since the days of the Roman Empire.

Thus, in Toronto in the 1980s it is interesting to see that quite separate interests began to converge on the issue of the sustainability of the city; some were concerned about atmospheric change, others about public health. But the goal for both began to focus on the same area—'ecological sanity and social justice' (Hancock 1992: 45). This is an important reinforcement of the idea that the health of the people, the health of the city, and the health of the planet are inextricably bound up together. In the Toronto context the concerns about climate change and the health of the citizens are clearly coincident. These are the issues that were introduced separately in this book in Chapter Two, 'Environmental Change', and Chapter Four, 'Urban Pathology'. A pathological condition in a city is one in which people die, or suffer, unnecessarily. They have not lived out their natural span, but have been reduced by circumstances that could have been prevented if different decisions had been taken. That is the focus of the Healthy Cities Movement—understanding how we can reduce morbidity and mortality by making different decisions.

The other themes of this book can readily be traced in Toronto. There is no full-scale study of the metabolism (Chapter Three) of the city, yet, but some important elements are in place, such as the measurement of energy flows made by the Metro Toronto Government, as illustrated in Figure 3.4. Concern about discharges to the air (Chapter Five) is the main drive behind attempts to reduce energy wastage. While concern about discharges to the ground (Chapter Six) is putting increasing pressure on the metropolitan government to internalise its waste management system, with mixed results so far. How far does Toronto meet the standards for an 'ecological city' (as proposed in Chapter Seven)? Well, obviously there is still a very long way to go; but, at least, one has a strong sense that this is a city that has begun to understand James Lovelock's message, and it is gearing itself up to make the move towards an urban form which has a less destructive impact on the environment.

Toronto: a city, its organisation and its problems

Spatially, there are three Torontos—the City, the Metropolitan Government, and the Greater Toronto Area, the latter being a statistical, rather than administrative unit which includes the surrounding regions of Halton, Peel, York, and Durham. The respective populations of these three Torontos are 610 000, 2.2 million and 3.6 million (Figure 8.1a). They will be referred to in this chapter as the City, Metro, and the GTA. Metro is responsible for water treatment and delivery, sewage, the police, regional planning issues, arterial roads, the subway and bus system (Toronto Transit Commission), some social housing, the ambulance service, and waste disposal. The City (like the other constituent cities and boroughs that make up Metro—see Figure 8.1a) is responsible for local planning, roads and parklands, street lighting, some social housing, public health, the inspection of buildings, the fire brigade, and waste collection. Natural gas is provided by Consumers Gas, which is an 'investor-owned public utility that is regulated by the Ontario Energy Board' (City of Toronto 1991: 10); and electricity is supplied by Ontario Hydro (a Crown Corporation) and distributed by Toronto Hydro, which is 'owned and controlled by the City of Toronto' (City of Toronto 1991:10). Very significant powers which relate to urban management lie in the hands of the federal and provincial governments, especially relating to taxation and to environmentally relevant regulations. For example, the standards for the energy efficiency of buildings are set by the province—not by Metro or the City. The province supports the GO (Government of Ontario) system of light commuter railways. The federal government controls one of the two railway companies which own 80 hectares of former railway lands in the downtown core, the redevelopment of which has been the focus of heated debate for 30 years (Crombie 1992: 363–77).

As in all cities there is an interplay between public and private sector operations as well as an interplay between different levels of government. In Toronto there is constant interplay between the four levels of government—City, Metro, provincial and federal. All have significant roles to play in the search for improved standards of urban environmental management, although the federal role is more indirect than it commonly is in Europe.

Unlike many major urban centres in the rich countries of the North, the population of the City of Toronto is fairly stable

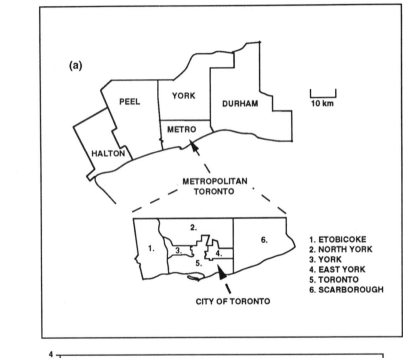

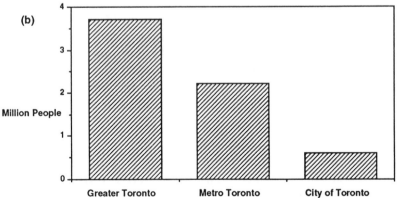

Figure 8.1(a)   The Greater Toronto Area; (b) Relative Population Size, 1986.
Source: Canadian Urban Institute, 1991

although there was a time in the 1960s when it looked as if the reduction of the resident population was about to follow the North American trend, with the centre jammed with commuters' cars in the daytime, and emptied of people at night. At that time attempts to retain a suburban green belt and contain urban sprawl faltered in the face of the pressure for new land for low-density suburban sprawl. A provincial document, *Design for Development*, was published in 1966, and this duly called for the containment of urban sprawl by concentrating growth in a hierarchy of settlements and creating a Parkway, or green belt, around the existing built-up area. But the pressure for development simply over-ran the provincial guidelines and:

> 'within a decade the Parkway Belt had been battered into little more than a thin grey servicing corridor. Any restraint to development north of Metro in the Yonge Street corridor was lifted' (Sewell 1993: 212).

Of course, the growing suburban population needed an expressway system to carry them round their sprawling city and into the downtown core. Meanwhile, the old residential neighbourhoods in the City were being demolished to make way for office skyscrapers and tower blocks of apartments. The first two blocks of apartments of the St Jamestown complex were built in 1959 and more than a dozen more were completed on the site by the mid-1960s. The official city plan of 1969 was to replace the old downtown neighbourhoods with hundreds of these blocks (Sewell 1993: 167–9). The first two commuter expressways were built and three more expressways were planned.

But the movement to modernise the city with tower blocks and expressways was halted. As John Sewell, former Mayor of the City of Toronto, explained:

> 'Suburbanites thought it entirely reasonable that the existing city should be demolished to make way for the new city, including building roadways necessary to join the downtown office towers where people worked to the suburban houses where they lived.
>
> City residents didn't quite see it that way. They argued that their homes were important to them and shouldn't be destroyed; that the cost of the expressway was unreasonable; that the time savings were minuscule; that the downtown would be one giant parking lot; that public transport was a much better investment than roads for more cars' (Sewell 1993:179).

The struggle to save the inner city neighbourhoods went on for four years, until a group of reformers was elected to the City Council. With more elections in the offing in 1971, the Ontario provincial government supported the City viewpoint, against that of Metro, which was then dominated by suburban interests (Sewell 1993: 179). As provincial political support and finance were needed for the expressway programme, the modernising movement ran out of steam and, as a result, Toronto's downtown neighbourhoods are still inhabited by people rather than cars.

Of course, no story is that simple. Jane Jacobs, in her foreword to John Sewell's recent book, *The Shape of the City*, identifies three 'virtues of omission—a mirror image, as it were, of sins of commission' which explain why the outcome was different in Toronto to Detroit, Chicago, and other American cities where the day was won by the suburban viewpoint (Jacobs 1993). She cites the fact that the Canadian banks did not follow the American practice of designating downtown neighbourhoods ineligible for mortgages, and thereby hastening their dilapidation, and subsequent conversion to other uses. Neither were racial ghettos deliberately created by the real-estate industry to drive fearful whites to new houses in the suburbs. Third, the expressway programme was to be financed by the provincial and local governments, rather than the federal government, as in the United States, and hence the issue was more sensitive to local opinion. Fourth, by the time the Canadian federal urban renewal agency was in business the tragedy of the public housing tower block was already becoming apparent in Europe and south of the border; so the movement to replace all the old housing stock was reconsidered and comparatively few tower blocks were built.

Other coincidental factors certainly helped. The 1950s and 1960s had seen a great influx into downtown Toronto of immigrants from southern Europe, many of whom had moved into the old neighbourhoods with their families, and there they invested their own labour and borrowed capital in the housing stock; which is probably why the banks saw downtown housing mortgages as a useful source of profit. Also, as Sewell notes in his book, the downtown neighbourhoods included some wealthy areas, home to the financial élite of the city, who also felt threatened by the expressway spectre. In London terms, it was as if Hampstead were to make common cause with Islington and Tower Hamlets. All of these factors helped to tip the balance against the modernist conception of the city, based on downtown tower blocks for housing and offices, expressways into the city and mono-functional land-use zoning to isolate suburban residential areas from other parts of the urban fabric.

Of course, halting the expressway programme did not entirely reverse the other land-use trends in the region. The GTA continued to grow, and nearly all of that growth, in the last twenty years, has been on the periphery, where highways are constantly being widened and residential densities remain low. More and more of Canada's limited stock of first class farmland is being cemented over. After years of steady increases the use of the bus and subway system has stalled and has now begun an alarming decline (Gilbert and Di Mascio 1993: 3). The daily traffic jam of commuters gets worse. The lakeshore beaches have become too polluted for swimming. Vigorous attempts to reduce the waste stream have paid dividends, but high tipping fees have diverted disposal to the United States, so the waste problem has been shelved rather than solved. Furthermore, the various levels of government in the Toronto area are trying to come to grips with the problem of reducing the urban area's ecological footprint (to use William Rees's term), at a time when the population in the region is increasing, and the country is still mired in recession.

Land-use planning

Toronto is still growing onto greenfield sites, and it is also renovating and intensifying land-use within the existing built-up area; so it is dealing with the conditions a, b, and c in Figure 7.1. The situation is complex, however, because although new policies emerge the old policies have considerable inertia. In Toronto we can now identify three main policy phases related to land-use. The first is the post-war period up to 1971, when the full force of modernistic planning threatened to transform 'the shape of the city' (in John Sewell's phrase). The second phase ran from 1971 to 1988, when modernism was halted, but nothing coherent emerged in its place in Metro, and growth continued unchecked, to produce very low densities on the periphery, in what became known as the Greater Toronto Area. Post 1988 has seen the emergence of policies which signify a vigorous search for more environmentally benign urban forms, when managers at all levels of government are trying to edge the system back towards higher densities and to a re-orientation towards public transportation.

Although the housing stock in North America tends to be replaced or renovated more rapidly than is the case in Europe, it still changes slowly, at about 2% per year in Toronto. In the meantime we are stuck with a very large, and expanding, area of low density, car-dependent, suburban sprawl. Table 8.1 summarises the implications of this for car-use. One way to encapsulate the implications of this table is to note than even the least-polluting cars produce two and half kilograms of carbon dioxide for each litre of petrol used (Crombie 1992: 326). The combination of the suburban single-family dwelling and reliance on the private car are a big part of the reason why Canada's large cities are not environmentally sustainable. Unfortunately, stating the problem is only the first step in the search for a solution. As Richardson observed:

'The low-density suburb places a heavy burden on resources and the environment'

and, despite the fact that:

'suburbs made up of single detached houses are a suitable habitat only for the households in a particular demographic and income category ... this typical urban form is so bound up with a complex of cultural values and

Table 8.1 Residential Densities, Car Use, and Carbon Dioxide Emissions in the Toronto Region (Autumn 1986)

	Core	Inner Suburbs	Outer Suburbs
Persons per km^2	5300	2780	1440
Vehicles per 1000 people	407	526	572
Percentage of trips made by car	55	70	81
Average car trip length (km)	8.7	9.0	11.8
Grams of CO$_2$/person/day	2100	2940	4520

Source: Adapted from Gilbert, R. (1991), in McCulloch, J. (Ed.) *Cities and Global Change*.

with financial, commercial, and political interests that even a growing public "environmental consciousness" has not yet brought about any general recognition that it constitutes one of Canada's principal environmental issues' (Richardson 1992: 159).

The same writer notes that the low-density suburb not only has implications for space-heating and car use, but also energy demands for snow-removal in winter and air-conditioning and powered lawn-mowers in the summer, plus water use for the lawns and the cars, and the resources used in the infrastructure required by urban sprawl in the form of new roads, water-mains, sewers and lighting.

Although there may be no general, or public, recognition of environmental problems posed by low-density suburbs, it is certainly widely appreciated at the planning level in many of the authorities in the Toronto area. Many problems appear simultaneously as the residential density falls, especially in monofunctional residential zones—public transit becomes uneconomical, thus forcing people to rely on cars; all services become more expensive to deliver, including the removal of solid and liquid wastes. The energy demands, especially for space-heating, go up, and more water is required to water private lawns and grassed open spaces around apartment blocks. In the Canadian climate open spaces are vulnerable to the wind in winter and desiccation in summer. Trees, which provide both shade and shelter, are more easily integrated into neighbourhoods comprised of denser, low-rise housing.

Two further factors have shaped a change of opinion regarding the desirability of the low-density suburb as the preferred form of residential land-use, both of them financial. The first is the cost to a new home-buyer. The average suburban house in Metro now costs much more than the average for Metro as a whole. Even more ominously this suburban house price is now four times the average family income. (See Figure 8.2.) The second financial setback began in the early 1970s when the two-tier fare system for transit was converted to a single fare, as a concession to the suburban communities in compensation for the cancellation of the expressway programme (Sewell 1993: 217). After 50 years of operating on a break-even basis, without any public operating

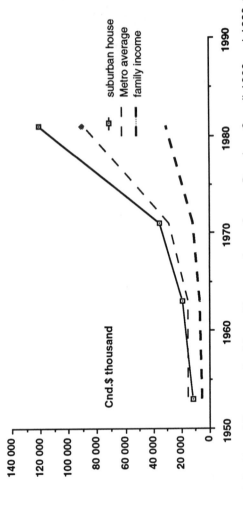

Figure 8.2 House Prices in the Metro Toronto Area. *Source:* Based on Sewell 1992 and 1993 (p. 214)

subsidy, the Toronto Transit Commission began to run at a loss; in 1991 its deficit exceeded Cnd.$200 million. The combination of environmental and economic problems posed by urban sprawl has led one observer to state:

> 'The suburban form of urban development has no future. It is simply not a viable urban form in either economic or environmental terms ... It is simply inconceivable that the environmental challenges we face can be met without stopping the spread of new suburbs and without rapidly transforming those that already exist into higher density urban communities through redevelopment and intensification' (Martin 1991: 175).

As the 1970s unfolded it became clear that stopping the proliferation of expressways and tower blocks was only the first step in the search for a more sustainable urban form in the Toronto area. Circumstances in both the countryside and the city underlined the fact that suburban sprawl was not in the long-term public interest. In 1978 the provincial Ministry of Housing had produced a paper on Urban Development Standards to encourage a doubling of the density of lots per acre; but this was largely ignored in the townships surrounding Toronto. Farmers wanted to sell their land; developers wanted to make their profits; and there was a demand for the houses. In the same year the City of Toronto produced a new Central Area Plan which encouraged a more diverse, low- and medium-rise approach to building in the City, but the changes were contested by developers who saw more profit in multi-storey buildings. Two years later the provincial Ministry of Agriculture made a similar argument for a more compact form in order to preserve first class agricultural land. Again the province's guidelines were resented and resisted by the local planning authorities. However all of these factors reinforced the idea that there was a need to move toward a more compact urban form, both by encouraging new developments at higher densities and by infilling, or intensifying, existing residential areas.

All of these processes—the unaffordability of the suburban home, the growing deficit of the TTC, the continuing loss of the best agricultural land, the need to develop an urban form to meet a greater diversity of needs—converged on the same solution, namely a denser form of settlement, which did not dictate that the vast majority of the people would spend an appreciable part of their lives driving around the suburbs and into and out of the city core. This lifestyle was not healthy for the people or for the land from which they drew their sustenance. However, the Healthy Cities Movement did not derive from these concerns about the suburbs at all, but rather from the more immediate problems emerging in the City.

The Healthy City initiative

The focus here is on the public health responsibilities of the City of Toronto's Board of Health, which was instrumental in promoting the WHO Healthy Cities Project mentioned above. Whereas the public health problems found in the City of Toronto are small compared with conditions in cities in the countries of the South, there is no room for complacency. Indeed there are signs that the very prosperity that characterised Toronto in the 1970s and early 1980s exacerbated inequalities in income and access to a healthy environment. The Board of Health's 1988 report, *Healthy Toronto 2000*, noted that:

> 'There is an increasing sense ... that our generally favourable situation is under severe pressure. While Toronto is economically prosperous, this hides pockets of poverty, hunger and homelessness; while Toronto has a reputation for being clean and safe, it is becoming more crowded, over-developed, polluted and unsafe; while we have had an effective City government, good health and social services, and a culturally diverse population living in harmony, these benefits can only be maintained by dint of hard work and careful thought; and while life expectancy is high, infant mortality low, and health status good, these figures disguise dramatic inequalities in health' (City of Toronto 1988: 61–2).

The sources of pressure which threaten the situation are diverse. They include global factors such as the economic recession which undermines the tax base at a time of increasing social need. They also include local processes referred to earlier in this chapter, such as the modernisation policy of the 1960s which destroyed old neighbourhoods, and also the later trend to preserve the neighbourhood by converting it to occupancy by higher income groups. As Figure 8.2 shows, the cost of the average home in the

Metro Toronto in relation to average income has changed dramatically. As Toronto as a whole has become wealthier, other components of the cost of living, such as food prices, have risen faster than the rest of the country. These trends have made life more difficult for people in lower income groups and those dependent on welfare. The 'Healthy Toronto' report estimated that 5% of the City's population depended on food banks regularly; 30–40 000 were on waiting lists for social housing; and 10–25 000 were actually homeless and dependent on hostels or living on the street.

Other trends add complexity to the problem and warnings for the future. As is the case throughout the North, the population is aging, and this will raise new demands for suitable housing and access to services, while reducing the relative size of the working population contributing to the tax base. Family structure continues to change with more single-parent families, and more families with both parents working outside the home. Again this changes and increases the needs of the population. Toronto continues to become less British and more multicultural. So far this process has proceeded quite well (compared with other cities in the North), but it makes the delivery of services more complicated (through the variety of languages required to deliver services and the cultural preferences to which the health sector must be sensitive), and it may raise additional points of conflict if the overall social and economic environment deteriorates. As the report noted, harmony is not something that we can take for granted; it requires careful thought and hard work.

Some physical environmental factors add further complexity to the situation. For example, there are several initiatives under way to provide additional affordable housing within the City and to reintroduce residential units to what were formerly purely commercial lots. Problems exist however in the conversion of old industrial sites (including disused railway lands) to residential use in the cost of decontaminating sites containing lead and PCBs, especially. The increase in vehicular traffic continues to pose a threat to air quality, even though most vehicles now use lead-free petrol. This increase in traffic runs counter to the goal of switching from private to public transport where possible. Vehicular congestion also discourages people from walking and cycling. Problems of water quality and waste management have already been mentioned.

The City established an Environmental Protection Office in 1986 to coordinate all these public health concerns. The *Healthy Toronto 2000* report was accepted unanimously by City Council in 1989 and a Healthy City Office was created in the same year. The EPO secured an early victory to regulate smoking indoors and this has so far been implemented without formal opposition. Improvements have been made in the quality of ante-natal care especially for high-risk groups such as the young and low-income families. On a more general front the movement has gained acceptance for the idea that all urban planning proposals should be assessed for their human health impact, just as we include environmental impact assessments in such decisions. Furthermore, the Healthy Cities Movement has strengthened the perception that urban management decisions must be treated in a holistic context if they are to have a positive impact on the health of the people.

Discharges to the air

Reference has been made in Chapter Five to some aspects of the City of Toronto's proposals to reduce emissions to the air of carbon dioxide and other residuals. These include the use of cool water from the depths of Lake Ontario to run a district cooling system in the downtown core, to reduce demand for heating and cooling. Retrofitting old buildings and defining higher standards for new buildings will further reduce demand. Mention was also made of the impact of car use on carbon dioxide, as it varied with residential densities. Thus, although individual households downtown have less impact on the air than do suburban households, the downtown core itself, from the cluster of multi-storey office blocks, has a considerable impact.

These proposals are only part of the City's plan to reduce emissions of carbon dioxide, and other greenhouse gases, including ozone-depleting CFCs (City of Toronto 1991). Other elements of the plan are summarised in Figure 8.3. The proposal is to reduce energy use, and hence carbon dioxide emissions by 20% (compared with the 1985 level) over the next ten years, even though

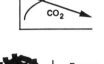 1. Set a target of of a 20% reduction in CO_2 emissions by the year 2005 (compared with the 1985 level), at a time when population is expected to rise by 20%.

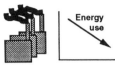 2. Targets set to reduce energy use for the gas and electrical utility companies , with a service role to increase efficiency, rather than the traditional production role. Tariff structures to be changed to encourage efficiency. Set up an Energy Efficiency Office to do life-cycle analysis of all new projects and conversions.

 3. Water to be drawn from the lower levels of Lake Ontario to provide cooling for an extended district heating system in the downtown core.

 4. Encourage the use of public transport, bicycles and walking by increasing the price of parking and decreasing its availability. Increase land-use density to provide support for public transport; establish bus lanes.

 5. Plant trees in the City to provide shade and shelter. Plant trees in southern Ontario to increase CO_2 uptake and provide 'migration corridors' for plants and animals. Plant trees in the tropics to promote sustainable development.

Figure 8.3 The City of Toronto Proposal for the Reduction of Carbon Dioxide Emissions. Summary based on The City of Toronto, *The Changing Atmosphere: Strategies for Reducing CO_2 Emissions*, (2 vols.), March 1991

the population is expected to grow in that time by 20%. An important element in this plan is the switching of people from private to public transport, walking, and cycling. In general, more of the road-bed will be given over to collective use, as opposed to motorised individual transport (or MIT). This may take the form of reducing the availability of parking, in complete contrast to the former policy which was to insist that every new building include provision for parking for all its potential users. Priority bus lanes are already appearing, and these will visually reinforce the message that public transport is preferable to travelling in congested, slow-moving MIT. This message can already be seen from the main expressway running along the lakeshore, as the stalled vehicles are passed by the suburban (surface) commuter train system run by the provincial government. Since the carbon dioxide reduction report was accepted by City Council bicycle paths have begun to appear in the City, although there is no connected network in place, yet. Additional tree-planting is underway in the City to provide shade and shelter, and tree-planting outside the city is planned, partly to increase carbon dioxide uptake.

All of this can be seen as the antithesis to the modernist vision of the 1960s where people would sweep from low-density suburb to downtown tower block in their cars, or, at best, dropping their car off at the park-and-ride station on the periphery of Metro and taking a subway to complete the journey.

Following the report of the Special Advisory Committee on the Environment the City set up an Energy Efficiency Office which works in liaison with Ontario Hydro, Toronto Hydro, and Consumers Gas to prepare energy efficiency and conservation plans, to retrofit all City-owned buildings and to convert street and lane lighting to a more energy efficient system. About 20 of the city's buildings are involved in the first two phases of the retrofit programme, and between them the improvements should reduce annual carbon dioxide production by 7500 tons; more than half of this will come from City Hall itself, the rest from community centres and sports arenas (City of Toronto 1993). When the annual energy savings are set against the costs of retrofitting, the average payback period is 3.2 years. What had been completed by July 1993, in this and other programmes, would already produce 3% of the 20% target by the end of 1994. Some of the costs are met from a fund proposed by the Committee called the Toronto Atmospheric Fund.

The main activities for the City, so far, in the first phases of implementation, (apart from city-owned buildings and street lighting), are a new procurement policy for the City's vehicle fleet (to achieve a fuel efficiency standard of 5.2 litres per 100 km for all new purchases and leases), the evaluation of a variety of proposals for cogeneration in the downtown core, proposals for retrofitting city-owned housing, data collection (including an energy audit of all the City's buildings), computer modelling, and liaison with other cities tackling these problems.

The scope of the problems facing the Municipality of Metropolitan Toronto, or Metro, is suggested by the energy flow diagram, Figure 3.4 in Chapter Three. The most striking feature of this diagram is that it shows that barely half the raw energy input is turned into usable energy output in the form of motion for vehicles, space heating and cooling, and electrical motive power. The efficiencies of the various conversion processes are: hydroelectricity, 100%; natural gas to heat, 78%; oil to heat, 71%; nuclear power to electricity, 30%; coal-fired power to electricity, 30%; oil to vehicular motion, 25%.

With this information as a starting point, Metro has identified a detailed set of programmes for reducing the demand for raw energy, including the following:

- use the energy that is presently being wasted:
  —through cogeneration of heat for a district heating system;
  —through burning methane that is presently leaking from landfill sites;
- reduce demand for raw energy:
  —by constructing and maintaining vehicles and buildings more efficiently;
  —by recycling materials, and thereby reducing the energy used in the production process for glass, aluminium, paper, etcetera;
  —by fostering greater energy production efficiency, through district heating and cooling;
  —by reducing demand for petroleum-fuelled vehicles, by switching to public transit, bicycling, and walking, including the creation of a network of lanes for high occupancy vehicles;
- use raw energy inputs more efficiently:
  —by switching to those technologies that convert energy more efficiently;
  —by switching from petroleum-fuelled vehicles to vehicles powered by gas, and even electricity, especially where the latter entails a switch from MIT to public transport, thereby transporting far more people for the amount of energy used.

Detailed calculations have been made to show how much each such initiative contributes to the reduction of greenhouse gas emissions and the use of CFCs. It is significant to note that:

> 'The waste heat from Ontario Hydro generating stations at Pickering and Lakeview alone could replace all other energy consumed for heating of interior building space in Metropolitan Toronto which cost approximately $1.4 billion in 1988, and would eliminate its impact on our local and global environment' (Metropolitan Toronto Government 1993: 4).

In the 1960s and 1970s members of the public and their urban governments were most concerned with local air quality, and to a lesser extent, with acid deposition. Then the goal was seen as emission reduction, rather than the reduction of energy use, and different solutions come into play such as scrubbers on power station stacks, catalytic converters on car exhausts, and other end-of-pipe technologies. Today's decision-makers are faced with a broader problem and must, of necessity, adopt a broader approach to meet it.

Metro, as a government for 2.2 million people (compared with 600 000 in the City of Toronto), clearly has a larger problem to focus on, and a more dispersed target to reach. The City's very density makes certain options immediately apparent, such as district heating and cooling, reduction of MIT, retrofits of buildings within the City's jurisdiction, and so on. Recent reports of the Metropolitan Works Department make it clear that the linked ecosystem nature of both the problems and the solutions is steadily becoming more apparent. They also underline the necessity for closer integration between the planning and provision of services and infrastructure by the different levels of government. For example, the Metro Government is involved in the financing and the evaluation of studies related to the deep water cooling proposal, and the district heating and cooling schemes within the City of Toronto (as the City is a member of Metro). There is an additional Metro benefit from reducing the need to use fossil fuels to generate electricity because 'in the prevailing southwesterly summer winds, air emissions from the Lakeview Generating Station are directed over Metropolitan Toronto' so the introduction of district cooling and to the City should improve air quality for wider areas of Metro (Metropolitan Toronto Government

1992). The Metro Commissioner of Public Works sees additional benefits of the deep lake water scheme if water can be drawn from that depth for water supply, because water drawn from deeper levels may not require the use of chlorine to keep zebra mussels from clogging the intake pipe, as is presently the case in the nearby water filtration plant, where water is drawn from a shallower depth (Metropolitan Toronto Government 1992).

Once links of this kind are made then we are moving towards the implementation of a conserver society, reducing Daly's throughput, and reducing Rees's ecological footprint. Finally we can look at the connections between emissions to the air and intakes from the water, and the problems of waste discharges to the ground. In this matter Metro must deal with the surrounding regions of the GTA (which are outside its jurisdiction), because the major water users are the power stations which lie outside Metro. The landfill sites used by Metro lie outside its boundaries also.

Discharges to the ground

One concern about the Deep Lake Water Cooling System was the environmental implications of the amount of water that it would draw from Lake Ontario, and the similar amount of warmer water that it would return to it. This is calculated at 178 million cubic metres annually, which compares with the 543 million m^3 which is currently drawn off by the Metro Water Supply System. Yet these figures are dwarfed by the more than 3 billion m^3 that are extracted for cooling the Lakeview and Pickering Generating Stations. Indeed 70% of all withdrawals from Ontario's lakes and streams are taken for cooling purposes. This would suggest that using the waste heat from the generating stations to supply district heating will produce an environmental benefit (by reducing the need for additional generating capacity, and reducing the need for cooling water) with no additional environmental cost. This approach to internalising the flows of energy and materials (so as to minimalise the external disruptions) is exactly what ecosystem planning is supposed to do.

The discharge of solid wastes provides a less encouraging

scenario, although the pace of change is rapid and much has been achieved in a short time. Metro produced about 4.7 million tons of solid waste in 1988, about half of which came from industry, commerce, and institutions (ICI), and the rest from households. Of this total about 1.5 million tons was recycled (mostly metals in the private sector), 3.1 million went to two landfill sites in surrounding regions within the GTA and about 100 000 tons was incinerated within the City, on a lakeshore site. The landfill sites were close to capacity with only two or three years left. Alternative sites were proving difficult to find as a result of powerful NIMBY forces in the other regions, and due to the time required to comply with the province's environmental regulations for new sites. The City incinerator was due to be closed down. Three possibilities were in the air. Energy-from-waste derived from improved incinerators was favoured in some quarters; an unused mine, a 12-hour train trip away in Northern Ontario had much support as a landfill site; while the province had contributed towards the start-up costs of a pilot scheme for kerbside collection of recyclable newspapers, cans, and glass from blue plastic boxes —hence known as the Blue Box programme. The provincial goal was to reduce the waste stream by 50% by the year 2000, and (like the carbon dioxide emission reduction target) this allowed for an expected increase in population. Nobody expected the Blue Box programme to handle 50% on its own, and the spirit of the times was still very much in favour of burning the rubbish or shipping it elsewhere. Both of these 'solutions' would create jobs, make a profit, and solve the 'landfill problem'. Note that this was seen as a landfill problem, rather than as a waste problem. Holistic thinking about the environment was still not very widespread in 1988.

The following year produced a more hopeful sign with the meeting of the chairmen of the five regions of the GTA—Metro and its four neighbours, the latter all being formerly rural areas in the throws of rapid urbanisation and suburbanisation. Landfill costs were rising, new sites were difficult to find, and the five regions saw possible benefits from cooperating, especially in the emerging field of recycling. Events south of the border were forcing the pace of change in local thinking as 14 American states had already passed legislation requiring recycled paper in newsprint, a major Canadian (and Ontario) export. Ontario was only just setting up its paper recycling plants and might lose some of its share of the American market. The problem lay in matching the supply of waste newsprint to the scale of the output the plants required to make a profit. The recycling plants might have to import waste newspapers from the United States to make up the supply. This was a chicken-and-egg problem, with quite large chickens and eggs at stake.

A provincial election added pressure from the environmentally-minded voters. Despite controversy on most other fronts, everyone seemed to be in favour of environmental integrity. The Blue Box experiment had proved very popular and enjoyed an 80% participation rate from households, thereby catering for a population of two million people. There were promises made to extend the programme to the more difficult area of apartments and businesses, and to extend the range of recyclable materials to include plastics and cardboard. The municipalities also promised to collect and compost all garden wastes that households did not absorb themselves. With the election won the new provincial government cancelled the Northern Ontario landfill proposal and subsequently banned any new proposals for incinerators. While some engineers believed that a properly designed and managed incinerator posed no environmental threat, the public perception linked incinerator emissions with smog, acid rain, greenhouse warming, and threats to human health through respiration and contamination of the food chain. Even the cleanest flue ash, produced by incinerators, was contaminated and required special treatment before shipping to a hazardous waste facility, at costs up to ten times the disposal costs of 'normal' waste. Meanwhile, the most combustible material, such as plastics and paper, had been diverted to the recycling stream. So perhaps even if inciner-ation could pass the environmental tests, it might fail the eco-nomic test.

Thus the disposal options narrowed very rapidly, and landfill costs soared, with the result mentioned in Chapter Six. There was a diversion of waste from Metro landfills to landfills south of the border, as far afield as Montana and Tennessee, estimated to amount to 1.6 million tons annually by 1993, mostly from the pri-vate sector. This was not what the government intended or what the people wanted, yet the provincial government said it had no control over the movement as the international border traffic came under federal jurisdiction.

The next stage in this saga is difficult to predict, although new landfill sites are being considered within the GTA and efforts are being widened all the time to reduce what goes into the waste stream and to divert to recycling more of the material that does go in it. At this point, however, the interplay between economic and environmental forces may well throw another twist in the tale, because the handling of the Blue Box materials costs about $180 per ton, while the average market value of the recovered materials is only $30 per ton. The provincial government plans to phase out its financial contribution to the programme in the near future, at which point the cost will fall on the municipalities, the private sector, and the households.

At the moment households in Toronto pay a flat fee for waste collection, as a portion of their property tax assessment, so the cost is not really visible unless you read the small print on the back of your bill. It would seem likely that a charge per quantity collected (as is found in some jurisdictions in Europe and the United States) might be applied, and thus households will be encouraged to internalise some of this environmental impact themselves, either by paying more or wasting less. In turn, households may then put more pressure on retailers to reduce packaging materials, and so the system will continue to evolve. The Blue Box is a very visible symbol of the change in people's attitudes to the environment, so maybe it just needs an equally visible financial symbol to strengthen its impact on the public consciousness.

What is interesting is how quickly all these changes have taken place. Only five years ago the choice of solutions for Toronto's waste were energy-from-waste incinerators and a 12-hour train ride to an abandoned iron ore mine in Northern Ontario. In the meantime waste management has become the province's fifth largest economic sector, worth $2.5 billion a year in turnover, and providing 32 000 jobs.

Conclusion

The experience in Toronto is not offered as unique in any way, neither as the world's 'worst offender', in terms of original level of resource use, nor as the 'most improved', in terms of current moves towards environmental stewardship. It is offered because it illustrates one of the main contentions of this book, and that is that it will fall to urban governments to put their own ecosystems in order, calling on higher levels of government and regional partners when circumstances, both physical and legislative, require it to do so.

At least in the case of the kind of urban governments that belong to an organisation like the International Council for Local Environmental Initiatives (both the City and Metro are members), there is a willingness to deal with the environmental challenge. A recent report from Metro noted:

'Carbon dioxide is accumulating in the atmosphere and contributing to the global warming effect and climate destabilization ... The change over the next 50 to 80 years will be sudden ... and will not allow the ecosystem to adapt. The potential result will be that forests and other vegetation that absorb CO_2 now will be damaged and will not absorb as much CO_2. This will compound the effect of CO_2 produced from human activity and potentially accelerate the global warming effect ... There is a consensus in the world community of climatologists that the atmospheric CO_2 concentration must be stabilized to prevent global warming' (Metropolitan Toronto Government 1992d: 2).

Despite the scale of the possible disruption of the climate and hence global patterns of food production and trade, the initial investigations and pilot schemes have been encouraging. Indeed, much of what has been found so far in terms of recommended responses falls in the 'no regrets' category mentioned earlier— these are actions that should be taken whether global warming were likely or not. As the same Metro report went on:

'The main objective of the Urban CO_2 Reduction Project is to use raw (primary) fossil energy more efficiently. Participating cities have learned from comparison of the way energy is used in other world cities that there is great potential to reduce energy use without reducing the standard of living' (Metropolitan Toronto Government 1992d: 3).

For Toronto this realisation seems light years away from the not-so-long-ago 1960s when the planners and developers were poised to run expressways through old neighbourhoods, and relocate the population in tower blocks and in an ever-widening expanse of low density suburbs.

Further reading:

Canadian Urban Institute (1993). *Cooling Buildings in Downtown Toronto.* Final Report of the Deep Lake Water Cooling Investigation Group. Canadian Urban Institute.

City of Toronto (1988). *Healthy Toronto 2000.* Toronto, Department of Public Health.

City of Toronto (1991). *The Changing Atmosphere: Strategies for Reducing Carbon Dioxide Emissions.* Volume 1, Policy Overview; Volume 2, Technical Volume. Special Advisory Committee on the Environment.

Crombie, D. (1992). *Regeneration. Toronto's Waterfront and the Sustainable City: Final Report.* Ottawa, Ministry of Supply and Services.

Gilbert, R. (1991). Cities and global warming. In *Cities and Global Change.* Ed. J. McCulloch. Washington, DC, The Climate Institute. 182–91.

Hancock, T. (1992). The development of the healthy cities project in Canada. In *Healthy Cities.* Ed. J. Ashton. Milton Keynes, Open University Press. 43–8.

Hancock, T. (1992). Toronto. In *Healthy Cities.* Ed. J. Ashton. Milton Keynes, Open University Press. 175–85.

Harvey, L. D. D. (1993). Toronto's CO_2 emission reduction programme: a bottom-up approach. *Environment*, September: 16–20, & 38–45.

Martin, D. (1991). The suburban dilemma. Regional transit issues and the global environmental crisis. In *Cities and Global Change.* Ed. J. McCulloch. Washington DC, The Climate Institute. 174–9.

Metropolitan Toronto Government (1991). *Strategic Plan, May 1991.* Metropolitan Toronto Government.

Richardson, N. and H. (1992). Canada. *Sustainable Cities.* Eds. R. E. Stren, R. R. White and J. W. Whitney. Boulder, Westview Press. 145–167.

Sewell, J. (1993). *The Shape of the City: Toronto Struggles with Modern Planning.* Toronto, University of Toronto Press.

9

Postscript

'We arrived very suddenly at the edge of the abyss, beyond which lies a very brutal ecological denouement' (Atkinson 1991: 172).

'It is now widely accepted that the planet Earth is in danger of becoming uninhabitable and that urgent measures, at every level, are essential to protect the global environment' (Metropolitan Toronto Government 1991: 16).

The average global temperature (at the earth's surface) fell from 15.41°C in 1991 to 15.13°C in 1992; and the 1991 temperature was itself lower than the record 1990 average of 15.47 (Brown et al. 1993: 68–9). Nor have temperatures risen as expected in the polar regions where the earliest confirmation of a warming trend is expected. For those people who are sceptical about the models which predict a warming trend in response to increasing greenhouse gas emissions this is welcome news. For those who prefer to wait until the evidence is irrefutable this seems like a justification for their caution. However, for the modellers who predict a warming effect, the interruption of the upward trend in the 70s and 80s is entirely explicable due to the cooling effect of the sulphate aerosols put into the atmosphere by the eruption of Mount Pinatubo in the Philippines in June 1991. Indeed they see the cooling response as a useful confirmation of the accuracy of their models (Harvey 1993b, personal communication). The cooling effect of the aerosols is expected to last until the end of 1993, and then the warming trend is expected to resume. In the meantime the more prudent urban governments, who have the means to do so, are making preparations to reduce their impacts on the atmosphere. As has been said many times, even without the threat of global warming and stratospheric ozone depletion, there are many good reasons to reconsider—from the bottom up—many practices relevant to aspects of urban environmental management.

As was emphasised in Chapter Two the environmental challenge facing our cities is multi-faceted and it encompasses the whole broad field of the human use of resources, the production of residuals, and the uneven distribution of wealth which lies behind the continued rapid growth of the human population. As the human impact on the planet has steadily increased we see more clearly the interlinked nature of many of our problems in the use of the planetary store of materials. This awareness is no longer confined to scientists or people involved in global decision-making bodies like the United Nations, or policy advisors such as the Centre for Our Common Future. The evidence of this impingement of one process on another is clearly visible on the streets of many of our cities, certainly in the largest cities of the North. The economic and social problems (described in Chapter Four) are tightly interlocked with the physical environmental problems, although it is the latter that take up much of this book.

I have emphasised these physical problems because I submit that there is an important distinction to be made between conditions in a country where people find themselves without the opportunity to provide for themselves because of the peculiarities of the economic and political system, and conditions in a country where a family is without food because there is insufficient water to grow their own grain or pasture their livestock. However, at the close of the twentieth century we are in a situation where not only do the two worlds coexist but they also physically impinge on one another through the international flows of environmental refugees. These flows—some legal and tolerated, some illegal and resisted—bring face to face the landless, waterless peasant from the South and the unemployed urbanite from the North. The mixture is potentially explosive. On top of this human factor lie the environmental changes that humanity's increasingly onerous occupation of the planet imposes.

One way of conceptualising the complex inter-linkages between these problems is to focus on the evolution of urban systems as they have gradually extended their environmental impact from the immediate locality, to the region, and finally to the globe, as exemplified by the atmospheric problems of air quality, acidification, and the build-up of greenhouse gases, respectively. This extension of the scale of urban impacts has posed increasingly complex questions for the governance and administration of the urban areas which will soon be the home for half the world's rapidly expanding population. Interestingly, these environmental impacts are now having their own impact on the organisation of urban government, as local authorities struggle to find some operational understanding of the implications of the concept of sustainable development as it relates to their own part of the world (Maclaren 1992). The response of urban governments is taking place on two fronts. First, is the spontaneous response to the increasing complexity of 'managing' the urban environment at a time of climate change, economic recession, and the intensification of many of the traditional environmental problems, such as the provision of water and the disposal of wastes. Second, is the response to new environmental regulations—some handed down from higher levels of government and others drafted at international meetings such as the Earth Summit in Rio de Janeiro in 1992. Thus—not for the first time in human history—the higher authority takes a decision, and leaves the subsidiary authority to find the means to implement it. As it happens there is some evidence that this familiar situation may be quite appropriate in this context, because the 'bottom-up' approach to CO_2 reduction, for example, appears better able to 'identify the full economically attractive potential for emission reduction and to achieve a significant fraction of this potential' (Harvey 1993a). What is to be desired is that the experience gained by urban planners and managers will increasingly inform the decisions that are taken by the higher levels of government as they grapple with the international dimensions of the problem.

There is some reason to hope that information will flow upwards from the urban experience to the national level because the urban situation is really a metaphor for the larger issues of global environmental management. The international aspects of the situation are not ignored, even by decision-makers who normally work on the local scale. Furthermore, difficult and urgent as the CO_2 and energy issues (for example) are for urban managers, they are less urgent than the global population explosion which threatens to engulf human society. Unfortunately, it is difficult for the global community to even *discuss* the matter, let alone deal with it. Some of the reasons for this incapacity are well known. The South resents interference in its most personal affairs. And the North does not want to analyse the main reasons for continued rapid population growth in the South, as these are rooted in abiding poverty, which in turn is rooted in a global economic system which steadily intensifies the economic gulf between the North and the South. So the population issue remains the unmentionable skeleton in the global family closet. Yet it is the combination of the North's resource-intensive lifestyle and the South's poverty, and associated rapid population growth, that are the driving forces behind atmospheric change, desertification, deforestation, and the rest of the global environmental *problématique*. All of these aspects of the situation must be changed if humanity is to establish a sustainable niche for itself on the planet. The challenge is summarised in Figure 9.1.

I do not know how we can move from this *impasse*. Some writers believe that many members of the public, and even decision-makers, are still unaware of the dynamics of exponential population growth (Ehrlich and Ehrlich 1993: 5). Certainly, there is a rear-guard still defending the assumption that economic growth, encouraged by the free play of market forces, provides the best hope of creating material progress, for all people (Beckerman 1991; Simon and Kahn 1984). People may also assume that economic downturns and recessions, and even the deterioration of the biosphere, are part of the normal workings of this system.

However, there was a time when slavery was considered to be part of the natural state of affairs, and more recently people assumed that 'mutual assured destruction' through all-out nuclear war, was the best guarantee of peace between the superpowers. Society has managed to move away from these alarming states of 'normalcy', so perhaps one day (before it is too late) 'population and environment' will be seen to be an issue that must be addressed, even though it means restructuring the global economy in such a way that the gap between rich and poor will be narrowed, rather than widened. Fortunately, there is now some evidence that the interplay of the various factors that link population, environment, and economy are well understood at the highest levels of government. For example, see Gore, Chapter 15, 'A Global Marshall Plan', and Hall and Hanson, Chapter 10, 'A New Dialogue' (Gore 1993; Hall and Hanson 1992).

Certainly there is a new sense of urgency with which the global problem is being addressed, both in print and in international debate. Furthermore, it is increasingly accepted that in order to address environmental change constructively we must be

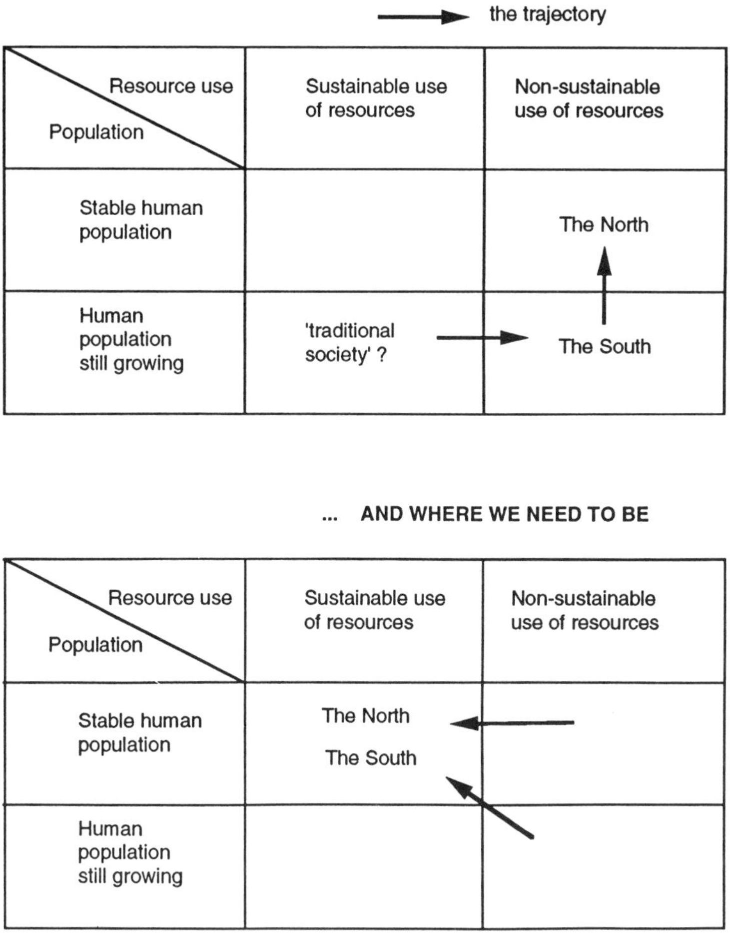

Figure 9.1 Where Countries of the North and South are Today ... and Where We Need to Be

prepared to re-examine even the most basic assumptions about the way our societies are organised. This should not come as a surprise because it has been argued, for many years, that economic growth did not automatically alleviate poverty and that the basic needs of the poor had to be addressed directly through government intervention (Sandbrook 1982). Fortunately, this proposition was eventually accepted by the World Bank in 1990, in the *World Development Report* which was devoted to the poverty issue. However, even in this *Report*, the issue of continued rapid population growth was scarcely mentioned (World Bank 1990). It was not until its 1992 *World Development Report* that the Bank did address the issue of population growth directly:

'There is strong evidence that economic stagnation is delaying declines in fertility.'

And:

'Stagnant incomes and the absence of improvements in human welfare have impeded the demographic transition' (World Bank 1992: 27).

There was also recognition of the need to address basic needs, such as health and education, in the demographic context:

'Evidence from a cross-section of countries shows that where no women are enrolled in secondary education, the average woman has seven children, but where 40% of all women have had a secondary education, the average drops to three children, even after controlling for factors such as income' (World Bank 1992: 29).

It is significant that it was this 1992 *World Development Report* that was devoted to the environment. The size and the rate of growth of the human population have become the most important factors to influence large-scale, often irreversible, environmental change. This fact will become increasingly difficult to ignore. This is especially so in the cities, in which a steadily increasing percentage of the world's population will be living. Thus it is essential to address the fundamental problems of cities—political, economic and environmental. It is ironic that population, environment, and the cities—all topics that have been studiously ignored by mainstream theories of economic development—should now coalesce and force themselves on the world's attention.

We must labour in the hope that the pressures of these converging problems are now intense enough to force some realism into the global debate. If this does happen then it may be due to efforts made at the urban scale to deal with the long-term deficiencies of our cities, because in the last few years it is urban governments rather than national governments that have appeared more ready to respond to these problems, both physical and social. I hope this book can make some contribution to this effort.

Although some of the problems we face today are unique in human history, it is sobering to note that other problems have been with us since ancient times. For example:

'It would be simplistic to state categorically that the fall of the Roman Empire was due to abuse of the environment. There were undoubtedly many other reasons—political, social, military, medical, perhaps even climatic. Suffice it to say that environmental degradation must have been an important contributing factor. Ironically, the very achievements which most impress so many observers to this day, and of which the Romans themselves were most proud (namely, the grandeur and scale of their works), were the most destructive of the natural environment and hence most likely to have hastened the decline of their empire' (Hillel 1991: 107).

The Roman achievement was illustrated by the expansion of their empire over much of Europe, North Africa and parts of the Middle East. Like our modern cities the Romans extended their hinterland to bring in goods from all over the known world. Our problem today is that we have reached the limits of that kind of extension of our domain to new regions and untapped resources. We can no longer increase our rate of resource use by annexing new places nor by extruding the residuals from fossil fuel consumption into the atmospheric sink. We are not masters of the world, nor even stewards, but simply one species among many. Thus, we must re-evaluate our cities as outgrowths of, and dependent on, the natural world. We must accept that we depend on daily food, water and energy supplies from the biosphere, just like any other species. Unlike most other species we have been given the ability to take a long-term view of our situation. We must avail ourselves of this gift while there is still time to use it.

Glossary

Environmental work is inescapably interdisciplinary. This is what makes it both stimulating and frustrating. One of the frustrations is the difficulty of communicating across disciplines, a difficulty which is compounded when one worker borrows a term from another's discipline and uses it to mean something rather different. I hope I have not committed too many of these sins of commission. In order to reduce any confusion I may have caused in this way, I have assembled a brief glossary to explain how certain terms have been used in this book. If a reader finds a lot of the vocabulary unfamiliar, I recommend using an environmental dictionary such as the *HarperCollins Dictionary of Environmental Science* which contains more than 2000 entries (Jones et al. 1992). Items described elsewhere in the glossary are bolded.

Acidification, acid deposition The combustion of fossil fuels produces sulphur oxides and nitrogen oxides as a gaseous residue, most of which is deposited on the ground a few days after emission. While in the air, these gases mix with water vapour to produce weak acids which have very detrimental effects on aquatic life, plants and soils.

Agglomeration economies The concentration of people in cities provides an opportunity for producers of goods and services to take advantage of scale economies, thus being able to produce at a lower cost per unit.

Agricultural revolution The term is most commonly applied in this book to that period of agricultural innovation that began in Western Europe in the late seventeenth century, when an awakening interest in science was applied to agricultural operations, such as plant and animal breeding, sowing, harvesting, storage, and the practice of rotating crops to preserve soil fertility. It is also applied to other periods of agricultural innovation from the **neolithic** to the twentieth century Green Revolution in the South. See also **North, South**.

Air-shed   An odd, inelegant, but necessary word that is being used as the atmospheric equivalent to the terrestrial watershed, the land drained by one river system. It signifies the air above a large urban system, the primary recipient of the pollutants discharged from the urban system below. Some air-sheds are closely defined by topography, and tend to hold the pollutants; others are more open and, thus, permit the dispersion of the pollutants over a wider area.

Anthropogenic   Due to human agency.

Anthropomorphic   This refers to the human habit of analysing situations with the assumption that human interests are paramount.

Aquifer   Strictly speaking, this is a porous geological strata (such as sandstone) into which groundwater percolates and resides. Sometimes (as in this book), it is used more loosely to refer to a body of groundwater. If the water is pumped out of the ground faster than it is replenished, by seepage from the surface, then the level of the water table (the highest level of the groundwater) falls. Unconfined aquifers are those aquifers that are relatively open to recharge from the surface. However, they are more prone to contamination from urban and agricultural **residuals**.

Atmosphere   A layer of gases that surrounds the earth to a depth of approximately 45 kilometres, 99% of which consists of nitrogen and oxygen. The lower 10 km is known as the troposphere, the upper 35 km as the stratosphere.

Bio-accumulation, bio-magnification   Some organic and inorganic materials persist and accumulate in various **environmental media**, including the bodies of plants and animals. As the various members of the food chain consume one another they tend to accumulate, or magnify, the quantities of these materials. In this way the materials may build up in various parts of the body in sufficient quantities to impair its function.

Bio-geochemical cycles All materials continually circulate through the earth's **environmental pathways**, as matter is neither created nor destroyed. Recently there has been renewed interest in how these global *biological, geological* and *chemical cycles* interact, at a global scale, because some elements are accumulating in one part of the pathway system, and this could change the operation of other parts of the system. The principal concern at this time is that carbon is accumulating in the atmosphere, and this could cause widespread changes in the climate. (See also **carbon cycle** and **sinks**.)

Bio-region Etymologically this is a simple term, meaning *biological region*. It is similar to the geographers' concept of a natural, or physiographic region. Currently, it is being used by political ecologists to explore the possibility of each city limiting its resource demands to an adjacent region, such as a watershed, as opposed to taking its resources from all over the globe, governed only by the economic rules of demand and supply.

Carbon cycle, carbon dioxide Carbon dioxide is the gaseous portion of the carbon cycle which describes the passage of carbon from the **atmosphere** as it is taken up by plants and converted into fibre, and then released back to the atmosphere when the plant rots or is burned. A portion of the carbon is buried in the ground and eventually may turn into carboniferous strata (coal, lignite), or reside underground in gaseous form (natural gas) or in liquid form (petroleum). Another portion of the cycle is routed through marine creatures who use carbon in their shells, and eventually sink into the ocean to form limestone and other carboniferous strata. Human beings have disrupted this natural cycle by burning fossil fuels, thereby significantly increasing the amount of carbon dioxide in the atmosphere. As carbon dioxide is a **greenhouse gas** this disruption is expected to lead to a rapid heating of the lower atmosphere.

Carbon tax Carbon taxes have been proposed as a means of encouraging consumers and producers to reduce energy use and/or to switch to fuels with the lowest quantity of carbon **residuals** per unit of energy produced. The proposed tax on fuels would reflect the quantity of carbon released when the fuel was used. Despite the elegance of the concept its adoption has been delayed in those countries which produce a substantial amount of coal or lignite—the fuels which give off the most carbon. At the **Earth Summit** such a tax was also opposed by members of OPEC. Furthermore, many governments feel that any such legislation must not be drafted in a way that provides an incentive to use nuclear power (which is carbon-free), because of outstanding concerns regarding operational safety and the safe disposal of wastes.

Carrying capacity   Originally the term was used to delimit the optimum population density for a particular species in a particular **ecological niche**. It has been applied to the human population in relation to the globe, but this application is controversial because carrying capacity will vary greatly according to the efficiency with which humans use the resources around them.

Clean Air Acts   These Acts were passed in most countries of the **North** in the 1950s and 1960s to control smoke emissions from domestic premises. Separate regulations were usually passed to cover emissions from industrial activities.

Climate change   Before the current environmental crisis the term was applied to climate studies throughout the history of the earth, to understand events such as the onset and retreat of the ice ages. Now it is often used more narrowly to refer to the anticipated impacts of human activities on climate such as the enhanced **greenhouse** effect associated with burning fossil fuels.

Climate change commitment   This is the phrase used by atmospheric scientists to refer to the amount of global warming to which the planet is already committed, due to the existing increase of **carbon dioxide** and other **greenhouses gases** in the atmosphere.

CFCs   Chlorofluorocarbons are a group of synthetic chemicals which have been produced since the 1930s to serve as coolants, solvents, foam packaging, and aerosols for spray cans, among others uses. As far as human comfort is concerned, their coolant function in refrigerators and air-conditioners is the most important. Since the 1970s it has been known that CFCs destroy the stratospheric **ozone layer** which screens out incoming ultra-violet radiation, an excess of which damages fauna and flora. In 1987 a protocol was signed in **Montreal** to phase-out the production of CFCs.

Cost-benefit analysis, discounting   This is a technique which compares the discounted costs and benefits of a project over a period of several years. The rate of discount reflects the commercial rate of interest, although it may be set below this for projects that produce benefits in addition to financial benefits. Its relevance to projects that have important environmental repercussions is small if these repercussions take place over a long time period, as both costs and benefits are heavily reduced by discounting over time.

Demographic transition   This is the transition of the human population from a stage of high birth rates and high death rates (when the population will grow slowly, if at all), through a stage when death rates fall faster than birth rates (when the population grows very quickly), to a later stage, when both death rates and birth rates are low, and the population becomes fairly stable.

Densification   See **intensification**.

Earth Summit   An international conference held in Rio de Janeiro in June 1992, at which most of the participants signed treaties on climate change and biodiversity, a statement of forest principles, the Rio Declaration on the environment, and an action plan, titled Agenda 21. The conference produced less than what most environmentally-concerned people wanted, but it did mark an important step in the evolution of a global commitment to facing up to the environmental crisis.

East, West   The terms are used in this book to distinguish between parts of the North. (See **North, South**.) In the early 1980s it was recognised that the material quality of life in the communist countries of Central and Eastern Europe, and the former Soviet Union was much closer to that of the industrialised West, than to the South. Hence industrialised countries, both communist and capitalist, were grouped together as 'the North'. Since the collapse of Communism the predicament of the former communist regimes of Europe has become starkly apparent. In particular, very serious environmental and health problems have come to light. In this book, the terms North and South are still used in the

1980s sense, while the terms East and West distinguish between European countries which were formerly grouped as the North.

Ecological cities It is too soon to imagine cities that have *no* negative impact on the physical environment, in the sense of playing a neutral role in the cycling of energy and nutrients. The phrase is used in this book, in a preliminary sense, to describe cities in which important steps have been taken to reduce the city's parasitic role in the planet's ecology.

Ecological footprint A term used by William Rees to describe the areal extent of the environmental impact of a city, or a country.

Ecological niche That part of the biosphere on which a species depends for its sustenance.

Energetics A method of analysis which estimates all the energy inputs and outputs of a particular activity, such as mechanised agriculture.

Energy audit An assessment of energy use and dissipation by processes operating within an activity.

Energy transition This is the recent transition in the use of different fuels, which industrial countries have passed through, especially in the last 200 years. At the beginning of that period they depended on human and animal labour, burning biomass (mostly wood and charcoal), and they made some use of falling water and wind power. The industrial revolution in the nineteenth century saw the switch to coal, which was progressively displaced, in this century, in the first industrial countries, by hydroelectric power, petroleum, natural gas, and nuclear power. It is hoped that we are now in a new stage of the transition to the use of renewable energy sources—solar, wind, tidal, and some biomass. However, many major industrial economies of the South—such as India and China—are still increasing their use of coal.

Enterprise zone A term used in the United Kingdom and the United States to designate certain depressed parts of a city which are entitled to special tax concessions and grants to create employment.

Environmentalism   This term can be used, neutrally, to mean simply 'an interest in environmental matters'. But it can also be used pejoratively to imply that some person, or institution, is content to treat the superficial environmental symptoms, without attacking the root causes of the environmental crisis. Thus, in its pejorative form, it has a similar meaning to the term 'instrumentalism' in planning.

Environmental change   This term refers generally to the dynamics of the environment, but it is currently being used to mean the change in those elements of the environment which poses some threat to the human occupancy of the planet, such as species extinction, desertification, deforestation, marine pollution, global warming, acidification, and stratospheric ozone depletion. (See also **climate change**.)

Environmental media   When used by natural and environmental scientists this refers to the different components of the biosphere, such as the atmosphere, the hydrosphere (rivers and oceans), the lithosphere (the land, the crust, and outer mantle of the earth), and the cryosphere (glaciers and the polar ice caps).

Environmental pathways   These are the routes followed by elements and compounds as they circulate through the various components (or **media**, as above) of the biosphere. The term is related to the 'chemical fate' of elements and compounds which determines where they will come to rest, and what form they will then take.

Feedback, positive and negative   These are terms developed in systems analysis. Positive feedbacks are those processes which encourage a system, or process, to grow. For example, global warming may encourage people to install air-conditioning in their homes, the increased use of which (through CFCs and energy consumption) will enhance the greenhouse effect, which in turn, etcetera. Negative feedbacks are those that dampen a process, so returning it to its original condition. For example, beyond a certain level, higher incomes and urbanisation encourage people to limit their family size, thus acting as a negative feedback on population growth.

Gaia hypothesis   This hypothesis has been put forward by James

Lovelock (see the list of references and the index) to explain why conditions on the planet seem ideal for plant and animal life. The main element of the hypothesis is that the earth, seen as a single organism, is able to regulate changes in the composition and temperature of the atmosphere (for example). Gaia is the Greek goddess of earth.

GHGs, greenhouse gases   These are gases which trap outgoing radiation, thereby increasing the temperature at the earth's surface. The principal, natural greenhouse gases are carbon dioxide, methane, nitrous oxide, and water vapour. People have created artificial greenhouse gases, the **CFCs**, and they have greatly increased the output of the natural greenhouse gases, thereby enhancing the greenhouse effect.

Global sourcing   This is the commercial practice of seeking the cheapest goods and services on a global scale, irrespective of national boundaries.

Global warming   Surface temperatures are expected to rise as a result of the enhanced **greenhouse** effect, which is attributed to human activities. Global warming will lead to sea-level rise as a result of the thermal expansion of the ocean, and perhaps the melting of glaciers and polar ice-caps.

Groundwater   See **aquifer**.

Hadean, Archean, Proterozoic, Phanerozoic periods   These are the major periods of earth history. The first lasted a billion years, saw the earth cool and acquire its first atmosphere of carbon dioxide and hydrogen. Bacteria in the Archean period (another billion years) produced oxygen which combined with hydrogen to form water. The Proterozoic was a time of increasing oxygen in the atmosphere and the evolution of more complex cells. The Phanerozoic runs from 700 million years ago to the present. Plants and animals evolved and carbon dioxide was reduced to a **trace gas** (0.03%) in the **atmosphere**.

Heat island, urban   The urban heat island is an area of higher than natural temperatures which forms around the centres of urban areas. It is caused partly by the fact that buildings and roads absorb more heat than rural land uses such as forests and agricultural land.

Hinterlands, urban Originally this was a term used in geography to denote the tributary trade area for a port, that is the area from which it drew goods for transshipment. It is now used more generally to refer to the area from which any urban system draws the resources on which it depends. Generally, the hinterlands of the richer urban systems of the North are global in extent. See also **ecological footprint**.

Hydrological cycle This cycle traces the global flow of water, from precipitation, through surface runoff and underground drainage, to the sea, and from evaporation from the surface of the sea and the land, back to the atmosphere. See also **biogeochemical cycle**.

Hypothermia Death due to lack of adequate warmth. People, especially the elderly, die of hypothermia in inadequately heated houses.

Industrial revolution The period when industrial activities became a significant source of employment, usually reaching a peak at 30% of the workforce. Industrial revolutions have been taking place since ancient times, but the term is usually used to denote that revolution which began in Britain in the early eighteenth century, first based on falling water and wind power, shifting gradually to the widespread use of coal. This, in turn, fuelled a transportation revolution which led to the construction of railway networks around the world. See also **energy transition**.

Informal sector A term used in development studies to refer to those economic activities which do not rely on the formal operating rules of the modern economy, such as book-keeping, paying taxes, and paying a regular workforce. It includes hawkers and traders, waste-pickers, and small groups of crafts-men and -women. There was a time when it was assumed that such workers would eventually be absorbed into the formal economy, either directly as employees, or indirectly by adopting formal means of operation. Instead, the informal sector has proliferated in the **South** and has become an important type of activity in the **North**.

Input–output analysis A measurement technique which showed how one sector of the economy fed into, and made demands upon other sectors of the economy. It was used to estimate the multiplier effect of the rise in demand in one sector, through the demand it passed on to the sectors on which it was dependent for inputs. In the 1970s attempts were made to add environmental goods (like clean air and water), and outputs (like pollutants), onto these input–output tables.

Intensification   This is a planned attempt to intensify land-use especially in low-density suburbs, where population is insufficient to make public transport viable. Intensification includes adding retail outlets and other services to areas that had once been purely residential, and encouraging the building of more housing units per hectare. It is also applied to downtown areas which may have been losing business and residents. It is an important set of initiatives to encourage a more compact urban form, thus reducing the energy requirements for transportation, for example.

Labelling, i.e. **environmental labelling** The practice of describing the environmental attributes of products is now becoming accepted in business, in response to consumer demand. It has been suggested that the practice should go much further to embrace major items such as houses and cars.

Managing the transition Projections of the effect of the enhanced greenhouse effect on the earth's climate are usually made for a time when the amount of **carbon dioxide** in the atmosphere will be double what it used to be before human interference. This is the 'doubled CO_2' scenario referred to by the climate modellers. The time it will take to reach that point depends on human action and unknown atmospheric responses. It is recognised that even if human emissions of greenhouse gases are then eliminated and atmospheric conditions become more stable again there will still be a period of rapid (and, as yet, largely unpredictable) environmental change. This period is referred to as the 'transient scenario'. The phrase 'managing the transition' has also been used in Chapter Seven of this book to refer to the urban management challenge of moving from the present situation to a more stable, future state when we live in **ecological cities**.

Market forces These are the result of the interplay between the demand and supply for any good or service. Under the assumptions of perfect competition, demand and supply will continually interact to provide an equilibrium price, at which demand is fully satisfied. In practice, lack of information, government intervention in the market place, and the presence of monopoly suppliers, cartels, and protectionism between nations, very often hinder the free play of market forces. In the last 15 years there has been a worldwide tendency to reduce government intervention in favour of market forces.

Materials balance approach This is an approach to the analysis of regional-scale environmental problems which attempts to estimate the key material flows in a regional economy, such as water, soils and minerals, and the outflow of residuals. As an approach it is similar to 'residuals and environmental quality management' and the concept of **urban metabolism**. (See below.)

Metabolism, urban metabolism This concept is based on a metaphorical comparison of an urban system with a living organism. Although it cannot really be used to identify a life-cycle for a city, the concept is very useful for describing the major daily material inflows and outflows of a city, such as water, fuel and food flowing in, and waste heat, sewage, solid waste, and air pollutants flowing out. In this book, the term 'metabolic intensity' is used to compare the relative environmental impacts of two cities.

Methane This is the common name for natural gas, CH_4, which is produced naturally through fermentation by bacteria. It is extracted as a fossil fuel and is an important **greenhouse gas**.

Modal split This term refers to the allocation of the travelling population (especially the commuting population), to the different modes of transportation—train, bus, car, bicycle, and foot. Planners sometimes try to influence the modal split by regulation, pricing, and the provision of improved services.

Montreal Protocol on ozone depletion The Protocol was signed in 1987 to commit the signatories to phase out the use of CFCs. Additional countries have since signed, and the number has now reached 56. Some of the signatory nations have since committed themselves to more stringent goals than those required by the protocol. See **CFCs**.

Neolithic The early stage in human history, beginning about

10 000 years ago, when people developed agriculture and fixed settlements to supplement their hunting and gathering activities.

Niche   See **ecological niche**.

NIMBY   The *Not-In-My-Backyard* syndrome which evolved since the late 1970s as neighbourhood groups began to oppose landfills and other unwanted activities in their own neighbourhood, or backyard.

'No-regrets' policies   These are environmental policies that provide other, non-environmental benefits, and therefore can be undertaken without regret, even if the environmental problem subsequently is perceived to be less important than first expected. For example, energy-efficient systems will save the consumer money, apart from reducing the problematic emissions to the air.

North, South   Roughly speaking, these terms distinguish between the richer countries, which are mainly in the northern hemisphere, and the poorer countries, many of which are in the South. However, the term was very imprecise even when first popularised by the Brandt Commission in 1980, and much has changed since then to make it even less useful. It is used for want of anything better that is as brief. See **East, West**.

Nutrients   These are the chemical elements that nourish plant life, the principal ones being nitrogen, phosphorous, calcium, potassium, magnesium, and sulphur. However, plants require specific amounts of these nutrients, so too much can be as damaging as too little. In excessive quantities, nutrients become contaminants. For example, overloads of phosphorous, used in detergents and fertiliser, pollute waterways and harm aquatic life.

Ozone, ozone layer   Ozone, O_3, is a **trace gas** that plays two very different roles in different parts of the **atmosphere**. In the troposphere, or lower atmosphere, it is an irritant which harms human eyes and skin and causes damage to crops and trees. The natural quantity of ozone in the troposphere is now being greatly augmented by human activities, especially emissions from motor vehicles in cities, where vehicles are concentrated. In the stratosphere, or upper atmosphere, the naturally occurring ozone layer screens out harmful ultra-violet radiation. The thickness of the ozone layer in the stratosphere is measured in terms of millimetres that it would occupy if compressed to the pressure found at sea-level, at 0°C. Unfortunately, this protective shield has been weakened by the arrival of man-made **CFCs**. See also **Montreal Protocol**.

Political ecology In his book, *Principles of Political Ecology*, Adrian Atkinson defines the primary concern of the book as being 'the establishment of a way of thinking and acting which is congruous with an understanding of the natural world, through the framework of ecology' (page 4). Towards the end, he cautions: 'political ecology has so far been no more than a few sketchy lines on an enormous canvas' (Atkinson 1991: 215).

Product life-cycle In the environmental context this phrase refers to a new approach to designing products. The new approach considers the use and disposal of the product, and the residuals from the fabrication process, instead of just the fabrication process itself. For example, for an car, the product life-cycle approach to design would take into account the materials used to produce it (plastic, metals, rubber, etcetera), the energy used to procure and produce those materials, the discharges to ground, air and water entailed in assembling and processing these materials, the resources needed to use and maintain it, the residuals thus produced, and, finally the cost and efficiency of the recovery of the spent materials when the product life-cycle comes to an end.

Residuals Residuals are waste products—materials and energy —from the human activities relating to the production and the use of resources. The term replaced the word 'pollution' in many academic and planning circles because 'not all materials discharged into the environment result in adverse environmental conditions' (Bower, no date: 8).

Retrofitting This means refitting buildings and vehicles to reduce the amount of energy they consume and the quantity of residuals they produce. Much can be gained by retrofitting building and vehicle stocks, but the costs are generally higher, and the gains lower, than what can be expected from 'best practice' new products.

Sick building syndrome In the last 20 years experience has shown that certain buildings are so poorly heated and ventilated that occupants are often sick, most commonly with respiratory complaints. In the 1970s the move to insulate buildings more thoroughly, coupled with the proliferation of air-conditioning even in temperate cities (like London), produced more and more cases of the syndrome. Finally, this has become recognised as a serious problem that should receive more attention in the design of new buildings.

Sinks   Sinks are those parts of the biosphere that soak up certain elements as they cycle through various **environmental media**. For example, the atmosphere acts as a sink for the gases discharged to it from both natural and **anthropogenic** sources. Eventually, these gases fall back to the earth and the ocean. (See **biogeochemical** cycles, and **environmental pathways**.) Problems may occur when human beings inject **residuals** into a sink at a rate which exceeds the rate at which that sink passes the residuals on to the next stage in the cycle. When that happens the residuals build-up in the first sink, hence the build-up of **greenhouse gases** in the atmosphere.

Steady-state economy   This term was used by Herman Daly in a book titled, *Towards a Steady-State Economy* in 1973. It is a concept that is sometimes misunderstood, as people assume that it means that the economy will come to halt and that the world will be plunged into a deep recession. Nothing of the kind is implied by the term. What Daly was, and is, concerned to do is reduce 'throughput-growth', or growth which depends on the ever-increasing use of resources. It is now widely appreciated that this type of growth cannot go on much longer. The steady-state economy implies a reduction of waste, not a reduction of employment, and an improvement, not a deterioration, in the quality of life.

Trace gases   This term refers to those gases that occur only in very small quantities in the atmosphere. Carbon dioxide (without human additions) generally accounts for 0.03%. Other gases, such as hydrogen, helium, **ozone** and **methane**, each account for less than 0.01%. Despite their small quantity, certain trace gases play a key role in the atmosphere by screening out ultra-violet radiation and by trapping heat radiated from the earth's surface, thereby creating the greenhouse effect.

Traffic calming Traffic calming refers to roadway designs which reduce the amount of space dedicated to vehicular traffic in towns. This has the dual effect of reducing the number of vehicles in an area and reducing the speed of those that do use it. These changes make the areas more attractive and practical for pedestrians and cyclists, and they also reduce the noise and emissions produced by vehicles.

Utopia This is the title of Thomas More's book, first published in Latin in 1516 and first translated into English in 1551. It is a Greek word which means 'elsewhere' or 'nowhere'. It does not mean 'impractical' or 'impossible' or 'absurdly idealistic', although it is commonly misused like this today. More chose the word to signify to the readers that he was not writing about the contemporary world of Tudor England, but of a place of the imagination where life might be lived very differently, with justice, meaningful work, and equality for all.

Ultra-violet radiation See **ozone**.

Water balance Most parts of the earth's surface have water flowing in, being used by various organisms, and then flowing out or evaporating, or sinking into the ground. The concept of the water balance, for a given watershed or administrative area, attempts to quantify the inflows, uses, and outflows of water.

Zones of transition These are parts of the city that are declining in wealth, and suffering some degree of physical and social blight. The concept was proposed by E. W. Burgess to describe the life of new waves of immigrants to Chicago in the 1920s. The purpose of the concept is to understand the social evolution of the immigrants within their new society, rather than to understand urban morphology.

References

Acres, G. J. K. (1990). Catalyst systems for emission control from motor vehicles. *Pollution. Causes, Effects and Controls*. Ed. R. M. Harrison. Cambridge, The Royal Society of Chemistry. 221–236.

Adams, B. (1993). Personal communication.

Akbari, H., Davis, S., Dorsano, S., Huang J. and Winnett, S., Eds. (1992). *Cooling Our Communities. A Guidebook on Tree Planting and Light-Colored Surfacing*. Washington DC, United States Environmental Protection Agency.

Arrhenius, S. (1896). On the influence of carbonic acid in the air on the temperature on the ground. *Philosophical Magazine*.

Ashton, J., Ed. (1992). *Healthy Cities*. Milton Keynes, Open University Press.

Atkinson, A. (1991). *Principles of Political Ecology*. London, Belhaven Press.

Atkinson, A. (1992). *The urban bioregion as sustainable development*. Paper presented at a conference on Planning for Sustainable Urban Development. Cities and Natural Resource Systems in Developing Countries, Cardiff, July 13–17.

Bach, W., Lechtenboehmer, S., Oppermann, F., Bonhoff, C. and Luther, T. (1993). Municipal climate protection concept. Possibilities of achieving the German Government's 30% CO_2–reduction target in the City of Muenster. Center for Applied Climatology and Environmental Studies, Department of Geography, University of Muenster.

Barde, J.-P. and Pearce, D. W., Eds. (1991). *Valuing the Environment*. London, Earthscan Publications Ltd.

Basta, D. J. and Bower, B. T., Eds. (1982). *Analyzing Natural Systems. Analysis for Regional Residuals and Environmental Quality Management*. Washington DC, Resources for the Future.

Basta, D. J., Lounsbury, J. L. and Bower, B. T., Eds. (1978). *Analysis for Residuals–Environmental Quality Management*. Washington DC, Resources for the Future.

Bayliss-Smith, T. P. (1982). *The Ecology of Agricultural Systems*. Cambridge, Cambridge University Press.

Beckerman, W. (1991). Global warming: a sceptical economic assessment. *Economic Policy Towards the Environment*. Ed. D. Helm. Oxford, Basil Blackwell. 52–85.

Benedick, R. E. (1991). *Ozone Diplomacy. New Directions in Safeguarding the Planet*. Cambridge, Harvard University Press.

Blake, N. P. (1991). Water and the city: lessons from history. *Water and the City. The Next Century*. Eds. H. Rosen and A. Keating. Chicago, Public Works Historical Society. 59–67.

Boardman, B. (1991). *Fuel Poverty. From Cold Homes to Affordable Warmth*. London, Belhaven Press.

Bookchin, M. (1982). *The Ecology of Freedom: the Emergence and Dissolution of Hierarchy*. Palo Alto, Cheshire Books.

Borkiewicz, J., Mieczkowska, E., Aleksandrowicz, A. and Leitman, J. (1991). *Environmental Profile of Katowice*. Washington DC, The World Bank.

Bower, B. T., Ed. (1977). *Regional Residuals Environmental Quality Management Modeling*. Washington DC, Resources for the Future.

Bower, B. T. (1993). Personal communication.

Bower, B. T. (no date). Seminar on Integrated Coastal Management.

Bower, B. T. and Koudstaal, R. (1986). Managing Coastal Waters: Why, Who, What, How. *Analyzing Biospheric Change. Final Report*. Solna, Sweden, IFIAS. 38–61.

Boyden, S. (1979). *An Integrative Ecological Approach to the Study of Human Settlements*. Paris, UNESCO.

Boyden, S., Millar, S., Newcombe, K. and O'Neill, B. (1981). *The Ecology of a City and Its People: the Case of Hong Kong*. Canberra, Australian National University Press.

Bradbury, I. (1991). *The Biosphere*. London, Belhaven Press.

Brown, L. R., Flavin, C. and Kane, H. (1992). *Vital Signs 1992. The Trends That Are Shaping Our Future*. New York and London, W. W. Norton and Company.

Brown, L. R. and other contributors (1993). *State of the World 1993*. New York, W.W.Norton.

Burton, I. (1983). The vulnerability of cities. *Approaches to the Study of the Environmental Implications of Contemporary Urbanization*. Eds. R. R. White and I. Burton. Paris, UNESCO. 111–120.

Campbell, M. and Glenn, W. (1982). *Profit from Pollution Prevention*. Toronto, Pollution Probe.

Canadian Urban Institute (1993). Cooling Buildings in Downtown Toronto. *Final Report of the Deep Lake Water Cooling Investigation Group*. Toronto, Canadian Urban Institute.

Canadian Urban Institute (1993). Intensification on the national agenda. *The Intensification Report*. 1 (2): 1–2.

City of Toronto (1988). *Healthy Toronto 2000*. Toronto, Department of Public Health.

City of Toronto (1991). *The Changing Atmosphere: Strategies for Reducing*

Carbon Dioxide Emissions. Volume 1, Policy Overview; Volume 2, Technical Volume. Toronto, Special Advisory Committee on the Environment.

City of Toronto (1993). Third Annual Status Report on the Work Programme of the Energy Efficiency Office. Commissioner of Public Works and the Environment.

Crombie, D. (1992). *Regeneration. Toronto's Waterfront and the Sustainable City: Final Report.* Ottawa, Ministry of Supply and Services.

Crosby, A. (1986). *Ecological Imperialism: the Biological Expansion of Europe 900–1900.* Cambridge, Cambridge University Press.

Daly, H. E. and Townsend, K. N., Eds. (1993). *Valuing the Earth. Economics, Ecology, Ethics.* Cambridge, MIT Press.

Davidson, J., Myers, D. and Chakraborty, M. (1992). *No Time to Waste. Poverty and the Global Environment.* Oxford, Oxfam.

Davison, A. and Barnes, J. (1992). Patterns of air pollution: critical loads and abatement strategies. *Managing the Human Impact on the Natural Environment.* Ed. M. Newson. London, Belhaven Press. 109–29.

Deelstra, T. (1992). Western Europe. *Sustainable Cities.* Eds. R. E. Stren, R. R. White and J. B. Whitney. Boulder, Westview Press. 60–82.

Deelstra, T., Koning, T. and Beeker, C. (1990). *Human Settlements and Sustainable Development in the Third World.* The Hague, Ministry of Housing, Physical Planning and the Environment.

Dekker, L., Bower, B. T. and Koudstaal, R. (1987). *Management of Toxic Materials in an International Setting: a Case Study of Cadmium in the North Sea.* Rotterdam, A. A. Balkema.

Delft Hydraulics (1988). *Impact of Sea Level Rise on Society. A Case Study for the Netherlands.* Delft, Delft Hydraulics Laboratory.

Douglas, I. (1983). *The Urban Environment.* London, Edward Arnold.

Durr, B. (1992). Chicago's reputation washed away. *Financial Times.* London, April 21, 29.

Ehrlich, P. R. and Ehrlich, A. H. (1993). Why isn't everyone as scared as we are? *Valuing the Earth.* Eds. H. E. Daly and K. N. Townsend. Cambridge, MIT Press. 55–67.

Ekins, P., Hillman, M. and Hutchinson, R. (1992). *Wealth Beyond Measure. An Atlas of New Economics.* London, Gaia Books Limited.

Elkin, T., McLaren, D. and Hillman, M. (1991). *Reviving the City. Towards Sustainable Urban Development.* London, Friends of the Earth.

Environment Canada (1986). *Preliminary Study of the Possible Impacts of a One-metre Rise in Sea Level at Charlottetown, Prince Edward Island.* P. Lane and Associates Limited for Atmospheric Environment Services, Atlantic Region.

Environment Canada (1987). *Effects of a One-metre Sea-level Rise at Saint John, New Brunswick, and the Lower Reaches of the Saint John River.* Martec Limited for Atmospheric Environment Services, Atlantic Region.

Environment Canada (1988). *The Changing Atmosphere: Implications for Global Security.* Conference Statement. Ottawa, Environment Canada.

Environment Canada (1990). *Water. No Time To Waste. A Consumer's Guide To Water Conservation*. Ottawa, Ministry of Supply and Services.

Federal Republic of Germany MAB National Committee (1980). *The Development and Application of Ecological Models in Urban and Regional Planning*. Bonn, FRG MAB National Committee.

Firor, J. (1990). *The Changing Atmosphere. A Global Challenge*. New Haven, Yale University Press.

French, H. F. (1990). *Green Revolutions: Environmental Reconstruction in Eastern Europe and the Soviet Union*. Washington DC, Worldwatch Institute.

Friday, L. and Laskey, R., Eds. (1989). *The Fragile Environment. The Darwin College Lectures*. Cambridge, Cambridge University Press.

Friends of the Earth (1990). *Warm Homes—Cool Planet. A Programme for Action on Cold Homes and Global Warming*. London, Friends of the Earth.

Frosch, R. and Gallopoulos, N. (1990). Strategies for manufacturing. *Managing Planet Earth. Scientific American*. New York, W. H. Freeman.

Furedy, C. (1992). Garbage: exploring non-conventional options in Asian cities. *Environment and Urbanization*, 4 (2, October): 42–54.

Garbesi, K., Akbari, H. and Martien, P., Eds. (1989). *Controlling Summer Heat Islands*. Berkeley, Applied Science Division, Lawrence Berkeley Laboratory.

Gilbert, R. (1991). Cities and global warming. *Cities and Global Change*. Ed. J. McCulloch. Washington DC, The Climate Institute. 182–91.

Gilbert, R. (1992). The future of cities. Paper presented at a conference on Economic, Social and Environmental Problems of Cities, organised by the OECD, Paris, November 18–20.

Gilbert, R. (1993a). Attracting, sustaining and keeping business in downtown. Toronto, Canadian Urban Institute.

Gilbert, R. (1993b). Personal communication.

Gilbert, R. and Di Mascio, P. (1993). Transit Planning in the Greater Toronto Area. Canadian Urban Institute.

Girardet, H. (1992). *The Gaia Atlas of Cities. New Directions for Sustainable Urban Living*. New York, Anchor Books published by Doubleday.

Glacken, C. J. (1967). *Traces on the Rhodian Shore. Nature and Culture in Western Thought from Ancient Times to the End of the Eighteenth Century*. Berkeley, University of California Press.

Goodland, R. and Daly, H. E. (1992). Ten reasons why Northern economic growth is not the solution to Southern poverty. *Population, Technology and Lifestyle. The Transition to Sustainability*. Eds. R. Goodland, H. E. Daly and S. El Serafy. Washington DC, Island Press. 128–46.

Goodland, R., Daly, H. E. and El Serafy, S., Eds. (1992). *Population, Technology and Lifestyle. The Transition to Sustainability*. Washington DC, Island Press.

Goodwin, P. B. (1991). Efficiency and environment—possibilities for a green–gold coalition. Paper presented at ESRC/SERC Seminar on Transport and the Environment, Pembroke College, Oxford, September 12–13.

Goodwin, P. B. (1992). Transport and CO_2 reduction. Paper presented at the Environmental Change Unit seminar, University of Oxford.

Gore, A. (1993). *Earth in the Balance. Ecology and the Human Spirit*. New York, Plume.

Goubert, J.-P. (1989). *The Conquest of Water. The Advent of Health in the Industrial Age*. Cambridge, Polity Press.

Goudie, A. (1986). *The Human Impact on the Natural Environment*. Cambridge, MIT Press.

Graedel, T. E. and Crutzen, P. J. (1990). The changing atmosphere. *Managing Planet Earth. Scientific American*. New York, W. H. Freeman and Company.

Grant, J. (1992). Mexican blast cause sought. *Financial Times*. London, April 24, 7.

Gribbin, J. (1990). *Hothouse Earth. The Greenhouse Effect and Gaia*. New York, Grove Weidenfeld.

Grubb, M. (1993). United Nations Framework Convention on Climate Change. *The Earth Summit Agreements*. Grubb et al., London, Earthscan Publications. 63–73.

Grubb, M., Koch, M., Munson, A., Sullivan, F. and Thomson, K. (1993). *The Earth Summit Agreements. A Guide and Assessment*. London, Earthscan Publications, for The Royal Institute of International Affairs.

Guerra, L. M. (1991). Urban air quality and health. Paper presented at a conference on Cities and Global Change, Toronto, June 12–14.

HABITAT (1987). *Global Report on Human Settlements 1986*. Oxford, Oxford University Press.

Hall, J. D. and Hanson, A. J. (1992). *A New Kind of Sharing. Why We Can't Ignore Global Environmental Change*. Ottawa, International Development Research Centre.

Hall, P. (1988). *Cities of Tomorrow*. Oxford, Basil Blackwell.

Hancock, T. (1992a). The development of the healthy cities project in Canada. *Healthy Cities*. Ed. J. Ashton. Milton Keynes, Open University Press. 43–8.

Hancock, T. (1992b). Toronto. *Healthy Cities*. Ed. J. Ashton. Milton Keynes, Open University Press. 175–85.

Hardoy, J. and Satterthwaite, D. (1989). *Squatter Citizen. Life in the Urban Third World*. London, Earthscan Publications.

Hardoy, J. E., Mitlin, D. and Satterthwaite, D. (1992a). *Environmental Problems in Third World Cities*. London, Earthscan Publications Ltd.

Hardoy, J. E. and Satterthwaite D. (1992b). *Environmental Problems in Third World Cities. An Agenda for the Poor and the Planet*. London, IIED.

Harrison, R. M., Ed. (1990). *Pollution: Causes, Effects and Control*. Cambridge, Royal Society of Chemistry.

Harvey, D. (1989a). *The Urban Experience.* Oxford, Basil Blackwell.

Harvey, D. (1989b). *The Condition of Postmodernity.* Oxford, Basil Blackwell.

Harvey, L. D. D. (1993a). Toronto's CO_2 Emission Reduction Programme: a Bottom-up Approach. *Environment,* September: 16–20 & 38–45.

Harvey, L. D. D. (1993b). Personal communication.

Henry, J. G. (1989). Water pollution. *Environmental Science and Engineering,* Eds. J. G. Henry and G. W. Heinke. Englewood Cliffs, Prentice-Hall. 409–70.

Hillel, D. (1991). *Out of the Earth. Civilization and the Life of the Soil.* Berkeley, University of California Press.

Hills, P. (1988). Environmental protection in a laissez-faire economy. *Environmental Quality Issues in Asian Cities,* Eds. P. Hills and J. B. Whitney. Hong Kong and Toronto, University of Hong Kong, IFIAS, and Project Ecoville, University of Toronto. 42–59.

Hills, P. and Whitney, J. B., Eds. (1988). *Environmental Quality Issues in Asian Cities.* Project Ecoville Working Paper. Hong Kong and Toronto, University of Hong Kong, University of Toronto, IFIAS.

Holdren, J. P. (1992). The energy predicament in perspective. *Confronting Climate Change. Risks, Implications and Responses.* Ed. I. M. Mintzer. Cambridge, Cambridge University Press. 163–70.

Hollander, J. K., Ed. (1992). *The Energy–Environment Connection.* Washington DC, Island Press,.

Hough, M. (1989). *City Form and Natural Process.* London, Routledge.

Houghton, J. T., Callander, B. A. and Varney, S. K., Eds. (1992). *Climate Change 1992. The Supplementary Report to the IPCC Scientific Assessment.* Cambridge, Cambridge University Press.

Howard, E. (1985 (1898)). *Garden Cities of Tomorrow.* Builth Wells, Attic Press.

IFIAS (1986). *Analyzing Biospheric Change. Final Report.* Solna, Sweden, IFIAS.

International Energy Agency (1991). *Energy Efficiency and the Environment.* Paris, OECD.

Isard, W. (1972). *Ecological-economic Analysis for Regional Development.* New York, Free Press.

Isin, E. F. (1992). *Cities Without Citizens. Modernity of the City as a Corporation.* Montreal, Black Rose Books.

ITALIA MAB (1981). *Urban Ecology Applied to the City of Rome.* Rome, Instituto di Botanica.

Jacobs, J. (1962). *The Death and Life of Great American Cities.* London, Jonathan Cape.

Jacobs, J. (1993). Foreword. *The Shape of the City.* J. Sewell. Toronto, University of Toronto Press. ix–xii.

Jones, G., Robertson, A., Forbes, J. and Hollier, G. (1992). *The HarperCollins Dictionary of Environmental Science.* New York, HarperCollins.

Kanté, B. (1986). Policies, constraints and opportunities for low- and no-waste technologies in developing countries. *Industry and Environment (published by UNEP)*, 9 (4): 15–18.

Kellogg, W. W. and Schware, R. (1981). *Climate Change and Society. Consequences of Increasing Atmospheric Carbon Dioxide.* Boulder, Westview Press.

Kharbenda, O. P. and Stallworthy, E. A. (1990). *Waste Management. Towards a Sustainable Society.* Aldershot, Gower Publishing Co. Ltd.

Krier, L. (1989). Master Plan for Poundbury Development in Dorchester. *Architectural Design Profile*: 46–55.

Kristensen, T. and Paludan, J. P., Eds. (1988). *The Earth's Fragile Systems. Perspectives on Global Change.* IFIAS Research Series. Boulder, Westview Press.

Leontief, W. W. (1970). Environmental repercussions and the economic structure: an input–output approach. *Review of Economics and Statistics*, 52: 262–71.

Linn, J. F. (1983). *Cities in the Developing World. Policies for their Equitable and Efficient Growth.* New York, Oxford University Press.

Lipton, M. (1977). *Why Poor People Stay Poor: Urban Bias in World Development.* Cambridge, Harvard University Press.

Lovelock, J. (1988). *The Ages of Gaia. A Biography of Our Living Earth.* Oxford, Oxford University Press.

Lovelock, J. (1991). *Gaia. The Practical Science of Planetary Medicine.* London, Gaia Books Ltd.

Lowe, M. D. (1989). *The Bicycle: Vehicle for a Small Planet.* Washington DC, Worldwatch Institute.

Lowe, M. D. (1990). *Alternatives to the Automobile: Transport for Livable Cities.* Washington DC, Worldwatch Institute.

McAuslan, P. (1985). *Urban Land and Shelter for the Poor.* London, Earthscan Publications Ltd.

McCulloch, J., Ed. (1991). *Cities and Climate Change.* Washington DC, The Climate Institute.

McHarg, I. L. (1969). *Design with Nature.* Garden City, New York, Doubleday and Company.

McKeown (1976). *The Modern Rise of Population.* London, Edward Arnold.

Mackay, D. (1991). *Multimedia Environmental Models. The Fugacity Approach.* Chelsea MI, Lewis Publishers.

Maclaren, V. (1992). *Sustainable Urban Development in Canada: from Concept to Practice. Volume 1: Summary Report.* Toronto, Intergovernmental Committee on Urban and Regional Research.

MacNeill, J. (1989). Strategies for Sustainable Development. *Scientific American*, September: 155–65.

MacNeill, J., Winsemius, P. and Yakushiji, T. (1991). *Beyond Interdependence. The Meshing of the World's Economy and the Earth's Ecology.* Oxford, Oxford University Press.

Mansfield, T. A. and Lucas, P. W. (1990). Effects of gaseous pollutants on crops and trees. *Pollution: Causes, Effects and Control*. Ed. R. M. Harrison. Cambridge, Royal Society of Chemistry. 237–261.

Martin, D. (1991). The suburban dilemma. Regional transit issues and the global environmental crisis. *Cities and Global Change*. Ed. J. McCulloch. Washington DC, The Climate Institute. 174–9.

Martinez-Alier, J. (1991). Ecological perception, environmental policy and distributional conflicts: some lessons from history. *Ecological Economics*. Ed. R. Costanza. New York, Columbia University Press. 118–36.

Martinez-Alier, J. (1990). *Ecological Economics. Energy, Environment and Society*. Oxford, Basil Blackwell.

Maunder, W. (1989). *The Human Impact of Climate Uncertainty: Weather Information, Economic Planning and Business Management*. London, Routledge.

Meadows, D., Meadows, D., Randers, J. and Behrens III, W. (1972). *The Limits to Growth. A Report for the Club of Rome's Project on the Predicament of Mankind*. Washington DC, Potomac Associates.

Meadows, D., Meadows, D. and Randers, J. (1992). *Beyond the Limits. Global Collapse or a Sustainable Future*. London, Earthscan Publications Ltd.

Meier, R. L. (1970). *Resource-conserving Urbanism: Progress and Potentials*. International Future Research Conference, Kyoto, Japan Society of Futurology.

Meier, R. L. (1972). Notes on the creation of an efficient megalopolis: Tokyo. *Human Identity in the Urban Environment*. Eds. G. Bell and J. Tyrwhitt. Harmondsworth, Penguin. 557–80.

Metropolitan Toronto Government (1991). *Strategic Plan, May 1991*. Metropolitan Toronto Government.

Metropolitan Toronto Government (1992a). *The Livable Metropolis. The Draft Official Plan*. Toronto, Municipality of Metropolitan Toronto.

Metropolitan Toronto Government (1992b). Deep Lake Water Cooling Project Investigation. Commissioner of Works.

Metropolitan Toronto Government (1992c). Report No. 17 of The Works Committee. Commissioner of Works.

Metropolitan Toronto Government (1992d). Urban CO_2 Reduction Project—Metropolitan Toronto CO_2 Reduction Strategy. Commissioner of Works. Report No. 24, December 9.

Metropolitan Toronto Government (1993). Committee for Energy Efficiency Planning for Metropolitan Toronto. Commissioner of Works. February 19.

Millar, S. (1979). *Hong Kong Human Ecology Programme. The Biosocial Survey of Hong Kong*. Canberra, Australian National University for the National MAB Committee.

Mintzer, I. M., Ed. (1992). *Confronting Climate Change. Risks, Implications and Responses*. Cambridge, Cambridge University Press.

More, T. (1974 (1516)). *Utopia*. New York, Washington Square Press.

Moroz, W. J. (1989). Air pollution. *Environmental Science and Engineering*. Eds. J. G. Henry and G. W. Heinke. Englewood Cliffs, Prentice-Hall. 471–537.

Munn, R. E. (1986). Global environmental prospects. *Geography, Resources and the Environment. Volume Two. Themes from the Work of Gilbert F. White*. Eds. R. Kates and I. Burton. Chicago, University of Chicago Press. 326–338.

Netherlands Ministry of Housing, Physical Planning and Environment (1985). *Environmental Program of the Netherlands 1986–1990*. The Hague, Central Department for Information and International Relations.

Newson, M., Ed. (1992). *Managing the Human Impact on the Natural Environment*. London, Belhaven Press.

Nilsson, A. (1992). *Greenhouse Earth*. Chichester, John Wiley & Sons.

Nisbet, E. G. (1991). *Leaving Eden. To Protect and Manage the Earth*. Cambridge, Cambridge University Press.

Odum, E. P. (1989). *Ecology and Our Endangered Life-Support Systems*. Sunderland, Sinauer Associates.

Odum, H. T. (1983). *Systems Ecology. An Introduction*. New York, John Wiley and Sons.

OECD (1991a). *Environmental Indicators*. Paris, OECD.

OECD (1991b). *State of the Environment*. Paris, OECD.

OECD (1991c). *Climate Change. Evaluating the Socio-economic Impacts*. Paris, OECD.

Oke, T. R. (1973). City size and the urban heat island. *Atmospheric Environment*, 7: 769–79.

Owen, S. (1991). *Planning Settlements Naturally*. Chichester, Packard Publishing Ltd.

Owens, S. (1986). *Energy, Planning and Urban Form*. London, Pion Limited.

Owens, S. (1991). *Energy-conscious Planning. The Case for Action*. London, Council for the Protection of Rural England.

Oxford University Press (1992). *A Concise Dictionary of Chemistry*. Oxford, Oxford University Press.

Parkhurst, G. B. (1992). U.K. transport policy developments in 1991: environmental relevance. University of Oxford, Transport Studies Unit.

Parry, M. L. and other contributors (1991). *The Potential Effects of Climate Change in the United Kingdom*. London, HMSO.

Pearce, D., Markandya, A. and Barbier, E. B. (1989). *Blueprint for a Green Economy*. London, Earthscan Publications Ltd.

Pearce, D., Barbier, E B. and Markandya, A. (1990). *Sustainable Development. Economics and the Environment in the Third World*. London, Earthscan Publications Ltd.

Postel, S. (1992). *Last Oasis. Facing Water Scarcity*. New York, W. W. Norton.

Pucher, J. (1990). Capitalism, socialism, and urban transportation. *Journal of the American Planning Association*. Summer.

Rabinovitch, J. (1992). Curitiba: towards sustainable urban development. *Environment and Urbanization*, 4 (2): 62–73.

Redclift, M. (1987). *Sustainable Development. Exploring the Contradictions.* London, Methuen.

Rees, C. (1992). Personal communication.

Rees, W. E. (1992). Ecological footprints and appropriated carrying capacity: what urban economics leaves out. *Environment and Urbanization* 4 (2): 121–30.

Reisner, M. (1986). *Cadillac Desert. The American West and Its Disappearing Water.* New York, Penguin Books.

Richardson, N. H. (1992). Canada. *Sustainable Cities.* Eds. R. E. Stren, R. R. White, and J. W. Whitney. Boulder, Westview Press. 145–67.

Roan, S. L. (1989). *Ozone Crisis. The 15-Year Evolution of a Sudden Global Emergency.* New York, John Wiley & Sons.

Rosenfeld, A. H. and Ward, E. (1992). Energy use in buildings. *The Energy–Environment Connection.* Ed. J. M. Hollander. Washington DC, Island Press. 223–57.

Rostrum, H. (1987). *Human Settlements in Canada: Trends and Policies, 1981–86.* Ottawa, Canada Mortgage and Housing Corporation.

Rowland, A. and Cooper, P. (1983). *Environment and Health.* London, Edward Arnold.

Sandbrook, R. (1982). *The Politics of Basic Needs: Urban Aspects of Assaulting Poverty in Africa.* Toronto, University of Toronto Press.

Schneider, S. H. (1990). *Global Warming. Are We Entering the Greenhouse Century?* New York, Vintage Books.

Scientific American (1990). *Managing Planet Earth. Readings from Scientific American.* New York, W. H. Freeman and Company.

Sewell, J. (1993). *The Shape of the City: Toronto Struggles with Modern Planning.* Toronto, University of Toronto Press.

Short, J. R. (1989). *The Humane City. Cities as if People Matter.* Oxford, Basil Blackwell.

Simon, J. L. and Kahn, H., Eds. (1984). *The Resourceful Earth, A Response to 'Global 2000'.* Oxford, Basil Blackwell.

Smil, V., Nachman, P. and Long II, T. V. (1983). *Energy Analysis and Agriculture. An Application to U.S. Corn Production.* Boulder, Westview Press.

Sopper, W. (1990). Forests as living filters for urban sewage. *Green Cities.* Ed. D. Gordon. Montreal, Black Rose Books. 145–58.

Spofford, W. O. J., Russell, C. S., et al. (1977). The Lower Delaware Valley Integrated Residuals Management Model: a Summary. *Regional Residuals Environmental Quality Management Modelling.* Ed. B. T. Bower. Washington DC, Resources for the Future. 52–107.

Starke, L. (1990). *Signs of Hope. Working Towards Our Common Future.* Oxford, Oxford University Press.

Statistics Canada (1993). *Environmental Perspectives 1993. Studies and Statistics*. Ottawa, Ministry of Industry, Science and Technology.

Stren, R. (1989). Urban Local Government in Africa. *African Cities in Crisis*. Eds. R. E. Stren and R. R. White. Boulder, Westview Press. 20–36.

Stren, R. E. and White, R. R., Eds. (1989). *African Cities in Crisis. Managing Rapid Urban Growth*. African Modernization and Development. Boulder, Westview Press.

Stren, R. E., White, R. R. and Whitney, J. B., Eds. (1992). *Sustainable Cities. Urbanization and the Environment in International Perspective*. Boulder, Westview Press.

Sylvan, J. (1992). Eastern Europe. *Sustainable Cities*. Eds. R. E. Stren, R. R. White and J. B. Whitney. Boulder, Westview Press. 83–104.

Thomas, K. (1983). *Man and the Natural World. Changing Attitudes in England 1500–1800*. Harmondsworth, England.

Tolley, R. (1990). Introduction: Trading-in the Red Modes for the Green. *The Greening of Urban Transport*. Ed. R. Tolley. London, Belhaven Press. 1–8.

UK Department of Energy (1991a). Energy in your home. HMSO.

UK Department of Energy (1991b). Insulating your home. HMSO.

UNEP (1987). *The Ozone Layer*. Nairobi, UNEP.

Union of Concerned Scientists (1992). World scientists' warning to humanity. 26 Church Street, Cambridge, MA 02238.

Vojnovic, I. (1992). Energy Conservation in New Subdivision Designs. Program in Planning, University of Toronto.

White, J. C., Ed. (1989). *Global Climate Change Linkages. Acid Rain, Air Quality, and Stratospheric Ozone*. New York, Elsevier.

White, R. R. (1992a). The road to Rio, or the global environmental crisis and the emergence of different agendas for rich and poor countries. *International Journal of Environmental Studies* (41): 187–201.

White, R. R. (1992b). The international transfer of urban technology: does the North have anything to offer for the global environmental crisis? *Environment and Urbanization*, 4 (2): 109–21.

White, R. R. (1993a). *North, South and the Environmental Crisis*. Toronto, University of Toronto Press.

White, R. R. (1993b). Convergent trends in architecture and urban environmental planning. *Environment and Planning D: Society and Space*, 11 (4): 375–8.

White, R. R. and Burton, I., Eds. (1983). *Approaches to the Study of the Environmental Implications of Contemporary Urbanization*. MAB Technical Notes. Paris, UNESCO.

White, R. R. and Whitney, J. B. (1992). Cities and the environment: an overview. *Sustainable Cities: Urbanization and the Environment in International Perspective*. Eds. R. E. Stren, R. R. White and J. B. Whitney. Boulder, Westview Press. 5–52.

Whitelegg, J. (1990). The Principle of Environmental Traffic Management. *The Greening of Urban Transport*. Ed. R. Tolley. London, Belhaven Press. 75–96.

Wolman, A. (1965). The metabolism of cities. *Scientific American* (September): 179–88.

World Bank (1984). *World Development Report 1984*. Oxford, Oxford University Press.

World Bank (1990). *World Development Report 1990. Poverty*. Oxford, Oxford University Press.

World Bank (1991). *Environmental Assessment Sourcebook. Volume 1, Policies, Procedures and Cross-Sectoral Issues*. Washington DC, World Bank.

World Bank (1992). *World Development Report 1992. Development and the Environment*. Oxford, Oxford University Press.

World Bank (1993). *World Development Report 1993. Investing in Health*. New York, Oxford University Press.

World Commission on Environment and Development (1987). *Our Common Future*. Oxford, Oxford University Press.

World Health Organization and the United Nations Environment Programme (1992). *Urban Air Pollution in the Megacities of the World*. Oxford, Basil Blackwell.

World Resources Institute (1992). *World Resources 1992–93*. New York, Oxford University Press.

Xoomsai, T. N. (1988). Bangkok: environmental quality in a primate city. *Environmental Quality Issues in Asian Cities*. Eds. P. Hills and J. B. Whitney. Hong Kong and Toronto, University of Hong Kong, University of Toronto, IFIAS. 1–23.

Zuckerman, W. (1991). *End of the Road; the World Car Crisis and How We Can Solve It*. Cambridge, Lutterworth Press.

Index